Blockchain with Artificial Intelligence for Healthcare

A synergistic approach

Online at: https://doi.org/10.1088/978-0-7503-5839-2

IOP Series in Next Generation Computing

Series editors

Prateek Agrawal
University of Klagenfurt, Austria and Lovely Professional University, India

Anand Sharma
Mody University of Science and Technology, India

Vishu Madaan
Lovely Professional University, India

About the series

The motivation for this series is to develop a trusted library on advanced computational methods, technologies, and their applications.

This series focuses on the latest developments in next generation computing, and in particular on the synergy between computer science and other disciplines. Books in the series will explore new developments in various disciplines that are relevant for computational perspective including foundations, systems, innovative applications, and other research contributions related to the overall design of computational tools, models, and algorithms that are relevant for the respective domain. It encompasses research and development in artificial intelligence, machine learning, block chain technology, quantum cryptography, quantum computing, nanoscience, bioscience-based sensors, IoT applications, nature inspired algorithms, computer vision, bioinformatics, etc. and their applications in the areas of science, engineering, business, and the social sciences. It covers a broad spectrum of applications in the community, including those in industry, government, and academia.

The aim of the series is to provide an opportunity for prospective researchers and experts to publish works based on next generation computing and its diverse applications. It also provides a data-sharing platform that will bring together international researchers, professionals, and academics. This series brings together thought leaders, researchers, industry practitioners, and potential users of different disciplines to develop new trends and opportunities, exchange ideas and practices related to advanced computational methods, and promote interdisciplinary knowledge.

A full list of titles published in this series can be found here: https://iopscience.iop.org/bookListInfo/iop-series-in-next-generation-computing.

Blockchain with Artificial Intelligence for Healthcare

A synergistic approach

Rishabha Malviya
Department of Pharmacy, Galgotias University, Greater Noida, India

Arun Kumar Singh
Department of Pharmacy, Galgotias University, Greater Noida, India

Sonali Sundram
Department of Pharmacy, Galgotias University, Greater Noida, India

Balamurugan Balusamy
Shiv Nadar University, Greater Noida, India

Seifedine Kadry
Noroff University College, Norway

IOP Publishing, Bristol, UK

ISBN   978-0-7503-5839-2 (ebook)
ISBN   978-0-7503-5837-8 (print)
ISBN   978-0-7503-5840-8 (myPrint)
ISBN   978-0-7503-5838-5 (mobi)

DOI   10.1088/978-0-7503-5839-2

Version: 20230901

IOP ebooks

British Library Cataloguing-in-Publication Data: A catalogue record for this book is available from the British Library.

Published by IOP Publishing, wholly owned by The Institute of Physics, London

IOP Publishing, No.2 The Distillery, Glassfields, Avon Street, Bristol, BS2 0GR, UK

US Office: IOP Publishing, Inc., 190 North Independence Mall West, Suite 601, Philadelphia, PA 19106, USA

Dear Healthcare Professionals,

We are dedicating this book to you. Our Love for our profession shall live forever.

Contents

Foreword

I've always been interested in the medical sector, and I've been fortunate to share many of the findings of my study with my professional friends and colleagues. I've also always wanted to write a book that would be useful to readers. So when Dr Balamurugan and Dr Rishabha informed me about their book, I was fascinated.

A crucial aspect of our society, healthcare is always evolving to fulfil the demands of both patients and healthcare practitioners. Blockchain technology has received a lot of attention recently due to its potential to transform the healthcare industry. But can blockchain actually improve healthcare, or is this simply marketing hype? There must be something to this technology, and it seems that it is not simply hype, as evidenced by the significant investments being made in blockchain research for healthcare by major organizations like IBM, Microsoft, and Google. The current healthcare infrastructure is generally unable to deliver a significant degree of data availability owing to a variety of factors such as interoperability challenges, data breaches, and so on. Due to its dispersed nature, this technology can offer continuous data accessibility and assist in improving the managing of electronic health records. More accurate diagnoses, more effective therapies, and simply better capabilities for healthcare organizations to offer cost-effective care are all results of improved data exchange amongst healthcare professionals. Blockchain technology offers numerous benefits to the healthcare industry, including data security, data monitoring, and many more. The advancement in the healthcare sector is highlighted in this book by Malviya *et al* as an example of some real-world blockchain uses. This book will, in my opinion, serve as a resource for readers and educate them that the healthcare sector will undergo a fundamental transformation in the coming year or even the year after that as a result of this technology. If any of you feel that your healthcare organization is ready to accept change, adopt modern theories, and put cutting-edge technology to use, you can browse *Blockchain with Artificial Intelligence for Healthcare: A Synergistic Approach*, a brief and informative book about blockchain development in the healthcare industry.

Ms Aradhana Galgotia
Director of Operations
Galgotias University, India

Preface

Artificial intelligence (AI) has already started to work wonders in the healthcare sector, which is enough to fascinate people who grew up in the mechanical era. Applications of AI in telemedicine are becoming increasingly popular. These programs enable doctors to immediately respond by keeping track of patients and providing them with essential information. Blockchain technology helps the healthcare sector by increasing its security and traceability. The most common blockchain healthcare use currently is keeping our critical medical data safe and secure, which is not surprising. Security is a key problem in the healthcare sector. Blockchain is a technology that is suitable for security applications because it can maintain an unchangeable, decentralized, and transparent ledger of all patient data. Furthermore, while blockchain is transparent, it is also private, masking any individual's identity with complex and secure protocols that can protect the confidentiality of medical data. The technology's decentralized structure also makes it possible for patients, physicians, and other healthcare professionals to exchange the same information easily and securely. By incorporating the most recent technological advancements, such as AI and blockchain, the healthcare sector will provide better service at lower prices and with more democratized healthcare. This book emphasises how blockchain and AI might be used in conjunction to improve patient safety, health management, and biomedical research. This book will also shed light on data security, specifically how blockchain is used to manage healthcare data in a secure and transparent manner. This book will focus on the use of blockchain technology powered by AI to advance scientific research, patient safety, health management, and patient data security. This book consists of 11 chapters, and the contents of the book give sufficient and the latest updates about application of AI and blockchain in the healthcare industry. This book provides a glimpse of the concept of smart contracts for performing advanced level scripting to create a blockchain network to provide a platform for the development of decentralized applications. This book should become a useful source for researchers and industrialists working in healthcare, data management, clinical research, and research scholars, blockchain consultants, digital transformation experts, medical technology professionals.

The authors

Acknowledgements

Having a concept and transforming it into a book is as difficult as it sounds. The experience is both challenging and pleasant. I want to express my gratitude especially to those who made this project possible. I'd like to begin by thanking the Almighty, whose continuous blessing and supreme power enable us to achieve all of our objectives. I would like to thank my co-author Dr Balamurugan Balusamy for his all-time support for this new edition and Professor Seifedine Kadry for his steadfast support.

After that, I would like to special thanks to the management of Galgotias University, whom I want to thank for letting me serve, for being a part of our amazing organization, and for giving motivation every day. Without the experiences and support from my peers and team at Galgotias University, this book would not exist.

Many thanks also go to all the authors who so kindly contributed to accomplish this book. Finally, I extend my deepest thanks to the publishers for their kind and continuous support, innovative suggestions and guidance in bringing out this edition.

Author biographies

Dr Rishabha Malviya

Dr Rishabha Malviya completed B Pharmacy from Uttar Pradesh Technical University and M Pharmacy (Pharmaceutics) from Gautam Buddha Technical University, Lucknow Uttar Pradesh. His PhD (Pharmacy) work was in the area of novel formulation development techniques. He has 11 years of research experience and has been working as Associate Professor in the Department of Pharmacy, School of Medical and Allied Sciences, Galgotias University for the past eight years. His areas of interest include formulation optimization, nanoformulation, targeted drug delivery, localized drug delivery and characterization of natural polymers as pharmaceutical excipients. He has authored more than 150 research/review papers for national/international journals of repute. He has 51 patents (12 grants, 38 published, 1 filed) and publications in reputed national and international journals with a total of 91 cumulative impact factor. He has also received an Outstanding Reviewer award from Elsevier. He has edited 50 books (Springer Nature, Wiley, CRC Press/Taylor and Francis, Apple Academic Press, River Publisher and OMICS publication) and authored nine book chapters. His name has been included in the world's top 2% of scientists list for the year 2020 by Elsevier BV and Stanford University. He is a reviewer/editor/editorial board member of more than 50 national and international journals of repute. He has been invited as author for 'Atlas of Science' and pharma magazine dealing with industry (B2B) 'Ingredient south Asia Magazines'.

Arun Kumar Singh

Arun Kumar Singh completed M Pharm (pharmaceutics) from Galgotias University, Greater Noida, India. His area of interest is in the areas of nanoformulation, blockchain, Internet of Things, machine learning, cancer, artificial intelligence and big data. He has published three chapters in the field of big data with prestigious River Publisher, Denmark. He has also published two review papers of which one is in *Biochimica et Biophysica Acta (BBA)—Reviews on Cancer* [IF: 10.68]. His strength is research skills, thinking innovation, leadership qualities, decision making, and positive thinking. His hard-working nature and devotion to his work has made him distinguished and extraordinary.

Professor Sonali Sundram

Professor Sonali Sundram completed B Pharm and M Pharm (pharmacology) from AKTU, Lucknow. She worked as a research scientist in a project of ICMR in King George's Medical University, Lucknow, after which she joined BBDNIIT, and currently she is working in Galgotias university, Greater Noida. Her PhD (Pharmacy) work was in the area of neurodegeneration and nanoformulation. Her areas of interest are neurodegeneration, clinical research and artificial intelligence. She has edited four books (Wiley, CRC Press/Taylor and Francis, River Publisher) She has attended as well as organized more than 15 national and international seminars/conferences/workshops. She has more than eight patents national and international to her credit.

Professor Balamurugan Balusamy

Professor Balamurugan Balusamy has served up to the position of Associate Professor in his stint of 14 years of experience with VIT University, Vellore. He had completed his Bachelor's, Master's and PhD degrees from top premier institutions from India. His passion is teaching and he adapts different design thinking principles while delivering his lectures. He has published 30+ books on various technologies and visited 15+ countries for his technical course. He has several top-notch conferences in his resumé and has published over 150 quality articles, conference papers and book chapters combined. He serves in the advisory committee for several start-ups and forums and does consultancy work for industry on Industrial IOT. He has given over 175 talks in various events and symposiums. He is currently working as a professor at Galgotias University and teaches students, and does research on blockchain and Internet of Things.

Professor Seifedine Kadry

Seifedine Kadry is a Professor of Data Science at the Faculty of Applied Computing and Technology at Noroff University College, Kristiansand, Norway. He is a published author of 12 books, with prestigious publishers like IGI, Elsevier, Springer and Bentham. Some of them are related to mathematical sciences, system simulation, system prognostic and reliability engineering. He has also published more than 200 articles and organized numerous conference tracks and workshops. Professor Kadry is the Editor-in-Chief of *ARPN Journal of Systems and Software* and *Maxwell Journal of Mathematics and Statistics*. He is an IEEE senior member. His specialized areas of research include computing, software engineering and systems reliability and safety.

IOP Publishing

Blockchain with Artificial Intelligence for Healthcare
A synergistic approach
Rishabha Malviya, Arun Kumar Singh, Sonali Sundram, Balamurugan Balusamy and Seifedine Kadry

Chapter 1

Blockchain and artificial intelligence: an overview

A novel strategy in the healthcare sector is to use blockchain and artificial intelligence (AI). Web of Sciences and other Google surveys are used to gather information on healthcare indices. This chapter is all about the study of how AI and blockchain technology may improve healthcare by increasing the use of widely applicable advanced analytics that can be incorporated into more complete risk-management systems. Blockchain, a distributed system for information exchange and approval, has been utilized in e-Health to demonstrate the variety of options for creating trustworthy AI models. The blockchain will allow healthcare providers to store patient medical data, and AI is going to utilize a variety of algorithms and a vast amount of data to make choices. AI relies on encrypted records that may be maintained on the blockchain, and by embracing the most recent advancements in these technologies, healthcare will be more efficient, more accessible, and more economical.

1.1 Introduction

There are several health informatics strategies based on conditional phases, which may be thought of as an ongoing set of patient care activities. There should be better internal controls, better performance, better compliance, and more consistency in healthcare organizations, and a reduction in the danger, time spent working, and costs incurred [1–4]. Smart contracts might well be utilized to handle patient data and simplify complicated medical procedures by using a thorough healthcare blockchain investigation and a sound healthcare management plan. We designed a blockchain-based solution for healthcare management after analyzing the latest and most current healthcare blockchain research. Governments and relevant corporate sectors are getting increasingly engaged in the digitization of healthcare

doi:10.1088/978-0-7503-5839-2ch1

systems, as shown by several projects in different nations and economies. If a company wants to succeed, blockchain, AI, as well as other readily available technology must be incorporated into the organization's DNA. If the medical industry uses technology to build representations or data-driven alternatives that are centered on the needs of patients and customers, it may progress medical research and improve patient care [5–7]. It is essential to identify and prioritize patients for medication monitoring or growth in order to reduce lead times for the distribution of medicine [8]. Repurposing commercial medication, investigating the effectiveness of prescription formulations, and quantifying dosages have all been studied using numerical drug design methodologies and AI. A continuously changing environment necessitates that governments figure out the most efficient methods to use resources and promote change while also guaranteeing consistency, compliance, and data security [9–11]. In figure 1.1, we discuss e-Health security measures using blockchain and AI. Data may be safely and automatically analyzed using blockchain technology, which enables the development and management of content blocks called 'ledgers.' Medical professionals, healthcare providers, and purchasers will be able to get rapid updates on all health-related data thanks to the secure storage and analysis of this information. By incorporating AI algorithms into the blockchain, this may be pushed to another level [12]. AI has started to think and learn like a physician in order to understand health trends and patterns. Unstructured data is gathered from many sources, particularly the radiologist as well as the patient [13, 14].

Moreover, AI has the capacity of performing complex computations and swiftly evaluating large amounts of patient information [14, 15]. Although AI has proven to be faster than humans at many constantly evolving cognitive activities, some physicians are still wary of deploying it in healthcare, especially in positions that

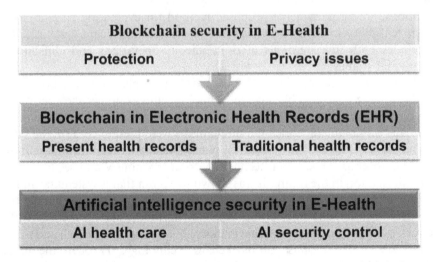

Figure 1.1. Blockchain and AI technology in e-Health. Reprinted by permission from Springer Nature Customer Service Centre GmbH: (Springer Nature) (Environmental Science and Pollution Research) [136], copyright (2021).

may have an impact on a patient's wellbeing. The auto sector has already shown that it can use AI to develop self-driving cars. Other organizations, on the other hand, have already identified methods to use machine learning (ML) to detect fraud or financial risks. Only a few aspects of AI's maturity can be shown.

1.2 Blockchain in e-Health

Hash links between blocks, a mechanism vulnerable to replicating state machines, are used to ensure integrity as well as immutability within a blockchain's transaction log. The distributed electronic money known as Bitcoin brought the blockchain idea to the world [16–21]. Implementing a blockchain that is independent of a third party to perform safe and trustworthy transactions over an untrustworthy network has been made feasible thanks to the success of Bitcoin. According to a number of sources, the blockchain's fundamental building components have been extensively covered. Blockchain can be considered as a collection of transactions, each block comprising an array of transactions with all of their details accurate and up to date [22]. A linkage of blocks is created by connecting the blocks using a hash value. The first and last blocks are known as genesis blocks, since they are the only two blocks that precede them [23]. Many industries are using blockchain technology to store and safeguard their data, from financial markets to IoT and nutritional research. Blockchain technology has acquired significant popularity and advancement in the healthcare industry and brain studies. One day, it may be possible to combine and show all of a patient's real-time clinical data in the latest and most reliable healthcare setting in order to help with tailored, believable, and safe treatment.

A blockchain platform that focuses on concurrent processing and AI healthcare networks may be utilized to identify a patient's healthcare condition. Patients' overall health, diagnosis, and recovery systems, as well as relevant surgical interventions, are all part of the proposed method for evaluating patient care and diagnosis feasibility in both real-world and simulated healthcare systems [24, 25]. This includes both investigations of simultaneous operations and clinical choice computational studies.

For this reason, Singh and Kim (2018) created CHIE, a platform for sharing medical knowledge in 2018 that uses blockchain technology and examines the conditions for sending medical data, including personal information, and electronic medical records. Both on- and off-chain authentication mechanisms were used to confirm the system's safety and privacy [26, 27]. More medical practitioners and healthcare organizations may be able to utilize blockchain technology to anonymously and securely transfer medical information in the future. It was shown by Cryan that a systematic and novel blockchain architecture could preserve sensitive patient information, handle fundamental data security challenges, and create a hospital-wide blockchain software framework by employing a comparable manner [28]. Biological research and therapies have also shown the promise of blockchain technology. Through the practical application of blockchain technology, clinical trials may be able to record all clinical approvals, schedules, and procedures even before they begin. There are a number of advantages to keeping clinical trial data current, secure, or time-stamped in this manner [29, 30].

1.3 Blockchain healthcare use cases in e-Health

1.3.1 Supply chain transparency

Healthcare items must be authenticated in the same way as many other products, just as in many other industries. With the use of a blockchain-based system, customers can track the journey of their products from the manufacturing facility to their doorstep. False information concerning the hazards of illegally obtained prescription drugs is common. Because of the development in the usage of remote health monitoring, more and more immoral actors are interested in medical equipment. In the pharmaceutical supply chain, MediLedger is a well-known blockchain technology for verifying the legitimacy of medications and their expiration dates.

1.3.2 Smart contracts

This may be done repeatedly and then enforced to maintain track of the progress of research in its many stages, all with the use of smart contracts [31–34]. The phrase 'smart contract' describes programs that run on a blockchain in the true sense of the term. Patients in remote areas may utilize a blockchain-based healthcare continuous monitoring system to identify and cure cancerous cells. In modern hospitals and outpatient facilities, smart contracts and blockchains may be widely used to safeguard the authenticity and security of patient data [35–38]. There has been some discussion about Dermonet, a blockchain-based online dermatological counseling system with remote monitoring capabilities to assist patients with dermatology, in a different study.

A blockchain-based network dubbed 'Proactive Aging,' on the other hand, tries to encourage older people to stay active and engaged in their community [33, 39–42]. For instance, the usage of blockchain technology may be advantageous for aging (like chronic illnesses) and cancer treatment (such as surgery). DNA information stored on blockchains may also be useful for pharma businesses, drug makers, and biomedical researchers to do sophisticated global genomic analysis.

Blockchain technology must be utilized by smart contracts in order to accelerate and enhance the effectiveness of data transfers. Nick Szabo was the first to introduce this idea back in 1994. Following the definition of 'smart contracts,' computers may transmit a contract's terms utilizing them. Contracts may be created in code, eliminating the requirement for parties to collaborate in groups [43].

Each smart contract on the blockchain has a unique identification. It is possible to easily create a smart contract for trading with the blockchain address. Depending upon the transaction data, each node in a network carries out this process manually [44].

1.3.3 Patient-centric electronic health records

Medical health data is increasingly being accessed digitally by physicians, clinics, and medical products because it facilitates better and faster decision-making and enables more access to the data for both patients and healthcare professionals. Electronic medical records are one of the most widely used applications of blockchain technology in medicine [45]. Due to personal circumstances that prohibit them from obtaining the data of one source through another, individuals are left with fractured records that are difficult to collect; as a consequence, they no longer have access to earlier data. In order to handle electronic health records (EHRs) in a novel way that allows patients to exchange both their present and historical health information, many scholars have advocated using blockchain application verification [46]. A 'MedRec' model makes use of unique blockchain characteristics to handle security, honesty, and quick data interchange. As an outcome, patients can access all of their medical records from various practitioners and healthcare facilities, and the system works on a decentralized basis to manage data and claims. Medical records would be lost if 'MedRec' were to be used. On a blockchain, a record label is stored, and it is sent to the patient who is responsible for where the form goes [47].

Due to issues such as lack of control, provenance, and monitoring of medical data during EHR adoption, the transfer or exchange of medical information also presents significant risks. These constraints guided the development of MeD Share, an encrypted blockchain architecture for sending medical data between unknown organizations [48, 49]. MeD Share is an excellent option if you're seeking for a solution to safely transfer medical data and store electronic medical records in the cloud while reducing the danger of privacy breaches. Patients' sensitive and vital medical information is transmitted between physicians, neurosurgeons, healthcare providers, doctors, scientists, and other healthcare professionals through EHRs [50–54].

It seems that most of the physicians at the hospital are already aware of the problem when a patient initially arrives. Drug mistakes, hypersensitivity, and medical solutions may be accepted on the blockchain without the requirement for complex kinds of compromise in pharmaceuticals [55–59]. There are several ways in which using a distributed ledger technology (DLT) like blockchain might enhance access to treatment and monitoring of medical data.

1.3.4 Medical staff credential verification

It is possible to monitor medical personnel's experience using cryptographic technologies in the same manner that a medical item's origin may be traced. Medical institutions and healthcare organizations may help healthcare enterprises speed up the credentialing process by documenting the credentials of their employees [56]. R3 Corda is a blockchain-based credential verification system for medical professionals created by ProCredEx, an American startup [57].

1.3.5 Key benefits of the blockchain system

The following are the key benefits of the blockchain system:

(a) During the employment process, healthcare organizations are going to be able to obtain certifications more quickly.

(b) The data they already have on previous and present employees can be used to their advantage by healthcare organizations and medical facilities.

(c) By sharing the experiences of medical professionals in developing virtual healthcare models, partners, such as businesses that subcontract locum tenens, gain trust and transparency.

There may be dangers to patients' wellbeing if this highly sensitive patient information is collected and distributed to various organizations, it could pose major threats to the patient's health and create a current picture of the patient. A long history of treatment, compliance, and recovery may make these hazards more prominent among chronically ill persons (e.g., patients with leukemia and HIV). Because of this, medical professionals must stay up to date on their education [58, 59]. Using blockchain technology, In 2016, Estonia became the first country in the world to securely store millions of health records and make them available to doctors and insurance providers all over the world. Blockchain technology in medicine is gaining traction globally because it gives patients an express promise that they may utilize the technology to generate their own records. When using a blockchain, any attempt to gain access to or alter data is immediately recorded. Because it discloses any unlawful conduct, such as large-scale fraud or record manipulation, this is critical to the safety of the patients involved [37, 60, 61].

1.3.6 IoT security for remote monitoring

The adoption of remote monitoring systems, which employ a variety of sensors to collect data on patients' vital signs and give clinicians a full picture of their patient's health, has witnessed some of the most significant breakthroughs in digital health.

Because of this, security is a major issue in health IoT, both in terms of preserving patient privacy and preventing data manipulation. Even when a connected device may be depended on to warn a caregiver of an old person who has fallen or had a heart attack, the supporting systems must still have high levels of resiliency against distributed denial of service (DDoS) and additional attacks halting service [62].

IoT devices could be monitored in the field more securely by using blockchain technology:

- The blockchain's distinct hash algorithm ensures that only authorized parties can access personal data. (Any modification to the source data will result in a different hash function; to decipher the hash function into the initial data, a user needs a certain set of cryptographic keys.)
- Since access to every copy of the patient data that has been stored (through a hash function) is required, tampering with the blockchain ledger is practically impossible.

1.3.7 Tracking clinical trials and pharmaceuticals

1. In the medical field, clinical trials are used to find and prevent illness. Preventing and diagnosing illness is now easier than ever before. Several issues with these systems may be resolved using blockchain technology. Data integrity and record-sharing, as well as data privacy and patient registration, are all part of this framework of standards [54]. There are a number of clinical healthcare systems that take privacy and confidentiality seriously. There is a token-based healthcare currency that tracks information about hospital staff, physicians, health plans, or insurance firms, as well as other items. Clinical healthcare data can be shared thanks to the blockchain-based smart health system FHIRChain [37].

2. Additionally, a blockchain-based record-sharing network called Connecting Care is now available in numerous British locations. In a diversified health-care industry, Connecting Care is utilized to protect hospitals and various other medical record data [63]. It offers a list of authorized users, guarantee-ing that the clinical system is only accessible to those on the list. The blockchain's smart contract functionality is implemented using an Ethereum-based architecture. The healthcare system uses an enrollment method to enroll new patients. Medical records and personal information may be accessed by the government, as well as by the patient [64].

There is little doubt that the application of blockchain technology within clinical settings will create new research opportunities in the field of medicine [65]. However, accurate, secure, and scalable data collection, storage, and retrieval in precision medicine applications will open up new avenues for the early detection and treatment of diseases in patients [66]. A database might be employed in cognitive frameworks. Neurotechnologies are still at an experimental stage, but they might be used to process a digital brain on a blockchain. Only a small number of companies have publicly stated their support for blockchain technology.

1.4 Blockchain in the healthcare industry

After nine years of operation, Bitcoin transactions currently rely heavily on block-chain technology, which was introduced in 2009. Many individuals were interested in blockchain technology in 2016. This technology, which is used to regulate or transfer electronic health data, can handle several basic healthcare challenges, such as confidentiality, interoperability, common infrastructure, and international stand-ards. If new technology is not thoroughly reviewed, the National Health Information Technology manager's office will pay the system a lot of attention and cost money, and people's health and safety might be put in danger [67, 68].

One of the most rapidly expanding sectors in the world is the pharmaceutical one. Experimental and maybe viable medicines can be brought to market with the support of this key player in patient outcomes. It assures the general public's safety and efficacy while using prescription devices and medication [69, 70]. As a result, patients' recuperation times are shortened during the diagnosis and processing of sterile medication. Pharma businesses sometimes have problems keeping an eye on their products rapidly to avoid counterfeit items from interfering with manufacturing or entering the supply chain. For this reason, even developed countries have become susceptible to counterfeit production and distribution [71].

To test, monitor, and verify the manufacturing processes of prospective drugs during the development of these therapies, blockchain may be a great option. Even in the short term, a digital drug control system (DDCS) may be an option. To research and evaluate experimental drugs, pharmaceutical companies have worked together on a blockchain-based DDCS experimental project.

The blockchain's capacity to securely and irrevocably record online financial transactions is among its most significant features. Transactions are digitally authenticated by all parties involved to verify their legitimacy and security on the blockchain. Consensus is the driving force behind the distributed ledger (smart contracts) [72]. To add a transaction to the chain, both parties must agree on the ledger to place it in a block and verify the block. Data and information may be found in each block. And since it is safeguarded by cryptographic techniques, that chain can never again be tampered with [16]. Because of the multiple copies of data stored on separate servers, no one can alter the transaction data on the blockchain. Cybercriminals have easy access to data kept on centralized servers. On the other hand, the decentralized nature of the blockchain ensures data protection and privacy. In recent years, the value of the blockchain technology has significantly increased [73]. All other record-keeping methods pale into comparison to blockchain's level of reliability and security. Every node in a distributed ledger has access to the same data. It is also used to increase speed and effectiveness by employing blockchain technology to automate the antiquated process. Since it does not require third-party transactions, it also saves money.

1.4.1 Immutability

Time stamping, linking, and retrieving earlier records form the foundation of the blockchain's data structure. The blockchain can be used to store any type of record because of its decentralized nature, including information on the supply chain, finances, and medical records.

1.4.2 Decentralized consensus

A blockchain's decentralization is its main strength. The immutability and encryption provided by the blockchain make it vulnerable to tampering [74]. A decentralized agreement is required for implementation. When one corporation or group controls all networks, this organization will transform the blockchain. A transaction may be approved by any number of nodes on the blockchain [75]. Due to the many parties participating and their different interests, it is far more difficult to damage the integrity of the blockchain because of the decentralized consensus process. Given that more than half of the nodes are very unlikely to agree to compromise the blockchain data in this way, the best approach is to have numerous companies each operating a few nodes.

1.4.3 Baked-in incentives

In order for the network to function properly, each network member must perform certain duties, such as storing information and verifying transactions. Distributed ledger system nodes are rewarded for their work in ensuring safe, decentralized, distributed information storage that is immune to tampering [76]. In a blockchain-based trustless system, a group of non-rusting people can cooperate and do commerce without the need for third-party approval, where hierarchical records management of processing transactions is replaced by a network of open networks.

Data from peers is duplicated, shared, and synced throughout the network using any consensus process. In order for transactions to be carried out over a vast number of computers situated in various regions, the digital currency relies on protocols [77]. Since 2000, the term 'blockchain e-Health' has been used to characterize the application of information and communication technologies (ICTs) within the healthcare industry (ICT).

Medical informatics, patient care, health practitioners, health employees, medicine, and other areas related to clinical insurance and medical information may all benefit from the use of the Internet and related technologies. Knowledge or data may be easily accessed by patients using mobile devices and software applications [78].

1.4.4 Securing e-Health system and efficient data

Consistent access control, authentication, and data immutability are necessary to assure the safety, privacy, and reliability of all wearable sensor findings and allow for a comprehensive patient treatment record. Role-based permissions are required for the upload and processing of medical records since they include highly sensitive and private information. Auditing methods may record and document requests and data access [73, 79]. Private/public networks may be established with ease thanks to a secure data access control mechanism provided by the blockchain. Numerous research has recently been conducted on blockchain technology, intending to create a decentralized, secure network for exchanging data. It is possible to utilize the Healthcare Data Gateway (HDG) with a private blockchain to reward clients to keep track of their medical records.

Scientists believe that the blockchain is a great place to store and verify medical records. Nevertheless, the use of blockchain data information is a natural byproduct of this new technology. Therefore, blockchain's promise as a catalyst for trustworthy healthcare networks has garnered so little attention. Data management was handled through digital currency and blockchain, not via the use of the blockchain itself. A blockchain-based decentralized user authentication method was employed for user authentication. FHIRChain is an example of a healthcare use case that does not put the necessary clinical data on the blockchain. Blockchain development has been hindered by issues with scalability, interoperability, and a scarcity of blockchain developers. In addition, it has been hindered by poor standards and excessive energy usage. Furthermore, there is a lack of clarity in the statutes. A safe blockchain-based EHR system must address these issues and challenges. Table 1.1 shows challenges and EHR solutions based on blockchain.

Table 1.1. Blockchain adoption challenges and the most important goals for building safe blockchain-based EHR solutions. Reprinted by permission from Springer Nature Customer Service Centre GmbH: (Springer Nature) (Environmental Science and Pollution Research) [136], copyright (2021).

Challenges	Bugs in the security system	Core priorities in deploying secure blockchain
Security	1. Harmful software may take advantage of security holes in the built-in blockchain to develop its decentralized apps. 2. To assist in data theft and identity theft, among other crimes, these malicious assaults exploit security holes in smart contract implementations.	Concerning the following, there are three requirements: 1. To ensure data security, only those with a legitimate need to see it are allowed access. 2. To protect the data's integrity, it must not be interfered with while in transit. 3. Legal users have never unjustly been denied access to information or services.
Privacy	1. There is a major difficulty in preserving patient data privacy when using a blockchain-based EHR that uses cryptographic technologies. 2. A patient's current account numbers can no longer be used to identify them. Patient data security issues should be addressed in any system of this kind. 3. Since installing blockchain-based frameworks inside EHR involves a significant amount of computational resources and takes a long time to perform each activity effectively, patients should first be able to easily exchange their data. 4. Before a new patient is introduced to the blockchain network as a new node, it is also required to do background checks on them to verify their reliability.	To ensure patient privacy on the public blockchain, the following conditions must be met: 1. Transaction links should not be visible or accessible in any way. 2. The specifics of a transaction should only be accessible to the persons involved. The security of patient data may be ensured by implementing an access control policy in a healthcare blockchain application, whether it be private or consortium. 3. When it comes to safeguarding transactions in a shared blockchain environment, it is a 'double-edged sword'. A well-behaved patient is very concerned about maintaining patient confidentiality. 4. Privacy protection systems, however, may be exploited by an opposing party to carry out an unlawful transaction. The security of public blockchains in smart healthcare may be limited to ensure the authority's legal traceability and responsibility. 5. Researchers should explore ways to keep tabs on a specific user and compile all of their communications while protecting the privacy of the person's crucial information.

	6. Enhancing confidentiality in a blockchain with false assumptions and low processing costs is one potential research area. 7. Untrusted third parties might be allowed to do computations on patient data using a secure multiparty computing technique.
Scalability	While medical data is increasing, researchers are looking at the scalability of blockchain in healthcare apps. 1. Another issue with IoMT devices is the lack of scalability and the increased use of computing resources. 2. An increase in overall processing needs may be a consequence of this difficulty. 3. There are many smart gadgets and sensors, but their computational power is much less than that of a normal computer. This makes the issue even more difficult. 4. IoT devices on the computationally intensive blockchain network generate data delays and significant processing power. 5. As a result, they may be unable to run both their original software and the blockchain-enabled capabilities that these devices are capable of, resulting in subpar or even exorbitant performance.
Anonymity	For public ledgers like the Bitcoin blockchain and Ethereum, all transactions must be made available by default to be useful. 1. A pseudo-anonymity feature of the Ethereum network is the use of public keys obtained from private keys, rather than usernames or passwords, for transactions. 2. With zk-SNARKS, or Ethereum, you may check the validity of a transaction without revealing any of the details of the transaction itself or connecting with the person who aired it. 3. To keep transactions private, zk-SNARKs employ the consensus protocol of a blockchain to validate them. 4. Once the public Ethereum blockchain is enabled, business transactions may be conducted in perfect secrecy on the same network as your competitors.

(Continued)

Table 1.1. (*Continued*)

Challenges	Bugs in the security system	Core priorities in deploying secure blockchain
Latency	1. The process of reaching consensus and validating transactions may be challenging when integrating blockchains with healthcare systems that demand immediate responses to data and occurrences. The length of time required for a blockchain to complete a transaction is known as transaction latency. 2. Each transaction on the **Bitcoin** blockchain, for example, is confirmed after a ten-minute wait. It is advised that each transaction be verified within one hour of the transaction being made, even though it may take five or six blocks to be added to the chain. Traditional database systems, on the other hand, require only a few seconds to confirm a transaction.	1. Lower latency has been achieved by connecting blockchain-based IoT devices, but the same ideas might be used for other applications based on blockchain as well. 2. A network with delay is required due to the vast number of devices linked to the IoT network at any given time. 3. Each block's transaction is confirmed using the consensus technique, considerably reducing latency and thereby impacting the overall speed of the program.

1.5 Artificial intelligence in e-Health

Additionally, any computer system that is capable of doing a job on its own is said to have AI. These computers use enormous amounts of data, a wide variety of algorithms, and decision-making abilities to respond to questions [80]. For the vast majority of people, technology is an essential part of daily life. It is easy to see how far health research and wearable technology have come together in the previous few years. The first sector where AI may improve people's lives is still expected to be healthcare, even while other businesses have made great progress.

Neurobiology of aging has released research suggesting that AI may be able to identify Alzheimer's disease indications early on in brain scans, even before clinicians. AI is presently being used to compare images of healthy and Alzheimer's patients' brains. An IBM news release claims that the company's Watson supercomputer was able to appropriately identify a 60-year-old lady with a rare type of leukemia [81]. Watson was able to provide her with a wide range of treatment alternatives as a consequence of this. Using Watson's insights, oncologists may make better treatment choices. Medical Sieve, a tool for cardiologists and radiologists, was also created [82].

1.6 Features of artificial intelligence in e-Health

As seen in figure 1.2, in addition to the healthcare industry, AI can advance many other industries. Health organizations should investigate whether or not any or all of these may be included in their AI journeys. These are the sectors in healthcare where AI is gaining popularity [83].

1.6.1 Virtual advisor for personal health

The utilization of personal digital assistants has increased in the United States, particularly among people who use smartphones. AI-powered assistants like Cortana and Siri have been created with well-designed systems. These structures have the potential to be very valuable in the field of healthcare. Drug warnings, patient educational material, and human-like experiences may be used to gauge a patient's emotional state at any given time [84]. By acting in the capacity of an executive secretary, AI can significantly improve the way patients are treated when their doctors or other medical professionals cannot attend to them in person.

1.6.2 Advanced data analysis and screening

AI's abilities go well beyond interpreting human commands and determining what type of response is appropriate. The application of AI for cancer, genomics, as well as precision medicine has enabled the detection of abnormalities in x-rays as well as magnetic resonance imaging (MRI) scans, as well as the development of highly customized treatments for specific individuals.

In the IBM Watson example, the AI has successfully expanded its capacity to interpret both structured and unstructured patient data. IBM Watson's role in oncology would be to offer patients with drug proof of recommendations.

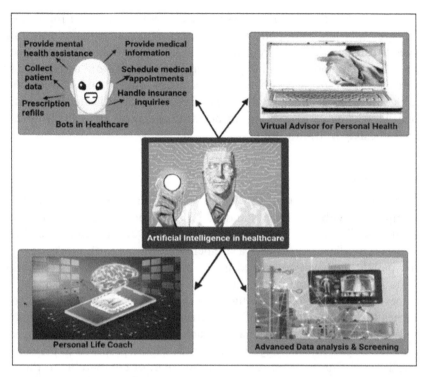

Figure 1.2. Features of artificial security in e-Health. Reprinted by permission from Springer Nature Customer Service Centre GmbH: (Springer Nature) (Environmental Science and Pollution Research) [136], copyright (2021).

1.6.3 Personal life coach

Patients with long-term diseases know how important it is for their doctors to stay in touch with them outside of the appointment room. Numerous clinics feature life-coaching programs as part of their overall offering [85]. In addition, reimbursements are decreasing, making it harder to keep up with the rising expenses of these services. But with today's powerful AI and smartphone applications, patients will have access to feedback on a variety of data elements they have collected on their phones or other connected electronic devices. AI may be used as a personal life coach, whether it is helping people keep to their medicine regimens or just providing a nice voice that urges them toward a healthy lifestyle and feedback to their physicians [86].

1.6.4 Bots in healthcare

Bots, which are AI software that patients may interact with through a chat session on a website or a mobile device to seek assistance with their needs, are expected to be accessible soon as part of healthcare institutions' services [87].

The reciprocity or openness of treatment that should take place in the partnership between healthcare professionals and their patients (whether it be a discussion or psychotherapy) is lacking in a second application of AI in mental health chatbots [88].

For example, a patient's doctor may utilize a bot to organize follow-up visits online. There are several questions about whether or not a customer's treatment or billing needs can be addressed by a bot. Care for patients is enhanced, operating costs are minimized, and essential applications like planning and accounting as well as various therapies are accessible 24 hours a day and 7 days a week. For the foreseeable future, AI is anticipated to play a key role in healthcare. For this reason, and since AI is capable of making an accurate diagnosis, it is likely to be used carefully and safely in healthcare [89].

1.6.5 Security and privacy

All patient health data is protected by federal legislation. The use of AI in healthcare needs compliance with the same standards that govern current applications and infrastructure facilities, which necessitates the use of AI in healthcare. Most AI systems are centralized and need a tremendous amount of processing power, therefore, patient data will be housed in the provider's data centers or sections of them. Data loss and damage may occur if the system was compromised.

Machines aren't always correct, and they may make errors, according to some critics of healthcare AI. However, if these errors are not remedied, they may have fatal repercussions, and AI will ultimately reach a position where it can be trusted to safeguard and prepare for therapy. The platform will be prepared to play an active part in healthcare if its error margins are lower than or comparable to those of its human equivalents. The development of AI is accelerating. It will be so strong and self-aware that it will be able to put its interests ahead of those of humans, according to Stephen Hawking, Bill Gates, and Elon Musk. However, robotics may be a danger to healthcare before it becomes a threat to healthcare itself. Healthcare AI may be used by doctors to uncover novel treatment options, spot cancer early, and improve communication with patients, among other things [90].

1.6.6 AI-based various tools used in healthcare

ML is an investigation of computer algorithms used to derive information from massive volumes of data and is an aspect of AI. For example, these technologies can analyze complicated data structures to build, customized for better individual health outcomes, a prediction model that enhances diagnosis, prognosis, monitoring, and treatment delivery. It's been a long time since we first saw clinical prediction models [91].

Computer algorithms may be used to learn from data, detect patterns, and predict future occurrences in the subject of AI [52, 92, 93]. Complex data structures may be examined to build a prediction model that is tailored and improves diagnosis, prediction, monitoring, and treatment administration for better individual health outcomes, which is one of the most exciting elements of these technologies. It has been a long time since clinical decision-making estimation techniques were first developed.

1.6.7 Framingham risk score

The Framingham risk score is used to determine a person's cardiovascular disease risk. These rating schemes are accessible online. In general, between 10 and 30 years from now, cardiovascular risk score approaches will assess a person's lifetime risk of developing cardiovascular disease [94–98]. They may help identify those most in need of cardiovascular disease prevention, based on their likelihood of contracting the condition. Based on cardiovascular risk ratings, preventive medication for blood pressure as well as cholesterol-lowering therapy can be given. High blood pressure (130/85) is the primary factor in nearly 30% of cases of coronary heart disease in both men and women, demonstrating the need of maintaining and controlling blood pressure for cardiovascular health.

1.6.8 MELD score

Systemic shuffling, the MELD model, can be used to determine a patient's odds of surviving surgery to implant an intrahepatic portosystemic shunt. MELD was initially approved by the United Network for Organ Sharing (UNOS) in 2002 because of its precision in predicting patients with cirrhosis' short-term survival [99–102]. In several patient groups with advanced liver disease, the MELD has now been demonstrated to be a reliable predictor of survival based solely on objective data. Since its introduction, it has become customary to utilize the MELD score to choose which organs to transplant: MELD scores are a stronger indicator of survival in cirrhotic patients with infections, severe liver failure, hemorrhage, and alcohol-induced hepatitis. The MELD score can be used to determine the best course of treatment and to pinpoint patients who require surgery besides liver transplantation for hepatocellular carcinoma. The MELD score can only accurately predict longevity in 15%–20% of patients, despite its many benefits. The ability of the model to forecast renal as well as liver function.

1.6.9 Nottingham prognostic index

Patients may utilize the Nottingham prognostic index (NPI) to determine their breast cancer risk at their treatment facility. The NPI approach (TNM stages I, II, and III) has three or more prognostic categories for patients with early-stage and locally advanced breast cancer. Because of its importance in clinical practice and research, NPI has been overtaken by more complex models. NPI and other prognostic models play a vital part in the clinical choice that patients and professionals must make for adjuvant chemotherapy following surgery [103–105]. In light of prior cohort studies, the NPI may be able to provide prognostic information to patients. Economic assessments and projections for individual patients are considerably aided by the NPI. In the economic evaluation of innovative medications, it is possible to estimate the additional costs and benefits of additional assessment and treatment options by using the overall survival rate as a crucial input for decision-analytic models [106–110]. Decision-analytic models serve an important role in appraising new technologies when clinical trials are neither feasible nor timely [111, 112].

1.7 Applications of AI in healthcare

In the early phases of an issue, AI allows for more accuracy. Because of AI, drug development and chemical selection are now both fully automated processes. Using AI and Keras, Peptone predicts protein quality and properties, enabling professionals to ease protein design, find production and depiction challenges, and reveal novel protein features [113, 114].

Computer models based on diverse biological and medical data are often employed in clinical studies. Using these models, doctors may determine which individuals are most likely to have various responses to medications, enabling them to mass-deliver individualized medication and therapy to everyone who needs it. In the field of pharmaceutical research, AI is also gaining ground. Helix, an AI engine that answers spoken questions and demands, may assist researchers in boosting lab security, increasing productivity, staying informed about important research issues, and managing inventory.

1.7.1 Radiology

Radiologists employ CT and MRI scans to conduct AI research to improve patient diagnosis and care. Based on the Radiography Community of North America (RCNA), the application of AI in radiology has rapidly increased in recent years. AI imaging has been successful in identifying and monitoring the progression of cancer abnormalities [108–111].

Radiology specialists must meticulously maintain scanners in between patients. Chest x-rays may be a better option in this situation because they can be cleaned more easily than other types of imaging. COVID-19 diagnosis has shown contradictory findings. Contrary to popular belief in other nations, x-rays are routinely used across the country for diagnostic purposes [80, 112–115].

1.7.2 Screening

When talking about anti-aging or anti-wrinkle procedures, one may bring up maxillofacial surgery or cleft palate repair (AI).

Research published in *Annals of Oncology* in 2018 suggests that an AI device (using a deep learning (DL) convolution neural network) may be able to detect skin cancer more correctly than the physician. Human dermatologists found 86.6% of skin malignancies, compared to 95% found by the CNN unit. To design an AI breast cancer screening device that surpassed doctors, researchers turned to Google Deep Mind [116, 117].

1.7.3 In psychology

To assess the efficacy of AI implementations, chatbots that replicate human behavior are being used to treat mental health issues such as depression and anxiety.

Different apps may be developed and used by commercial businesses to identify suicidal inclinations [118].

1.7.4 Principal care

Primary care has been a major growth area for AI technologies. Decision-making, statistical modeling, as well as market analysis have all been facilitated by the use of AI in primary care [119]. The perspective of healthcare professionals is quite constrained when it comes to the application of AI in primary care, focusing largely on organizational and reporting duties.

1.7.5 Diagnosis of illness

ML, logistic regression, and help vector machines are just a few instances of how AI has been applied to treat various diseases [120]. To guarantee that classifications are as accurate as possible, each of these approaches has a 'training objective.' There are two methods in which artificial neural networks (ANNs), as well as Bayesian networks (BNs), might be utilized to identify and categorize certain illnesses. There has been evidence that ANN is more intelligent and can accurately identify both diabetes and heart disease.

1.7.6 Telemedicine

The emergence of potential AI applications and the development of telemedicine, or doctor virtual diagnosis, are related developments. If their details are tracked by detectors, AI might enable them to care for patients from a distance. A wearable interface may allow for continuous monitoring and the capacity to spot changes that might not be immediately noticeable to the naked eye. Algorithms of AI may be used to connect the data and alert clinicians if any issues need to be brought to attention. When it comes to mental healthcare, some researchers believe patients and healthcare professionals should have more control over the therapy they get, which is why they're turning to chatbots for assistance (be it a conversation or psycho-therapist) [121, 122].

AI may be able to help with senior care when the population's average age grows due to better health. A caregiver may be alerted if an unusual activity or a computed vital is aberrant at any time throughout the technology's usefulness; nonetheless, there are still debates concerning monitoring's shortcomings [122]. Lei Xing and colleagues examined the present trends in medical AI research and development, as well as the consequences for healthcare in the future. All of the speakers from the medical community at the conference believed that AI has the potential to revolutionize the industry in many significant ways [123].

AI-based nanomedicine design has already been shown by many scientists to increase therapeutic efficacy by optimizing material properties based on forecasted interactions with the target drug, other biological fluids, and the immune system and vascular systems as well as with the cell membrane.

1.8 AI in drug discovery

AI may be utilized in a variety of ways in the pharmaceutical sector, including medicine creation, chemical manufacture, and drug screening, to name a few. AI can differentiate between hits and leads to analyze therapeutic targets and optimize structural design more quickly. However, despite its multiple advantages, AI has significant data concerns, such as the volume of data and its expansion, variety, and ambiguity.

Drug development sets of data may include millions of compounds that traditional ML algorithms cannot process. Quantitative structure–activity relationships (QSARs) can be used to swiftly predict large numbers of molecules or surface-level physicochemical characteristics like log P or log D [124–129]. These models, however, fall well short of accurately predicting the efficacy and negative effects of pharmaceutical treatments. QSAR-based models encounter many difficulties, including a lack of experimental validations, erroneous experimental data, and restricted training sets [54, 130–133]. To evaluate the efficacy and safety of pharmaceutical drugs, a variety of AI methods, including DL as well as its accompanying modeling studies, could be applied [134, 135]. To research the benefits of DL for the pharmaceutical sector, Merck held an ML competition in 2012. In a study of 15 medication candidates, DL models beat classical ML in predicting ADMET data [135–138].

To find potential pharmaceutical candidates, these methods include linear discriminant analysis (LDA), random forests (RFs), and decision trees. QSAR research may now be accelerated using AI-based approaches [139–141].

1.9 Conclusion

Patient medical information will be available to healthcare providers through the blockchain, and massive volumes of data, a variety of algorithms, and decision-making abilities are all used in AI [83, 142, 143]. The healthcare system will become more efficient, more accessible, and more inexpensive as a result of embracing the most recent advancements in these technologies. AI relies on encrypted records stored via blockchain [81, 144].

References

[1] Alotaibi Y K and Federico F 2017 The impact of health information technology on patient safety *Saudi Med. J.* **38** 1173

[2] Conway M, Hu M and Chapman W W 2019 Recent advances in using natural language processing to address public health research questions using social media and consumer-generated data *Yearb. Med. Inform.* **28** 208–17

[3] Campanella P, Lovato E, Marone C, Fallacara L, Mancuso A, Ricciardi W and Specchia M L 2016 The impact of electronic health records on healthcare quality: a systematic review and meta-analysis *Eur. J. Public Health* **26** 60–4

[4] Fotiadis D I, Liang J, Penders J, Pattichis C, Wang M D, Tourassi G and Xu W 2018 *Biomed. Health Inform.* Biomedical and Health Informatics and the Body Sensor Networks Conferences , Nevada, USA, 2018

[5] Nugent T, Upton D and Cimpoesu M 2016 Improving data transparency in clinical trials using blockchain smart contracts *F1000 Research* **5** 2541

[6] Lin C, He D, Huang X, Khan M K and Choo K K R 2020 DCAP: A secure and efficient decentralized conditional anonymous payment system based on blockchain *IEEE Trans. Inf. Forensics Secur.* **15** 2440–52

[7] Ferreira A 2021 Regulating smart contracts: Legal revolution or simply evolution? *Telecommun. Policy* **45** 102081

[8] Cong L W and He Z 2019 Blockchain disruption and smart contracts *Rev. Financ. Stud.* **32** 1754–97

[9] Pathak A D, Saran D, Mishra S, Hitesh M, Bathula S and Sahu K K 2021 Smart war on COVID-19 and global pandemics: integrated AI and blockchain ecosystem *Computational Modeling and Data Analysis in COVID-19 Research* (Boca Raton, FL: CRC Press) 67–94 pp

[10] Bohr A and Memarzadeh K 2020 The rise of artificial intelligence in healthcare applications *Artificial Intelligence in Healthcare* (New York: Academic) pp 25–60

[11] Han C, Rundo L, Murao K, Nemoto T and Nakayama H 2020 Bridging the gap between AI and healthcare sides: towards developing clinically relevant AI-powered diagnosis systems *Artificial Intelligence Applications and Innovations: 16th IFIP WG 12.5 Int. Conf., AIAI 2020 (Neos Marmaras, Greece)* pp 320–33

[12] Ilinca D 2020 Applying blockchain and artificial intelligence to digital health *Digital Health Entrepreneurship* (Cham: Springer) pp 83–101

[13] Ahuja A S 2019 The impact of artificial intelligence in medicine on the future role of the physician *Peer J.* **7** e7702

[14] Khan Z F and Alotaibi S R 2020 Applications of artificial intelligence and big data analytics in m-health: a healthcare system perspective *J. Healthc. Eng.* **2020** 8894694

[15] Wahl B, Cossy-Gantner A, Germann S and Schwalbe N R 2018 Artificial intelligence (AI) and global health: how can AI contribute to health in resource-poor settings? *BMJ Global Health* **3** e000798

[16] Mannaro K, Pinna A and Marchesi M 2017 Crypto-trading: blockchain-oriented energy market *2017 AEIT Int. Annual Conf.* pp 1–5

[17] Casado-Vara R, Prieto J, De la Prieta F and Corchado J M 2018 How blockchain improves the supply chain: case study alimentary supply chain *Procedia Comput. Sci.* **134** 393–8

[18] Khan P W and Byun Y 2020 A blockchain-based secure image encryption scheme for the industrial *Internet Things Entropy* **22** 175

[19] Jennath H S, Anoop V S and Asharaf S 2020 Blockchain for healthcare: securing patient data and enabling trusted artificial intelligence *Int. J. Interact. Multimed. Art. Intell.* **6** 15–23

[20] Yue X, Wang H, Jin D, Li M and Jiang W 2016 Healthcare data gateways: found healthcare intelligence on blockchain with novel privacy risk control *J. Med. Syst.* **40** 1–8

[21] Bryatov S R and Borodinov A A 2019 Blockchain technology in the pharmaceutical supply chain: researching a business model based on hyperledger fabric *Proc. of the Int. Conf. on Information Technology and Nanotechnology (ITNT)* vol 10 *(Samara, Russia)* pp 1613–73

[22] Omar A I, Bhuiyan A, Basu M Z A, Kiyomoto A and Rahman M S 2019 Privacy-friendly platform for healthcare data in cloud based on blockchain environment *Future Gener. Comput. Syst.* **95** 511–21

[23] Kannan A *et al* 2016 Mitochondrial reprogramming regulates breast cancer progression mitochondria in breast cancer *Clin. Cancer Res.* **22** 3348–60

[24] Dubovitskaya A, Xu Z, Ryu S, Schumacher M and Wang F 2017 Blockchain dans la eSanté: perspectives et une application pour le traitement quotidien *Swiss Med. Inform.* doi 10.4414/smi.33.00400

[25] Hylock R H and Zeng X 2019 A blockchain framework for patient-centered health records and exchange (HealthChain): evaluation and proof-of-concept study *J. Med. Internet Res.* **21** e13592

[26] Singh M and Kim S 2018 Branch based blockchain technology in intelligent vehicle *Comput. Netw.* **145** 219–31

[27] Feng Q, He D, Zeadally S, Khan M K and Kumar N 2019 A survey on privacy protection in blockchain system *J. Netw. Comput. Appl.* **126** 45–58

[28] Cyran M A 2018 Blockchain as a foundation for sharing healthcare data *Blockchain Healthcare Today* **1** 13

[29] Linn L A and Koo M B 2016 Blockchain for health data and its potential use in health it and health care related research *ONC/NIST Use of Blockchain for Healthcare and Research Worksho (Gaithersburg, Maryland, United States) ONC/NIST* pp 1–10

[30] Siyal A A, Junejo A Z, Zawish M, Ahmed K, Khalil A and Soursou G 2019 Applications of blockchain technology in medicine and healthcare: challenges and future perspectives *Cryptography* **3** 3

[31] Khan P W, Byun Y C and Park N 2020 A data verification system for CCTV surveillance cameras using blockchain technology in smart cities *Electronics* **9** 484

[32] Magazzeni D, McBurney P and Nash W 2017 Validation and verification of smart contracts: a research agenda *Computer* **50** 50–7

[33] Scekic O, Nastic S and Dustdar S 2018 Blockchain-supported smart city platform for social value co-creation and exchange *IEEE Internet Comput.* **23** 19–28

[34] Schechtman D 2019 Introdução e Guia Prático a smart contracts (introduction and practical guide to smart contracts) Available at SSRN: https://ssrn.com/abstract=3317504

[35] Taherdoost H 2023 Smart contracts in blockchain technology: a critical review *Information* **14** 117

[36] Kangbai J B, Jame P B, Mandoh S, Fofanah A B, George A, Briama A and McBrayer J L 2018 Tracking Ebola through cellphone, Internet of Things and blockchain technology *Curr. Res Integr. Med.* **1** 13–5

[37] Zhang P, White J, Schmidt D C, Lenz G and Rosenbloom S T 2018 FHIRChain: applying blockchain to securely and scalably share clinical data *Comput. Struct. Biotechnol. J.* **16** 267–78

[38] Khezr S, Moniruzzaman M, Yassine A and Benlamri R 2019 Blockchain technology in healthcare: a comprehensive review and directions for future research *Appl. Sci.* **9** 1736

[39] Ahmad S S, Khan S and Kamal M A 2019 What is blockchain technology and its significance in the current healthcare system? A brief insight *Curr. Pharm. Des.* **25** 1502–408

[40] Badr S, Gomaa I and Abd-Elrahman E 2018 Multi-tier blockchain framework for IoT-EHRs systems *Procedia Comput. Sci.* **141** 159–66

[41] Combining AI and blockchain to push frontiers in healthcare http://macadamian.com/2018/03/16/combining-ai-andblockchain-in-healthcare/ (accessed 1 October 2022)

[42] Evans J G 1993 Hypothesis: Healthy Active Life Expectancy (HALE) as an index of effectiveness of health and social services for elderly people *Age Ageing* **22** 297–302

[43] Chinnasamy P, Albakri A, Khan M, Ambeth Raja A, Kiran A and Jyothi Chinna B 2023 Smart contract-enabled secure sharing of health data for a mobile cloud-based e-health system *Appl. Sci.* **13** 3970

[44] Khan S N, Loukil F and Ghedira-Guegan C *et al* 2021 Blockchain smart contracts: applications, challenges, and future trends *Peer-to-Peer Netw. Appl* **14** 2901–25

[45] Dubovitskaya A, Xu Z, Ryu S, Schumacher M and Wang F 2017 Secure and trustable electronic medical records sharing using blockchain *AMIA Annual Symp. Proc.* p 650

[46] Wang H and Song Y 2018 Secure cloud-based HER system using attribute-based cryptosystem and blockchain *J. Med. Syst.* **42** 152

[47] Azaria A, Ekblaw A, Vieira T and Lippman A 2016 Medrec: using blockchain for medical data access and permission management *2016 2nd Int. Conf. on Open and Big Data (OBD)* pp 25–30

[48] Xia Q I, Sifah E B, Asamoah K O, Gao J, Du X and Guizani M 2017 MeDShare: trust-less medical data sharing among cloud service providers via blockchain *IEEE Access* **5** 14757–67

[49] Mandl K D, Markwell D, MacDonald R, Szolovits P and Kohane I S 2001 Public standards and patients' control: how to keep electronic medical records accessible but private *Brit. Med. J.* **322** 283–7

[50] Burki T 2019 The dangers of the digital age *Lancet Digit. Health* **1** 61–2

[51] Funk E, Riddell J, Ankel F and Cabrera D 2018 Blockchain technology: a data framework to improve validity, trust, and accountability of information exchange in health professions education *Acad. Med.* **93** 1791–4

[52] VoPham T, Hart J E, Laden F and Chiang Y Y 2018 Emerging trends in geospatial artificial intelligence (geoAI): potential applications for environmental epidemiology *Environ. Health* **17** 1–6

[53] Battineni G, Chintalapudi N, Amenta F and Tayebati S K 2019 Report on market analysis and preventions need to provide medications for rural patients of Italy using ICT technologies *Int. J. Innov. Technol. Explor. Eng.* **9** 5286–9

[54] Li H and Han D 2019 EduRSS: a blockchain-based educational records secure storage and sharing scheme *IEEE Access* **7** 179273–89

[55] Chapuis C, Roustit M, Bal G, Schwebel C, Pansu P, David-Tchouda S and Bedouch P 2010 Automated drug dispensing system reduces medication errors in an intensive care setting *Crit. Care Med.* **38** 2275–81

[56] Hamilton E C, Balogh J, Nguyen D T, Graviss E A, HeczeyA A and Austin M T 2018 Liver transplantation for primary hepatic malignancies of childhood: the UNOS experience *J. Pediatr. Surg.* **53** 163–8

[57] Feingold E 1987 Medical care, medical costs: the search for a health insurance policy *J. Publ. Health Policy* **8** 587–90 (book review)

[58] Chan H S, Shan H, Dahoun T, Vogel H and Yuan S 2019 Advancing drug discovery via artificial intelligence *Trends Pharmacol. Sci.* **40** 592–604

[59] Mathotaarachchi S, Pascoal T A, Shin M, Benedet A L, Kang M S, Beaudry T and Alzheimer's Disease Neuroimaging Initiative 2017 Identifying incipient dementia individuals using machine learning and amyloid imaging *Neurobiol. Aging* **59** 80–90

[60] Hang L, Choi E and Kim D H 2019 A novel EMR integrity management based on a medical blockchain platform in hospital *Electronics* **8** 467

[61] Sahoo M S and Baruah P K 2018 Hbasechaindb—a scalable blockchain framework on hadoop ecosystem *Supercomputing Frontiers: 4th Asian Conf., SCFA 2018 Singapore, March 26–29, 2018, Proc.* vol 4 pp 18–29

[62] Dwivedi A D, Srivastava G, Dhar S and Singh R 2019 A decentralized privacy-preserving healthcare blockchain for IoT *Sensors* **19** 326

[63] Peng Q Y, Wang X T and Zhang L NChinese Critical Care Ultrasound Study Group (CCUSG) 2020 Findings of lung ultrasonography of novel corona virus pneumonia during the 2019–2020 epidemic *Intensive Care Med.* **46** 849–50

[64] Narayanaswami C, Nooyi R, Govindaswamy S R and Viswanathan R 2019 Blockchain anchored supply chain automation *IBM J. Res. Dev.* **63** 7:1–11

[65] Andoni M, Robu V, Flynn D, Abram S, Geach D, Jenkins D and Peacock A 2019 Blockchain technology in the energy sector: a systematic review of challenges and opportunities *Renew. Sustain. Energy Rev.* **100** 143–74

[66] Zehravi M, Kabir J, Akter R, Malik S, Ashraf G M, Tagde P and Cavalu S 2022 A prospective viewpoint on neurological diseases and their biomarkers *Molecules* **27** 3516

[67] Fan K, Ren Y, Wan Y, Li H and Yang Y 2018 Blockchain-based efficient privacy preserving and data sharing scheme of content-centric network in 5G *IET Commun.* **12** 527–32

[68] Chamola V, Hassija V, Gupta V and Guizani M 2020 A comprehensive review of the COVID-19 pandemic and the role of IoT, drones, AI, blockchain, and 5G in managing its impact *IEEE Access* **8** 90225–65

[69] Nakamoto N 2017 Centralised bitcoin: a secure and high performance electronic cash system Available at SSRN: https://ssrn.com/abstract=3065723

[70] Zhou L, Wang L and Sun Y 2018 MIStore: a blockchain-based medical insurance storage system *J. Med. Syst.* **42** 149

[71] Pereira J C, Caffarena E R and Dos Santos C N 2016 Boosting docking-based virtual screening with deep learning *J. Chem. Inf. Model.* **56** 2495–506

[72] Big pharma builds blockchain prototype to stop counterfeits https://supplychaindive.com/news/big-pharma-blockchain-MediLedger-DSCSA-FDA/505563/ (accessed 5 October 2022)

[73] Kumar R, Wang W, Kumar J, Yang T, Khan A, Ali W and Ali I 2021 An integration of blockchain and AI for secure data sharing and detection of CT images for the hospitals *Comput. Med. Imaging Graph.* **87** 101812

[74] Mamoshina P, Ojomoko L, Yanovich Y, Ostrovski A, Botezatu A, Prikhodko P and Zhavoronkov A 2018 Converging blockchain and next-generation artificial intelligence technologies to decentralize and accelerate biomedical research and healthcare *Oncotarget* **9** 5665

[75] Lopes A R, Dias A S and Sá-Moura B 2023 Application of technology in healthcare: tackling COVID-19 challenge—the integration of blockchain and Internet of Things *Research Anthology on Convergence of Blockchain, Internet of Things, and Security* pp 108–31

[76] Pires D E, Blundell T L and Ascher D B 2015 pkCSM: predicting small-molecule pharmacokinetic and toxicity properties using graph-based signatures *J. Med. Chem.* **58** 4066–72

[77] Galvin R, Geraghty C, Motterlini N, Dimitrov B D and Fahey T 2011 Prognostic value of the ABCD2 clinical prediction rule: a systematic review and meta-analysis *Fam. Pract.* **28** 366–76

[78] De Filippi P and Mauro R 2014 Ethereum: the decentralised platform that might displace today's institutions *Internet Policy Rev.* **25**

[79] Tran V T, Riveros C and Ravaud P 2019 Patients' views of wearable devices and AI in healthcare: findings from the ComPaRe e-cohort *NPJ Digit. Med.* **2** 53

[80] Zou F W, Tang Y F, Liu C Y, Ma J A and Hu C H 2020 Concordance study between IBM Watson for oncology and real clinical practice for cervical cancer patients in China: a retrospective analysis *Front. Genet.* **11** 200

[81] Bragazzi N L, Dai H, Damiani G, Behzadifar M, Martini M and Wu J 2020 How big data and artificial intelligence can help better manage the COVID-19 pandemic *Int. J. Environ. Res. Public Health* **17** 3176

[82] Bai Q, Tan S, Xu T, Liu H, Huang J and Yao X 2021 MolAICal: a soft tool for 3D drug design of protein targets by artificial intelligence and classical algorithm *Briefings Bioinform.* **22** 161

[83] Jiang F, Jiang Y, Zhi H, Dong Y, Li H, Ma S and Wang Y 2017 Artificial intelligence in healthcare: past, present and future *Stroke Vasc. Neurol.* **2** 230–43

[84] Rallapalli S and Minalkar A 2016 Improving healthcare—big data analytics for *J. Adv. Inform. Technol.* **7** 65–8

[85] Timón S, Rincón M and Martínez-Tomás R 2017 Extending xnat platform with an incremental semantic framework *Front. Neuroinform.* **11** 57

[86] Lucas G M, Gratch J, King A and Morency L P 2014 It's only a computer: virtual humans increase willingness to disclose *Comput. Hum. Behav.* **37** 94–100

[87] Sapci A H and Sapci H A 2019 Innovative assisted living tools, remote monitoring technologies, artificial intelligence-driven solutions, and robotic systems for aging societies: systematic review *JMIR Aging* **2** 15429

[88] Adiwardana D *et al* 2020 Towards a human-like open-domain chatbot arXiv preprint arXiv:2001.09977

[89] Grosdidier A, Zoete V and Michielin O 2011 SwissDock, a protein-small molecule docking web service based on EADock DSS *Nucleic Acids Res.* **39** W270–7

[90] Casado-Vara R, Prieto-Castrillo F and Corchado J M 2018 A game theory approach for cooperative control to improve data quality and false data detection in WSN *Int. J. Robust Nonlinear Control* **28** 5087–102

[91] Prosser M 2020 How AI helped predict the coronavirus outbreak before it happened *Singularity Hub* February 5, 2020 https://singularityhub.com/2020/02/05/how-ai-helped-predict-the-coronavirus-outbreak-before-it-happened/#:~:text=BlueDot%20uses%20natural%20language%20processing,help%20predict%20virus%20outbreak%20patterns

[92] Adir O, Poley M, Chen G, Froim S, Krinsky N, Shklover J, Shainsky-Roitman J, Lammers T and Schroeder A 2020 Integrating artificial intelligence and nanotechnology for precision cancer medicine *Adv. Mater.* **32** 1901989

[93] Ciallella H L and Zhu H 2019 Advancing computational toxicology in the big data era by artificial intelligence: data-driven and mechanism-driven modeling for chemical toxicity *Chem. Res. Toxicol.* **32** 536–47

[94] Damen J A, Pajouheshnia R, Heus P, Moons K G, Reitsma J B, Scholten R J and Debray T 2019 Performance of the Framingham risk models and pooled cohort equations for predicting

10-year risk of cardiovascular disease: a systematic review and meta-analysis *BMC Med.* **17** 1–16

[95] Nakhaie M R, Koor B E, Salehi S O and Karimpour F 2018 Prediction of cardiovascular disease risk using framingham risk score among office workers, Iran, 2017 *Saudi J. Kidney Dis. Transpl.* **29** 608–14

[96] Hippisley-Cox J, Coupland C and Brindle P 2017 Development and validation of QRISK3 risk prediction algorithms to estimate future risk of cardiovascular disease: prospective cohort study *Brit. Med. J.* **357** j2099

[97] Ho J S Y, Rohra V, Korb L and Perera B 2021 Cardiovascular risk quantification using QRISK-3 score in people with intellectual disability *BJPsych Open* **7** S52–3

[98] Zheng Y Y, Ma Y T, Zhang J Y and Xie X 2020 COVID-19 and the cardiovascular system *Nat. Rev. Cardiol.* **17** 259–60

[99] Sacleux S C and Samuel D 2019 A critical review of MELD as a reliable tool for transplant prioritization *Semin. Liver Dis.* **39** 403–13

[100] Yip T C F, Chan H L Y, Tse Y K, Lam K L Y, Lui G C Y, Wong V W S and Wong G L H 2018 On-treatment improvement of MELD score reduces death and hepatic events in patients with hepatitis B-related cirrhosis *Am. J. Gastroenterol.* **113** 1629–38

[101] Piegat A and Sałabun W 2015 Comparative analysis of MCDM methods for assessing the severity of chronic liver disease *Artificial Intelligence and Soft Computing: 14th Int. Conf., ICAISC 2015 (Zakopane, Poland)* vol 14 pp 228–38

[102] Kamath P S, Wiesner R H, Malinchoc M, Kremers W, Therneau T M, Kosberg C L and Kim W R 2001 A model to predict survival in patients with end-stage liver disease *Hepatology* **33** 464–70

[103] Durrani S, Al-Mushawa F, Heena H, Wani T and Al-Qahtani A 2021 Relationship of Oncotype Dx score with tumor grade, size, nodal status, proliferative marker Ki67 and Nottingham Prognostic Index in early breast cancer tumors in Saudi population *Ann. Diagn. Pathol.* **51** 151674

[104] Gray E, Donten A, Payne K and Hall P S 2018 Survival estimates stratified by the Nottingham Prognostic Index for early breast cancer: a systematic review and meta-analysis of observational studies *Syst. Rev.* **7** 1–9

[105] Wong Z S, Zhou J and Zhang Q 2019 Artificial intelligence for infectious disease big data analytics *Infect. Dis. Health* **24** 44–8

[106] Daina A and Zoete V 2019 Application of the SwissDrugDesign online resources in virtual screening *Int. J. Mol. Sci.* **20** 4612

[107] Mishra S and Dahima R 2019 In vitro ADME studies of TUG-891, a GPR-120 inhibitor using SWISS ADME predictor *J. Drug Deliv. Ther.* **9** 366–9

[108] Bai H X, Hsieh B, Xiong Z, Halsey K, Choi J W, Tran T M L and Liao W H 2020 Performance of radiologists in differentiating COVID-19 from non-COVID-19 viral pneumonia at chest CT *Radiol.* **296** E46–54

[109] Hosny A, Parmar C, Quackenbush J, Schwartz L H and Aerts H J 2018 Artificial intelligence in radiology *Nat. Rev. Cancer* **18** 500–10

[110] Pianykh O S, Langs G, Dewey M, Enzmann D R, Herold C J, Schoenberg S O and Brink J A 2020 Continuous learning AI in radiology: implementation principles and early applications *Radiology* **297** 6–14

[111] Manapure P, Likhar K and Kosare H 2020 Detecting COVID-19 in X-ray images with keras, tensor flow, and deep learning *Assessment* **2**

[112] Abujamous L, Tbakhi A, Odeh M, Alsmadi O, Kharbat F F and Abdel-Razeq H 2018 Towards digital cancer genetic counseling *2018 1st Int. Conf. on Cancer Care Informatics (CCI)* pp 188–94

[113] Arora K and Bist A S 2020 Artificial intelligence based drug discovery techniques for COVID-19 detection *Aptisi Trans. Technopreneurship* **16** 120–6

[114] Basu S, Phillips R S, Phillips R, Peterson L E and Landon B E 2020 Primary care practice finances in the United States amid the COVID-19 pandemic: study estimates the potential impact of COVID-19 on operating expenses and revenues of primary care practices *Health Aff.* **39** 1605–161

[115] Zhang G Z, Deng Y J, Xie Q Q, Ren E H, Ma Z J, He X G and Kang X W 2020 Sirtuins and intervertebral disc degeneration: roles in inflammation, oxidative stress, and mitochondrial function *Clin. Chim. Acta* **508** 33–42

[116] Ardila D, Kiraly A P, Bharadwaj S, Choi B, Reicher J J, Peng L and Shetty S 2019 End-to-end lung cancer screening with three-dimensional deep learning on low-dose chest computed tomography *Nat. Med.* **25** 954–61

[117] Lowry O, Rosebrough N, Farr A L and Randall R 1951 Protein measurement with the Folin phenol reagent *J. Biol. Chem.* **193** 265–75

[118] DeLano W L 2002 PyMOL: an open-source molecular graphics tool *CCP4 Newsl. Protein Crystallogr.* **40** 82–92

[119] Gfeller D, Grosdidier A, Wirth M, Daina A, Michielin O and Zoete V 2014 SwissTargetPrediction: a web server for target prediction of bioactive small molecules *Nucleic Acids Res.* **42** W32–8

[120] Haq I and Esuka O M 2018 Blockchain technology in pharmaceutical industry to prevent counterfeit drugs *Int. J. Comput. Appl.* **180** 8–12

[121] Khurshid A 2020 Applying blockchain technology to address the crisis of trust during the COVID-19 pandemic *JMIR Med. Inform.* **8** e20477

[122] Marwala T and Xing B 2018 Blockchain and artificial intelligence arXiv preprint arXiv:1802.04451

[123] Xing L, Kapp D S, Giger M L and Min J K 2021 Outlook of the future landscape of artificial intelligence in medicine and new challenges *Artificial Intelligence in Medicine* (New York: Academic) pp 503–26

[124] McInnes, E *et al* 2020 Process evaluation of an implementation trial to improve the triage, treatment and transfer of stroke patients in emergency departments (T3 trial): a qualitative study. *Implementation Sci* **15** 99

[125] Behner P, Hecht M L and Wahl F 2017 Fighting counterfeit pharmaceuticals: new defenses for an underestimated and growing menace (accessed 12 December 2017)

[126] Taylor D 2015 The pharmaceutical industry and the future of drug development *Pharmaceuticals in the Environment* ed R E Hester and R M Harrison (Cambridge: Royal Society of Chemistry)vol 41

[127] Lombardo F, Obach R S, DiCapua F M, Bakken G A, Lu J, Potter D M and Zhang Y 2006 A hybrid mixture discriminant analysis—random forest computational model for the prediction of volume of distribution of drugs in human *J. Med. Chem.* **49** 2262–7

[128] Goldberg D, Mantero A, Newcomb C, Delgado C, Forde K A, Kaplan D E and Reese P P 2021 Predicting survival after liver transplantation in patients with hepatocellular carcinoma using the LiTES-HCC score *J. Hepatol.* **74** 1398–406

[129] Daina A and Zoete V 2016 A boiled-egg to predict gastrointestinal absorption and brain penetration of small molecules *Chem. Med. Chem.* **11** 1117–21

[130] Cha Y, Erez T, Reynolds I J, Kumar D, Ross J, Koytiger G and Laifenfeld D 2018 Drug repurposing from the perspective of pharmaceutical companies *Br. J. Pharmacol.* **175** 168–80

[131] Wang G, Weng Y C, Chiang I C, Huang Y T, Liao Y C, Chen Y C and Chou W H 2020 Neutralization of lipocalin-2 diminishes stroke-reperfusion injury *Int. J. Mol. Sci.* **21** 6253

[132] González A, Ramos J, De Paz J F and Corchado J M 2015 Obtaining relevant genes by analysis of expression arrays with a multi-agent system *9th Int. Conf. on Practical Applications of Computational Biology and Bioinformatics* pp 137–46

[133] Jain N, Gupta S, Sapre N and Sapre N S 2015 In silico de novo design of novel NNRTIs: a bio-molecular modelling approach *RSC Adv.* **5** 14814–27

[134] Mayr A, Klambauer G, Unterthiner T and Hochreiter S 2016 DeepTox: toxicity prediction using deep learning *Front. Environ. Sci.* **3** 80

[135] Paul D, Sanap G, Shenoy S, Kalyane D, Kalia K and Tekade R K 2021 Artificial intelligence in drug discovery and development *Drug Discovery Today* **26** 80

[136] Wang S, Wang J, Wang X, Qiu T, Yuan Y, Ouyang L and Wang F Y 2018 Blockchain-powered parallel healthcare systems based on the ACP approach *IEEE Trans. Comput. Soc. Syst.* **5** 942–50

[137] Zhu H 2020 Big data and artificial intelligence modeling for drug discovery *Annu. Rev. Pharmacol. Toxicol.* **60** 573–89

[138] Chen N, Zhou M, Dong X, Qu J, Gong F, Han Y and Zhang L 2020 Epidemiological and clinical characteristics of 99 cases of 2019 novel coronavirus pneumonia in Wuhan, China: a descriptive study *Lancet* **395** 507–13

[139] Bzdok D and Meyer-Lindenberg A 2018 Machine learning for precision psychiatry: opportunities and challenges *Biol. Psychiatry Cogn. Neurosci. Neuroimaging* **3** 223–30

[140] George D 2019 What can the brain teach us about building artificial intelligence? arXiv preprint arXi:1909.01561

[141] Hashimoto D A, Rosman G, Rus D and Meireles O R 2018 Machine learning in surgery: promises and perils *Ann. Surg.* **268** 70–6

[142] Khvastova M, Witt M, Essenwanger A, Sass J, Thun S and Krefting D 2020 Towards interoperability in clinical research-enabling FHIR on the open-source research platform XNAT *J. Med. Syst.* **44** 1–5

[143] Gole R and Lakshminarayana D C 2020 Seven level modular multilevel converter with Fft analysis *Int. J. Eng. Appl. Sci. Technol.* **5** 553–8

[144] McKinney S M, Sieniek M, Godbole V, Godwin J, Antropova N, Ashrafian H and Shetty S 2020 International evaluation of an AI system for breast cancer screening *Nature* **577** 89–94

IOP Publishing

Blockchain with Artificial Intelligence for Healthcare
A synergistic approach
Rishabha Malviya, Arun Kumar Singh, Sonali Sundram, Balamurugan Balusamy and
Seifedine Kadry

Chapter 2

Advancement in blockchain: revolutionizing healthcare

Blockchain has evolved from a fad to actual applications in industries like healthcare thanks to its built-in characteristics like distributed ledger, decentralized storage, authentication, security, as well as data integrity. Blockchain applications used in the healthcare industry are required by the Health Insurance Portability and Accountability Act of 1996 (HIPAA) to be more secure, interoperable, and able to share information. Blockchain technology is being utilized to build healthcare-related applications by researchers in both academia and business. Fraud detection and proof of identity are just two examples of how smart contracts may be put to use. The mining incentives, mining attacks, and key management still need to be addressed, even if considerable progress has been achieved. In addition, several of the blockchain trials now being examined do not meet the specific demands of many healthcare applications. In addition, this chapter touches on many additional research fields.

2.1 Introduction

Transparency and accountability are two possible benefits of adopting blockchain technology to handle electronic data. In a distributed ledger, everyone in the system has access to the same blockchain ledger. No one can alter or remove data after it has been recorded into the blockchain by network members [1]. When it comes to traditional financial institutions, such as banks and other middlemen, there is a lot of room for error. Pharmaceutical and medical device supply chains, monitoring permissions as well as improved facilities, medical records, or other health data by employees may also need transparent and continuous record-keeping in the healthcare industry. To guarantee that these transactions are secure, officials must determine whether or not the blockchain is essential. When compared to alternative technologies like centralized databases, how cost-effective is it? Digital solutions, on the other hand, do not have defined mechanisms for testing their efficacy. Healthcare systems may suffer as a result of software suppliers and buyers having uneven access to information. Blockchain-enabled solutions are also challenging to implement due to a lack of relevant healthcare knowledge. Blockchain technology has many benefits and disadvantages, as well as new and evolving applications in the health-care business and regulatory issues for using it. This short chapter will help you better grasp these aspects.

2.1.1 The old methods of data administration by blockchain technology

In a conventional database, there is just one database administrator, which implies that all of the data is kept on a single machine (or network of servers) [2]. However, the blockchain provides a decentralized system that does not require centralized record-keeping (figure 2.1).

A blockchain's blocks could contain information like records of business trans-actions or medical records. New blocks are created when the preceding one's data has been input. A blockchain network, like a global network of manufacturers and consumers of medical equipment, has no cap on the number of members [3]. In a blockchain, each node has access to the entire chain, which is constantly updated and synchronized. Nodes are computers that have access to a copy of the blockchain and are referred to as such. Those that join a blockchain network have access to all of the data. However, this is true for all blockchains, even if they are used in various ways. A blockchain can be private, where only network members with a specific set of privileges can access it, or it can be public, like the blockchain network.

2.1.2 Different characteristics and expense of blockchain technology

There is no single 'blockchain' when it comes to databases. Rather, there is a range of blockchain implementation alternatives, each with its own set of advantages and

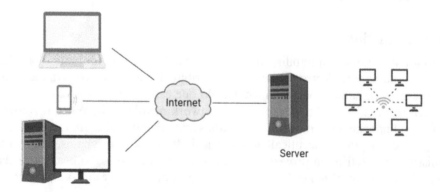

Figure 2.1. Centralized versus a distributed, peer-to-peer network. Created with BioRender.com.

disadvantages. Most blockchains have an 'append-only' structure. A block cannot be changed or removed after it has been included in the blockchain, however. It is possible to ensure the integrity of the blockchain by utilizing an 'append-only' structure, which enables every member to independently validate every new block as it is included in the chain of blocks. Every transaction recorded in a block of data in the chain is given a unique set of letters and numbers using a technique called cryptographic hashing. The hashing process would establish a new code that would be inconsistent with existing codes in the same blockchain and alert network users to a probable data tampering issue. The more participants in a network, the more difficult it is to modify a blockchain's blocks by hacking into many copies of the public ledger at the same time. Public blockchains for goods have significant operating expenses and energy usage; therefore, anybody may join and participate anonymously. According to one estimate, the typical US household consumes 718.53 kWh for each Bitcoin transaction, this is nearly what a US family utilizes in 24 h. For public blockchains to verify new blocks of data on the ledger, the process known as 'mining' is required. Nodes on the network compete to verify blocks, and those that participate in mining are rewarded as a result. Bitcoin transactions are reviewed against previous blocks to ensure that the same amount is not transmitted to the same address multiple times. A network agreement may be reached when mining discoveries are shared with the chain. If the block is made public, a transaction might finish in as little as ten minutes or as long as a day [4]. 'Proof of work' is the term used when a team agrees to add blocks. Private blockchains may not need a 'proof of work' technique since all nodes are authorized and know each other. Other consensus criteria include 'proof of authority,' which delegates network node validation responsibilities to specific nodes, and 'Byzantine high availability' which allows blocks to be created even if some sensor nodes fail to vote, which could be used by private networks of authorized users to verify the information and fix any discrepancies or conflicts.

2.1.3 Blockchain fits transparency and immutability of the data

The immutability and transparency of the blockchain make it ideal for storing transactions. You may also say that the data blocks are tiny and the network users have limited confidence in one another [5]. To enhance the supply chain or authenticate patient, doctor, and supplier identity, blockchain may be a viable option. As a result of the blockchain's processing and storage capacity limitations, high-volume data cannot be stored (node) [6]. Blockchain storage is inefficient and costly when it comes to storing large amounts of data, such as medical records and genetic information.

Privacy laws are in place in most OECD countries because health data is especially sensitive. Even if the data were de-identified, putting it on the 'chain' and making it accessible to the rest of the network would constitute a serious breach of privacy [7]. Even though it is technically conceivable, the inability to delete personal health data metadata creates privacy concerns since patient identities may be revealed. Concerns concerning privacy arise from this. If data on a blockchain is made publicly accessible, data minimization and use restrictions may be breached. There are ways to ensure compliance in a permissioned blockchain, in which all nodes are aware of one another and have been given permission to access and contribute to the network As an extra security precaution, a subset of the ledger may be accessible to several network nodes. Because the distributed ledger lacks a central data controller, like an organization that is accountable for the data and serves as its custodian, patients, and healthcare providers are unable to exercise their legal rights. Users of personal data have additional rights under the EU Data Protection Regulation (DPR) [8], which include the ability to access and amend their data. According to the Council for the Advancement of Science and Technology (2019), blockchain's 'append-only' feature, which prohibits data from being modified or removed from the chain, conflicts with the EU Data Protection Regulation's right to erasure. In comparison to traditional databases, distributed ledgers make it more difficult to find certain words or pieces of information. Because of this, their function as a repository for clinical and research data is limited. Blockchain-enabled ledgers' user interfaces are still under development; therefore they can't be widely deployed. In the future, new technological solutions may emerge as blockchain is adopted and used in more businesses [9].

2.2 Blockchain applications in the health sector

However, there is still a lot of work to be done before blockchain can be used in the healthcare industry. There is a lack of technical understanding and no prototype or trial implementation for the blockchain elements that are used in the majority of studies (figure 2.2). Blockchain technology has been adopted by just a few national health systems. Examples of ways in which blockchains may be used for good, such as data security as well as patient consent management, have been found in Estonia and Malta. The administration of the medical supply chain, patient participation in consenting, and authentication are three of the most promising blockchain uses in the healthcare sector [10].

2.2.1 Blockchain for identity management in healthcare

Excellent health outcomes necessitate the ability to accurately identify and verify the identities of other people and organizations. Patients, healthcare workers, and institutions like research institutes and universities are all included in this category [11]. When many versions of a person's identification are present, the use of a blockchain might aid in preserving the authenticity and veracity of that person's identity. A rise in wearable health devices and the IoT will lead to a rise in the importance of these data. This data, for example, will need to be linked to patients' electronic medical records appropriately.

It is critical for patients, accrediting organizations, and purchasers alike that healthcare providers give correct and up-to-date information to find and appropriately reimburse them. The use of a blockchain might improve information accuracy and authenticity.

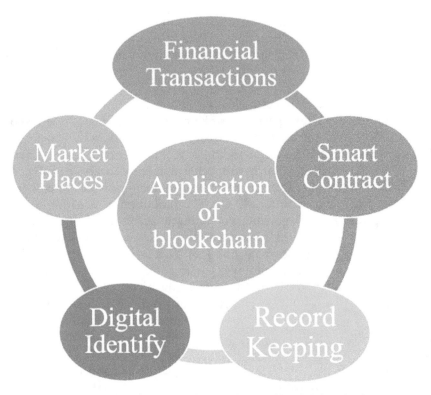

Figure 2.2. Schematic diagram of an application of blockchain technology.

The blockchain keeps an immutable record of every change made to a record. KSI, a blockchain program, protects official data, including electronic health information. It is possible to keep users' personal information secure and anonymous by employing KSI technology. You may compare an edited version of a record to its original version [12]. There is a much smaller transaction footprint associated with these instructions than there is with real-world health data. Blockchain, like other digital advances, works best when coupled with other technologies in a health information system.

2.2.2 Blockchain for management of the patient

Because of the transparency and audibility it provides, blockchain technology may be an attractive alternative to traditional methods for handling personal health information [13]. Medical professionals and other important actors should have access to patient data so that they may give direct care or so that secondary research or statistics can utilize the data (such as researchers and social workers, for example). Since electronic data may be used and reused indefinitely, using a 'dynamic' along with an 'incremental' consent model is an excellent substitute for 'blanket' as well as 'one-time-only' permission models. A person may insert a new block to overrule previous instructions if they want to change the terms of their approval or consent [14]. The Malta biobank handles individual authorization for the utilization of their biospecimens in research projects using the blockchain-based Dwarna system. The Dwarna web platform [15] records the consent of individuals on a blockchain permanently and irrevocably. The opportunity to select which research to take part in, revoke consent, and request the disposal of biosamples all help to increase people's trust in the biobank. As the name implies, MedRec makes use of blockchain technology, which was created by the MIT Media Lab to link medical records with other databases' access permissions and data retrieval instructions. It keeps records of patient–provider interactions via blockchain-based 'smart contracts'. Once a practitioner develops as well as certifies a medical record, patients are allowed access to their medical data. When a new medical record is created, the receiver receives an automated notification as well as an encrypted link [16]. Permissions may be found on the chain. With the help of this technology, patients may see and control their data. There have been some positive results from medications, blood tests, immunization records, and other treatments. RadBit allows patients to maintain ownership of their medical photos while ensuring that the chain of custody is immutable. Users of the blockchain may create 'tokens' that can be issued to healthcare providers and insurance firms so that they can have access to the blockchain [17]. Only permission instructions, which are subsequently confirmed and sent out as relevant reports, are included in a token's chain of custody. As a result of this, the message's integrity may be improved by using blind signatures, which are more secure than traditional signatures, using multiple authorities' signatures or while still confirming the sender's and user's identities. Data interchange and access permissions have improved with the usage of blockchain-based technologies for patient authorization and permits in biomedical research. The Blockchain Enabled Healthcare (IMI 2018) Project as well as the Pharmaceutical Users Software Exchange (PhUSEBlockchain Project) are the two main blockchain-supported pharmaceutical ecosystem initiatives. Blockchain technology may be able to keep clinical trial participants' sensitive information safe. The privacy of the person and the research team's trust in the quality of the data collected may both be safeguarded by a blockchain if it is set up appropriately [18]. Health records, information, software, code, as well as other materials associated with medical research, have been included in a new blockchain program called Research Foundry. This includes the study on the COVID-19 pandemic. Cross-border cooperation will be made easier by ensuring that participants adhere to the relevant data privacy regulations. Data that nodes on the network want to share with other solution users are controlled by them. In contrast, while the health data storage may be kept private from the blockchain nodes, its metadata can be shared with all members. Other nodes can make use of a repository if they agree to share all or part of it. Before accessing the repository, the data owner must grant the technology provider access.

2.3 Blockchain for managing medical and pharmaceutical supply chains

The management of supply networks for goods is the most typical use of blockchain in business. Blockchain technology is being used to monitor blood products, medical supplies as well as medical devices in the healthcare business [19].

The following are some examples of blockchain applications in this field:

- Product identification: faster and easier verification of a product's unique identity (e.g. in product failure cases).
- Tracing: distributed ledgers may be used by manufacturers, distributors, and dispensers to automatically verify pertinent information.
- Product verification: checks for counterfeit, unauthorized, or harmful items and makes it possible for both public and private actors to find them.
- Notification and response: enabling a safe procedure for reporting non-compliant items or transactions to the appropriate authorities.

Because of the enormous demand for medical supplies and equipment to battle COVID-19, healthcare systems are finding it difficult to get these items. From a breakdown in supply networks, there is a lack of trust. Concerns of new suppliers include standard compliance, customs certification, on-time delivery of products, and fraudulent activity. New vendors should be avoided. Suppliers' demands for upfront payment exacerbate these problems of trust. Assuring the authenticity of suppliers and tracking shipments might be done by using blockchain technology. To combat the COVID-19 pandemic, it was reported in April 2020 that IBM Rapid Supplier Link would connect governments and healthcare organizations with non-conventional providers of technology, apparatus, and supplies. The pharmaceutical supply chain is plagued by trust concerns. They include worries about intellectual property protection, quality control, piracy, and the selling of illegal drugs. Using the blockchain's immutability, it may be possible to authenticate the validity of suppliers and buyers. In the Counterfeit Medicines Project by Hyperledger, for instance, products are timestamped and entered into a blockchain for tracking and verification. It is becoming more difficult to keep up with demand and prevent medicine shortages, and blockchain technology may help with both of these issues. Blockchain technology has been used in Chinese hospitals to enable the precise monitoring and timely delivery of drugs to the homes of patients with COVID-19. Similar risks exist in the supply chain for medical devices. Safety as well as efficacy concerns, as well as high-risk gadgets with a history of security flaws, are all examples of these difficulties. A blockchain might provide additional security, transparency, and authenticity to these activities once agreed-upon standards and protocols are in place. ICU beds, Hospital beds as well as life-saving equipment are critical resources during the COVID-19 epidemic. Managing these resources is a major challenge for healthcare providers throughout the country. Blockchain may be a valuable tool in situations where trust is a problem or information exchange is restricted [20].

2.3.1 Policy considerations for deploying blockchain

Patients' consent, data sharing and access permissions, and the management of medicine and medical equipment supply chains are all examples of how blockchain might be utilized to enhance healthcare systems. A well-established healthcare information and data infrastructure, along with other technologies, should be used in conjunction with this one for the greatest outcomes possible. Using blockchain technology in healthcare may easily be overstated. When it comes to the healthcare industry's digital transformation utilizing blockchain, interoperability and data governance are two of its most challenging issues. As long as there is no central authority to keep data, blockchains do not remove the need for any authority whatsoever. The usage of blockchain technology will be required since healthcare data is so sensitive. A blockchain is governed by the agreement of its participants, not by technology. There will always be a need for rules to be established by a trustworthy authority (or, more precisely, 'rules that establish rules'). This information may have come from a government agency or an established institution. Standards Australia, for example, has produced a roadmap for the use of blockchain-enabled technologies. Legislators must take into account the expenses of technology development and deployment. Because blockchain technology is being used in Estonia's national healthcare system, the direct costs of technological development as well as implementation are cheap. Once the fundamental infrastructure is in place, additional applications can be added more cheaply. Resources must be spent to guarantee the technology can be utilized in the way that it was intended throughout any technological change. There is a direct correlation between how effectively the blockchain architecture works and how much data is retained 'on-chain' when it comes to operating the system. Traditional methods of data storage and administration will be rendered obsolete by the blockchain, which necessitates open lines of communication between all parties involved. Healthcare personnel must be educated and trained to get the most out of this resource. Patient's rights and responsibilities with their data will improve as a consequence of increased public involvement and education.

Since blockchains can't be changed, they might be dangerous. Health-related data cannot yet be deleted from a blockchain. Even if the data has been deleted off-chain, the chain record still exists and cannot be wiped. There is now a legal dispute about whether or not this information constitutes personal health data. Masking blocks that are related to a certain signature may lead to new solutions as the issue expands. However, this does not mean that the data in blockchain-based ledgers is correct or of acceptable quality. Users may be influenced by untrustworthy actors when it comes to approving the use of their data. As the population becomes older, there will be a rise in the number of people who are at risk for bodily and psychological harm. Effective governance, legislation, and enforcement are the only ways to deal with this problem. The OECD Council's Recommendation on Health Data Governance is a useful place to start when examining the effects of blockchain technology in the health sector. There are several procedures, such as security, privacy, and permission.

2.3.2 Four principles that assist policymakers with implementing blockchain technology in health

1. Appropriate for the task. Blockchain is a universally applicable digital technology that serves as an enabler. On its own merits, it should only be used in situations when it is the best answer for the issue at hand.
2. Alignment of governance and regulation. The compliance of blockchain-based solutions with laws, rules, and data governance frameworks must be reviewed in terms of the specific aspects of the system.
3. Integration is done step by step. Existing systems and technologies should be compared to those enabled by blockchain. Before a large-scale rollout, blockchain should be evaluated progressively in a controlled setting to ensure it complements and leverages current systems.
4. Involvement of the end-user in the design process. Blockchain necessitates a paradigm shift in data and information management. As a result of this technology's characteristics and ramifications for data ownership, access, and privacy, users, including patients and the general public, must be informed.

2.3.3 Healthcare industry

In the healthcare business, extra regulatory obligations to safeguard patients' medical information create significant security as well as privacy threats. As the utilization of cloud storage and mobile medical devices expands, so does the potential for malicious assaults and the exposure of private information. There are rising worries regarding the sharing as well as privacy of health information as smart devices make it simpler for consumers to acquire health data and as more people visit multiple doctors. Authentication, transparency, data sharing, medical information transfer, and concerns about mobile health are just some of the unique challenges confronting the healthcare business.

2.4 Healthcare industry application

2.4.1 System security

Many security measures are required to protect sensitive medical and healthcare data, including non-repudiation and access limitations to prevent it from being accessed or changed by unauthorized parties. Patient files and data collected from sensors are both types of health information that may be found in medical records. Security as well as role-based rights must be introduced to safeguard medical records as they transition from paper to digital medium. Data stored in healthcare databases should only be accessible by those who are properly authorized, and this access should be monitored and enforced [21]. The query should be audited and accessibility controls must be followed to prevent the modification or duplication of patient records. Because various encryption standards are used in various systems (such as electronic health records, digital medical records, and personal health records, or PHRs), there may also be issues with the encryption of medical records.

Unsecured medical records may have real-world repercussions (such as threats to patients' privacy from hostile assaults, which can affect their reputation and cost them money).

2.4.2 Interoperability

It is a security issue and a concern with civilian health records [10] that data is shared and accessed. It might be challenging to share medical records because of the many different places where a person's complete medical history can be kept [10]. This also applies to healthcare practitioners, who may not have up-to-date information on their patients if their records are distributed across many locations [10]. Due to a gap in record linkage, which refers to the idea of linking databases based on entities that might or might not share a common identifier, like a social security number, sharing healthcare data is difficult. When it comes to data interchange, interoperability is a significant problem [11].

2.4.3 Data sharing

There are many places where an individual's medical records might be held, making it difficult to share them with other healthcare providers [22]. Patients and healthcare practitioners alike are unable to obtain up-to-date information about their patients if their medical records are kept elsewhere [10]. Sharing healthcare information is challenging because there is a gap in record linkage, which is the notion of combining databases based on entities that may or may not have a common identifier, such as a social security number.

2.4.4 Mobility

Patient mobility and the need for their medical information to be portable are driving an increasing need for mobility in the healthcare business [23, 24]. The capacity to transmit data from increasingly common smart gadgets, sensors, as well as other internet-enabled devices, is becoming vital. The necessity for real-time sharing as well as access from any place on any device makes data security more challenging, which just increases the problem already there. In this chapter, there are three main types of mobility: wireless, mobile health, as well as Internet of Things (IoT).

2.4.5 Mobile health

Low-power body-area wireless networks, miniaturized sensors, as well as widespread smartphones are all part of the emerging field of mHealth (mobile health) in healthcare applications. In many ways, mHealth shares the issues that the vast majority of the healthcare industries' centralized server systems do. It's crucial to remember that these are but a few of the problems that require attention. Wireless sensor networks (WSNs) and IoTs need considerable resources to ensure privacy and security, yet unmanaged and compromised healthcare information may harm both patients and the future of mobile health applications [25, 26]. This is because healthcare institutions that employ technology may lack the ability to effectively protect patient information. Malware and other harmful assaults may also occur if a device is misplaced or connected to an unsecured network [27]. In addition to its use in the healthcare industry, wearable technology also has the potential to have security consequences. Wearable technology creates issues with privacy involving statutory protection and sensitive health information. Sensors, gadgets, and smart technologies pose privacy issues in the form of information disclosure, withholding of data or services, information modification, repudiation, nonavailability, as well as loss of authenticity/validity.

2.4.6 Wireless

With the proliferation of wearable body sensors in WBAN deployments, several new security concerns have emerged. These include the need to ensure that the data is precise and the latest while also ensuring that the WBAN network is always available to users [28]. Lightweight security solutions will also be needed for devices in a WBAN because of their limited resources [13].

Additional issues with wearable health technologies include damaged data, malfunctioning devices, and users tampering with the data for their profit. If life-saving medications like insulin are successfully compromised by implanted medical devices, major or even deadly health hazards may arise. The security and health issues related to health-related assaults must be addressed before wireless healthcare as well as healthcare applications may be actively investigated for large-scale applications [26].

2.4.7 Internet of Things

Increasing patient participation in healthcare decisions has led to an elevation in the usage of IoT technologies in healthcare [29, 30]. The upshot is a greater willingness on the part of patients to take a more active role in their treatment. Some doctors can remotely monitor their patients' chronic illnesses with the use of smart devices or sensor technologies that collect and communicate vital health data [31]. Wearable sensors, microchips in the skin, and contact lenses are examples of IOT technologies that help people make better health decisions [32–35]. Wireless systems that aren't as safe as more sensitive systems like databases, memory banks, and IoT technologies are vulnerable to a variety of attacks and weaknesses. There are two types of attacks on wireless IoT systems: aggressive and passive. As data packets go across the network, an attacker can alter their eventual destination [36]. The information included in packets could also be intercepted or 'sniffed' by an adversary as they move through a network or wireless range. To locate the operator of a device or network and get updated or personal information about the user, vulnerabilities may be used [37]. This is referred to as an active attack. A hostile actor may employ techniques including data manipulation, impersonation attack, eavesdropping, as well as replay to obtain health information from IoT devices. System security, administrator security, data security, plus information security are all vulnerable to hacking. Users of healthcare IOT apps must deal with problems related to protecting their identity, location, inquiries, footprints, and owner privacy [38]. Third-party cloud corporations sharing health data between healthcare institutions raise privacy concerns. Outside service providers use and management of the patient and medical data are at the heart of these privacy concerns [19]. Along with access control privacy flaws, IoT technologies also present inference assaults as a source of privacy concerns [39]. Wireless eavesdropping technologies and data mining may be used by hostile actors to determine the worth of communication or signal. The inferred data may then be utilized in a phishing attempt to further compromise an account [14]. Wi-Fi networks are vulnerable to a variety of assaults, some of which may be carried out actively and others of which can be carried out passively. Wireless networks as well as IoT applications raise new privacy issues. One of these worries is 'can healthcare data, such as a heart rate monitor, be obtained from a person without their consent in an emergency circumstance?'. Due to this issue, there are concerns about who will have access to emergency data and how it will be stored. It shouldn't be a surprise if cloud-based infrastructures grow more popular if these privacy concerns aren't resolved and patients have faith in the security of their records in the cloud. Data exchange as well as interoperability between medical experts and organisations grows more complicated as a result of these security issues.

2.5 Conclusion

Blockchain technology can address some of the problems facing the healthcare sector. Due to the global ledger plus block-related architecture, security, integrity, availability, decentralization, and authenticating principles [39] are among the most extensively researched applications of blockchain technology in healthcare. Internet-enabled gadgets, IoT, smart devices, and sensors are posing problems in the healthcare sector. Patient's medical records may be more easily accessed and copied by malicious actors, making it harder for hospitals to deliver better care to their patients in a more connected world. As a result of out-of-date records, patients may have health problems or misdiagnoses, as well as challenges confirming their identity. A wide range of healthcare issues might be resolved with blockchain technology, as shown by the reviews in this study. The main problems with present applications are identification, validity, record sharing, compatibility, IoT security, edge host protection, and patient empowerment. The ultimate objective is to support patients by providing them with authority over the sharing of their medical data and allowing them to conduct data analysis in a safe and secure setting.

References

[1] Clauson K A, Breeden E A, Davidson C and Mackey T K 2018 Leveraging blockchain technology to enhance supply chain management in healthcare: an exploration of challenges and opportunities in the health supply chain *Blockchain Healthc. Today* **1** 20

[2] Angeletti F, Chatzigiannakis I and Vitaletti A 2017 The role of blockchain and IoT in recruiting participants for digital clinical trials *2017 25th Int. Conf. on Software, Telecommunications and Computer Networks (SoftCOM)* pp 1–5

[3] Vazirani A A, O'Donoghue O, Brindley D and Meinert E 2019 Implementing blockchains for efficient health care: systematic review *J. Med. Internet Res.* **21** e12439

[4] de Vries A 2022 Bitcoin energy consumption index *Digiconomist* https://digiconomist.net/bitcoin-energy-consumption (accessed 15 October 2022)

[5] Hölbl M, Kompara M, Kamišalić A and Nemec Zlatolas L 2018 A systematic review of the use of blockchain in healthcare *Symmetry* **10** 470

[6] Taylor P 2016 Applying blockchain technology to medical traceability *Secur. Ind.* https://securingindustry.com/pharmaceuticals/applying-blockchain-technology-to-medicine-traceability/s40/a2766/#.V5mxL_mLTIV

[7] Burstiq https://burstiq.com/ (accessed 3 October 2022)

[8] Dubovitskaya A, Novotny P, Xu Z and Wang F 2020 Applications of blockchain technology for data-sharing in oncology: results from a systematic literature review *Oncology* **98** 403–11

[9] Blockchain Networks Overview https://himss.org/library/blockchain-networks (accessed 24 October 2022)

[10] Roadmap for Blockchain Standards https://standards.org.au/getmedia/ad5d74db-8da9-4685-b171-90142ee0a2e1/Roadmap_for_Blockchain_Standards_report.pdf.aspx (accessed 24 October 2022)

[11] Blockchain and the General Data Protection Regulation. PE 634.445. Brussels: European Parliament Research Service https://europarl.europa.eu/RegData/etudes/STUD/2019/634445/EPRS_STU(2019)634445_EN.pdf (accessed 24 October 2022)

[12] Mettler M 2016 Blockchain technology in healthcare: the revolution starts here *2016 IEEE 18th Int. Conf. on e-Health Networking Applications and Services (Healthcom)* pp 1–3

[13] Small A and Wainwright D 2018 Privacy and security of electronic patient records— tailoring multimethodology to explore the socio-political problems associated with role based access control systems *Eur. J. Oper. Res.* **265** 344–60

[14] 465k patients told to visit doctor to patch critical pacemaker vulnerability https://arstechnica.com/information-technology/2017/08/465k-patients-need-a-firmware-update-to-prevent-serious-pacemaker-hacks/ (accessed 23 October 2022)

[15] Mamo N, Martin G M, Desira M, Ellul B and Ebejer J P 2020 Dwarna: a blockchain solution for dynamic consent in biobanking *Eur. J. Hum. Genet.* **28** 609–26

[16] What is MedRec? https://medrec.media.mit.edu/ (accessed 24 October 2022)

[17] The MediLedger Network Retrieved from https://mediledger.com/ (accessed 24 October 2022)

[18] Sahi M A 2017 Privacy preservation in e-healthcare environments: state of the art and future directions *IEEE Access* **6** 464–78

[19] Al Ameen M, Liu J and Kwak K 2012 Security and privacy issues in wireless sensor networks for healthcare applications *J. Med. Syst.* **36** 93–101

[20] Ting D S W, Carin L, Dzau V and Wong T Y 2020 Digital technology and COVID-19 *Nat. Med.* **26** 459–61

[21] Abouelmehdi K, Beni-Hssane A, Khaloufi H and Saadi M 2017 Big data security and privacy in healthcare: a review *Procedia Comput. Sci.* **113** 73–80

[22] Mohan P and Singh M 2016 Security policies for intelligent health care environment *Procedia Comput. Sci.* **92** 161–7

[23] Tseng T W, Yang C Y and Liu C T 2016 Designing privacy information protection of electronic medical records *2016 Int. Conf. on Computational Science and Computational Intelligence (CSCI) (2016 December)* pp 75–80

[24] Al-Muhtadi J, Shahzad B, Saleem K, Jameel W and Orgun M A 2019 Cybersecurity and privacy issues for socially integrated mobile healthcare applications operating in a multi-cloud environment *Health Inform. J.* **25** 315–29

[25] Sinha S R, Park Y, Sinha S R and Park Y 2017 Dealing with security, privacy, access control and compliance *Building an Effective IoT Ecosystem for Your Business* (Cham: Springer) pp 155–76

[26] Sangpetch O and Sangpetch A 2016 Security context framework for distributed healthcare IoT platform *Internet of Things Technologies for HealthCare: 3rd Int. Conf. HealthyIoT* vol 18–19 pp 71–6

[27] Kotz D, Gunter C A, Kumar S and Weiner J P 2016 Privacy and security in mobile health: a research agenda *Comput* **49** 22–30

[28] Li H, Wu J, Gao Y and Shi Y 2016 Examining individuals' adoption of healthcare wearable devices: an empirical study from privacy calculus perspective *Int. J. Med. Inform.* **88** 8–17

[29] Ding D, Conti M and Solanas A 2016 A smart health application and its related privacy issues *2016 Smart City Security and Privacy Workshop (SCSP-W) (Vienna)* 1–5

[30] Top 3 Practical Innovations from Medical Hackathon https://cio.com/article/3161886/top-3-practical-innovations-from-yale-healthcare-hackathon.html (accessed 24 October 2022)

[31] Baskar P, Joseph M A, Narayanan N and Loya R B 2013April Experimental investigation of oxygen enrichment on performance of twin cylinder diesel engine with variation of injection pressure *2013 Int. Conf. on Energy Efficient Technologies for Sustainability* pp 682–7

[32] Recommendation of the Council on Health Data Governance. OECD/LEGAL/0433, Paris https://oecd.org/health/health-systems/Recommendation-of-OECD-Council-on-Health-Data-Governance-Booklet.pdf (accessed 24 October 2022)

[33] Dinev T, Albano V, Xu H, D'Atri A and Hart P 2016 Individuals' attitudes towards electronic health records: a privacy calculus perspective *Advances in Healthcare Informatics and Analytics* (Cham: Springer) pp 19–50

[34] Chowdhury E W R, Rahman M S, Al Islam A A and Rahman M S 2017 Salty secret: let us secretly salt the secret *2017 Int. Conf. on Networking Systems and Security (NSysS)* pp 115–23

[35] Fernando R, Ranchal R, An B, Othman L B and Bhargava B 2016 Consumer oriented privacy preserving access control for electronic health records in the cloud *2016 IEEE 9th Int. Conf. on Cloud Computing (CLOUD)* pp 608–15

[36] Al-Janabi S, Al-Shourbaji I, Shojafar M and Shamshirband S 2017 Survey of main challenges (security and privacy) in wireless body area networks for healthcare applications *Egypt. Inform. J.* **18** 113–22

[37] Sajid A and Abbas H 2016 Data privacy in cloud-assisted healthcare systems: state of the art and future challenges *J. Med. Syst.* **40** 155

[38] Jain P, Gyanchandani M and Khare N 2016 Big data privacy: a technological perspective and review *J. Big Data* **3** 1–25

[39] What is a protocol? http://prismastatement.org/Protocols/Default.aspx%20 (accessed 24 October 2022)

IOP Publishing

Blockchain with Artificial Intelligence for Healthcare
A synergistic approach
**Rishabha Malviya, Arun Kumar Singh, Sonali Sundram, Balamurugan Balusamy and
Seifedine Kadry**

Chapter 3

Decentralizing health data with blockchain technology

Data can be considered the most valuable asset in each type of company, and even though every firm is shifting to cloud storag
e, data protection is still a problem in different sectors. Since healthcare deals with the most sensitive personal data, it is one of the most important sectors. This is because patient medical information, prescriptions, health insurance, and other data are all included in the healthcare industry. Because of the sensitive nature of data kept in EHRs (electronic health records), the security of the data is essential. Because of their rising popularity, EHR systems, for instance, have been taken into consideration as potential blockchain implementation in the healthcare sector. To better understand blockchain options for EHR systems, this chapter is based on a systematic literature analysis that focused only on security and privacy issues. Before exploring the (potential) implementation of blockchain in EHR systems, this chapter begins with a review by presenting crucial background data concerning both EHR systems as well as blockchain. In this chapter, we describe how data may be accessed and kept safely in the healthcare industry.

3.1 Introduction

Many efforts are underway to digitally improve healthcare systems throughout the globe and in many sectors [1, 2]. The American Recovery and Reinvestment Act of 2009 involved the Health Information Technology for Economic and Clinical Health (HITECH) Act, signed by President Obama. With the HITECH Act, EHRs will be widely used, benefiting patients and society. The scientific community is interested in EHR techniques for many of these and additional reasons, including

doi:10.1088/978-0-7503-5839-2ch3

online patient access, public healthcare administration, as well as the exchange of patients' medical data [3–5].

In the ongoing 2019 novel coronavirus pandemic (commonly called 2019-nCoV or COVID-2019), EHRs have been widely utilized. Every new technology brings with it a slew of operational and research obstacles. For example, the server architecture is often centralized in conventional EHR systems, which raises concerns about security and privacy (e.g., single point of negligence as well as performance bottleneck) [6–8]. EHR use is increasing, and the public is becoming more aware of the reliability of data, especially healthcare data, the servers may be tempted to steal personal information from users while they are doing their normal duties.

Recently, the utilization of blockchain technology in various areas, including healthcare (like public health management and counterfeit medication detection), has increased. A trustworthy value chain may be built using blockchain, which is an immutable, transparent, and decentralized distributed database.

The healthcare system shown in figure 3.1 makes use of blockchain technology. A blockchain can be said to be a dispersed ledger that is constructed on top of a network of chronologically ordered blocks. These are distributed systems that are not controlled by any one person or organization (without relying on any third party) [9–11]. Mathematics and encryption are used instead of semi-trusted central organizations to build trust relationships among distributed nodes. By implementing blockchain-based solutions, a single point of negligence can be reduced [12]. In a blockchain network, all nodes may view the ledgers at any time and from any place, ensuring complete transparency and building confidence among the network's distributed members [13]. The capacity to maintain track of tamper-resistant records in the ledger also aids in data audit and accountability. It is possible to encrypt the data in the ledger using a variety of cryptographic algorithms, depending on the

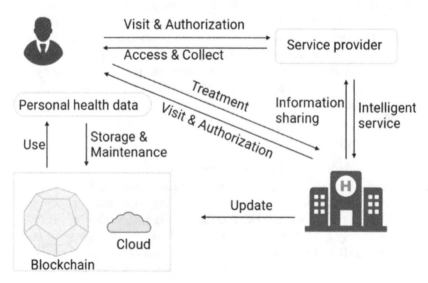

Figure 3.1. An example architecture for a healthcare system based on blockchain. Created with BioRender. com.

individual implementation. The use of pseudo-anonymity allows one to hide one's identity. Since smart contracts are self-executing programmed to be posted in the worldwide network of blockchain, they can be utilized to carry out a broad range of actions for a broad range of applications. A smart contract's terms will be honored if certain conditions are met. With this newfound power comes new responsibilities for data ownership. Gem, Guard time, and Health Bank are examples of blockchain healthcare systems that have been implemented in the real world.

As a result, the emphasis of this chapter is on healthcare blockchain systems. Specifically, researchers want to thoroughly analyze some prior work and identify current and future obstacles and research prospects. Before presenting our findings, we will go over the fundamentals of the blockchain and the EHR system in the section in the following part. This is followed by an examination of the current literature and a comparison of several existing systems.

3.2 EHR systems

When referring to an individual's electronic medical records (EMRs), the term 'electronic health record' is often used (EHR) [14]. Healthcare professionals at medical facilities (EHR) may use EMRs as an information source for AMRs. Patients' health records may contain information from wearable gadgets they own and use. Data gathered by people using personal health records (PHRs) may be shared with healthcare providers (patients).

Medical practitioners who need to view a patient's data to make a diagnosis may potentially access the EHR system's data securely [14]. If the system is appropriately constructed, it is feasible to decrease the risk of lost data. In addition, the expanding interconnection of these systems has made it more difficult to safeguard data in transit or at rest (e.g., more potential attack vectors). To aid in the stealthy exfiltration of sensitive data, hackers may exploit known flaws and install malware on hospital-issued mobile devices (such as patient health records, or PHRs) [15].

The massive amounts of data in EHR systems may be used for machine learning and other medical investigations. One example of how data might be used is to predict diseases (e.g., 2019 Novel Coronavirus) [16]. Smart as well as various Internet of Things (IoT) devices which collect plus upload relevant data, such as PHRs, could be advantageous for EHRs [17]. Because of the popularity of Bitcoin, the term 'blockchain' has become a household name to conduct safe transactions over an untrusted network without the necessity of a central authority. The following are some of the most important parts of the blockchain. A blockchain records all transactions that have taken place during a certain period. A linkage (a hash value) is used to connect each block to its forerunners in a chain. The block in the chain that comes before the genesis block is referred to as the parent block. Each block consists of a header and a body [18]. Figure 3.2 depicts the blockchain's organizational structure.

The following information may be seen in the block header:

- *Block version*: rules for validation of the block;
- *Previous block hash*: the hash value for a former block;

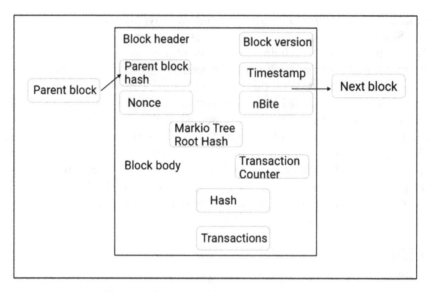

Figure 3.2. Design of a block.

- **Timestamp**: the formation period of the present block;
- **Nonce**: a 4-byte random field that is modified by miners after each hash computation for solving the PoW mining conundrum
- **Body root hash**: the Merkle tree root hash calculated from the block's transactions;
- **Target hash**: new valid block's hash value threshold. Defining the complexity of a PoW problem is based on the hash of the target.

Transactions that were verified within a certain period are involved in the body of the block [19]. Every leaf node in the Merkle tree symbolizes a transaction, whereas every non-leaf node serves as the unique identifier of its twin concatenated child nodes, because it is quicker to validate a transaction using the connected branches' hash values as opposed to the entire Merkle tree. Every time there is a new transaction at the top layer, the root hash is updated [20]. The size range of the block and the number of transactions it can hold determines the maximum number of transactions that can be stored in it. Append-only structures are created using a cryptographic hash function. Since previously confirmed data cannot be changed or removed, new data must be added as extra blocks linked to prior blocks. A fresh hash value or link relation is created each time a block is modified [21]. Secureness and immutability are gained as a direct result. It is possible to authenticate digitally using a digital signature. Transactions in an unreliable environment are frequently authenticated using digital signatures determined by asymmetric encryption [22]. The blockchain utilizes asymmetric cryptography for transmitting and verifying transactions. P2P network transactions are signed using a private key belonging to the sender. The present blockchain's most popular mechanism is the elliptic curve digital signature (ECDSA) [23].

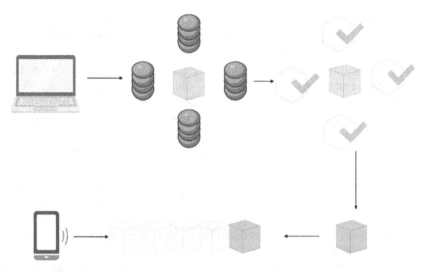

Figure 3.3. Transactions in the blockchain's operational order.

The network of peer-to-peer (P2P) broadcasts any transaction after it has been transmitted to all remaining nodes in the network. The sender's public key can only be utilized to validate a transaction's authenticity after all other nodes have received it [24]. The transaction will be sent to the following node to make sure that all nodes receive as well as validate it. If not, this process will destroy it. The blockchain network's new block can only contain valid transactions.

So, for example, let us say you want to transfer some coins (see figure 3.3). Alice dispenses some cash to Bob. To begin, she uses her private key to initiate a transaction. Using Alice's public key, it is feasible to validate the transfer [25]. In the network of P2P, each network node gets a duplicate of every transaction. Phase three of the verification procedure involves nodes comparing the transaction against a set of predetermined standards. Each verified transaction will be added to a new block after a miner has successfully solved the fourth step's challenge. Until all nodes have backed up the block, it will not be accessible.

3.2.1 Consensus algorithms

No reliable central authority exists in the network of blockchain. The Byzantine Generals (BG) problem, presented by researchers explains that it is transformed into a distributed network problem by obtaining agreement among untrustworthy nodes in the network (1982) [26, 27]. To win the war, the Byzantine army must be surrounded by a collection of generals, each of whom commands a different part of it. In a scattered setting, they are unsure whether any traitors may flee. As a result, they must come to terms with whether to attack. The blockchain network has the same problem [28].

A variety of protocols have been suggested to be created to gain consent from all dispersed nodes before an additional block is added to the blockchain:

- **PoW (proof of work):** Bitcoin uses the PoW agreement algorithm (PoW) to reach a consensus. Miners must first prove their innocence by mining to receive payment for a specified amount of processing power. The node must keep doing hash calculations until the hashed blockhead is minor than (or like) the necessary hash value to obtain an acceptable nonce value. Unattainable but straightforward to demonstrate in practice [29]. Because of the difficulty of the computations, the project is expensive (in terms of computational resources). Attackers may be able to take advantage of a weakness in the network of blockchain if a single miner or a small number of miners interferes with the creation of new blocks.
- **PoS (proof of stake):** PoS, an effective and far less resource-intensive substitute for PoW, has been introduced. Theoretically, a node that is most vulnerable to attack will be less likely to do so [30–33]. It is unfair to choose nodes dependent on the account balance as the richest node is prone to controlling a network.
- **DPoS (delegated proof of stake):** DPoS, is a type of consensus. Most of the time, DPoS selection is democratic, as opposed to the selection of PoS, which is dependent on all nodes. The community elects stakeholder representatives to create as well as verify new blocks. The lesser nodes need to verify the block, the quicker transactions are verified by the remaining nodes. Fraudulent delegates might be simply elected out, making it easier to keep everything running well.
- **PBFT (practical Byzantine fault tolerance):** Replication method PBFT is a three-phase technique for coping with Byzantine errors. The three phases of the process are pre-preparation, preparation, and commitment. It may be constructed if the new block receives responses from more than two-thirds of the entire number of nodes in each phase. Less than one-third of malicious Byzantine replicating nodes could ensure the accuracy of the entire network. An agreement mechanism known as PBFT is used by permission Hyperledger Fabric to verify the transaction.
- Using Raft's consensus technique, a cluster of computer nodes may better manage their replicated logs. Each term's designated leader must approve and duplicate all new transactions. If the leader gets feedback from an adequate percentage of followers who wrote down the transactions, they will turn out to be considered committed [34–38]. The raft should be used for a consortium or private blockchains that can sustain up to 50% of node failures.
- **PoA (proof of authority):** It saves a fair amount of time to use a PoA consensus technique. Only nodes which have been permitted to build new blocks can do so. Each node must first pass an authentication procedure. On the other hand, this approach tends to generate a hierarchical organization.
- **PoC (proof of capacity):** Instead of relying on computer power to prove its effectiveness, this consensus approach does so by using hard drive space. It is more likely that a new block will be formed the more storage you have because you can store more solutions.

- **PoET (proof of elapsed time):** PoET's objective is to randomly and equitably select a block producer based on how long every participant waited in a trustworthy execution environment.

Integrating several consensus techniques is becoming more commonplace to increase performance in various applications.

Smart contract: these self-executing programmers or employment of smart contracts is done in a broad range of sectors, involving finance, healthcare as well as government. An agreement-invoking transaction may be sent to the appropriate contract address to perform complicated programming tasks [39, 40]. The terms specified in the secure container will then be automatically carried out by the smart contract.

The first accessible blockchain with such a turning smart contract language allowed developers to construct arbitrary decentralized applications on top of it (DApps).

3.3 Taxonomy of blockchain systems

Can be split up into three groups depending on the rights granted to the network of nodes.

3.3.1 Public blockchain

Any individual can join the open blockchain on any occasion as well as take part as a miner or a node to earn rewards. Two of the most familiar public blockchains are Ethereum and Bitcoin.

3.3.2 Private blockchain

To join the private blockchain network, members must first be invited or granted permission to do so. Private blockchains like GemOS are common, but they are not unique.

3.3.3 Consortium blockchains-op

Businesses that have been thoroughly reviewed and approved by appropriate authorities may use blockchain, which lies on the 'semi-private' boundary between public and private blockchains. For corporations, Hyperledger Fabric is a block-chain platform. Ethereum is also capable of supporting the creation of consortium blockchains.

3.4 Motivations for blockchain-based EHR systems

EHRs frequently include an individual's medical history, demographic data (like weight and age), and the findings of laboratory tests. Therefore, sensitive information needs to be protected and kept secret [41–43]. As a result, hospitals in nations like the United States are subjected to stringent regulatory control. Healthcare system deployment and implementation face several difficulties. Because of the single-point attack constraints and hostile insider assaults, centralized server architectures are particularly susceptible. In most cases, users (such as patients) who have their medical records saved in these EHR systems have no idea who is accessing their information or for what reasons it is being used (i.e., violation of personal privacy) [44–47]. Another company's insurance coverage for a specific patient may be denied if a leak of the patient's medical history was discovered by an insider with malicious intent.

Data exchange is also growing more significant as our culture as well as people become much more mobile. By utilizing the connections in various healthcare groups, it is feasible to improve the delivery of medical services [48–52]. Due to privacy and regulatory concerns, it will turn out to be challenging to prevail over the 'Information as well as Resource Island' (information silo). Because of the information silo, more data is duplicated, and there is more red tape involved.

The Health Insurance Portability and Accountability Act (HIPAA) was approved by United States Congress in 1996 [53–55]. Regulations enacted to secure the confidentiality of private health information as well as prevent fraud and waste in the healthcare system include the following.

3.4.1 Privacy rule

In healthcare, the rules and laws that regulate the use and sharing of healthcare data.

3.4.2 Transactions and code sets rule

Healthcare transactions will be streamlined if all health plans are required to participate in them consistently.

3.4.3 Security rule

Complementing the privacy rule are controls on computer access and safeguards for communications across open networks.

3.4.4 Unique identifiers rule

Protecting the patient's identity requires just the National Provider Identifier (NPI) in normal transactions.

3.4.5 Enforcement rule

Investigations and fines for HIPAA violations.

ISO 27789 has been created to make sure that EHRs are capable of being verified across several systems and domains [56]. Each time the system initiates an operation following ISO 27789 requirements, an audit record needs to be produced. Researchers believe that an audit and post-incident inquiry need an interactive and transparent data-sharing method when an alleged infringement occurs (e.g. data leakage). Experts in the field of forensics also support this point of view (forensic-by-design).

For the authenticity, integrity, or confidentiality of patient health data, medical systems are obliged by Title 21 CFR Part 11 to implement methods such as document encryption and digitally signed standardization [57]. Based on the relevant criteria mentioned above and the above requirements, the following issues must be considered while creating the subsequent generations of secure EHR systems:

Quality as well as reliability of information (e.g. any unauthorized alteration is prohibited and detectable.)

- Data security and privacy;
- A streamlined method of exchanging information;
- Patients will be able to monitor their EHRs and get alerts if they are lost or accessed without their permission;
- In the case of forensic-by-design, data auditing, and accountability.

The following qualities may be obtained with blockchain:

- **Decentralization.** Unlike centralized systems, which depend on a third party with some level of confidence, blockchain systems do not have this problem.
- **Security.** The decentralized blockchain technology protects against single points of failure and insider assaults.
- **Pseudonymity.** To keep its identity a secret, each node is assigned a public pseudonymous address.
- **Immutability.** The one-way cryptographic hash algorithm used by the block-chain makes it computationally impossible to remove or edit any record in a block.
- **Autonomy.** Patients can modify the smart contract's specifications to control how their information is shared and are given the option to do so.
- **Incentive mechanism.** Medical services and research may be boosted by using the incentive mechanism of blockchain.
- **Auditability.** It is simple to maintain track of any activity since every transaction on the blockchain is recorded.

As a result, proper implementation of blockchain to EHR systems might improve data quality plus privacy, encourage businesses and individuals for sharing data as well as make auditing or accountability easier [58–62].

3.5 Blockchain-based EHR systems

Based on the necessity for an entirely new generation of protected EHR systems as well as the traits of blockchain, this section will concentrate on the primary goals for developing secure EHR systems based on blockchain.

1. **Privacy**: The essential data will only be accessible to authorized individuals.
2. **Security**: Secrecy, integrity, and the capacity to access information (CIA).
3. **Confidentiality**: Only authorized operators have access to the data.

4. *Integrity*: Correct data must be sent as well as not be tampered with by unauthorized parties (ies).
5. *Availability*: There are no unjustified restrictions on lawful users' access to information and other resources [63, 64].

The present focus of healthcare blockchain research is on the following key areas to accomplish the goals:

- *Data storage*: Various sorts of private healthcare data may be securely maintained on the blockchain, which operates as a trustworthy ledger. Personal data may be protected if a secure storage facility is in place [65]. However, in practice, the scale and variety of health records are rather considerable. Therefore, dealing with enormous volumes of data without significantly compromising the pace of the blockchain network is a big issue.
- *Data sharing*: Current healthcare systems place a heavy emphasis on the management of patient data by service providers. Healthcare data ownership is progressively being restored to the patient, who is then free to disclose or not disclose their data as they see fit. This is good news for people who believe in individual autonomy [66, 67]. Companies and domains must also be able to securely communicate data with one another.
- *Data audit*: Audit logs may be used as proof in a dispute to keep EHR users accountable for their actions [68, 69]. Certain systems rely on smart contracts plus the blockchain for keeping their audibility. The blockchain ledger keeps a follow-up of every transaction, so they may be recovered at any time.
- *Identity manager*: Every user's identification must be verified in the system. To put it another way, only authorized users can make the necessary requests to keep the system safe from intrusion.

3.6 Data storage

One method to ensure improved data security is the combination of blockchain technology with an EHR system. Sensitive information could still be exposed by statistical attacks, even if all raw or encrypted information in the public ledger is encrypted. EHR systems built on blockchain should contain additional privacy safeguards to protect patient data [70–75]. Cryptographic and non-cryptographic privacy-preserving solutions include encryption, anonymization, as well as access control systems. Two of the most common types of encryption are symmetric key encryption (SKE) and public key encryption (PKE). Blockchain-dependent MediBchain employs public-key encryption (ECC) to encrypt private data and transfer it via a secure channel. According to Lee and Yang, private and public keys should be utilized to upload biometric information to the blockchain network. Cloud servers should be secured using symmetric key schemes like Rijndael AES with a threshold encryption method before uploading data, according to Zheng and colleagues. Shamir's secret sharing system will spread the symmetric key into several shares among various key holders. The data applicant can only decode the cipher text if he has sufficient key shares. Data leaking would not occur if a small number of key keepers (less than the threshold) were compromised. Healthcare Data Gateway is a smartphone app-based on blockchain created using the multi-party computing approach by Yue et al [47]. (HDG). It is possible to run calculations on private blockchain data and get results without releasing raw data with this approach. As a further example, a signature system based on attributes having multiple authorities (MA-ABS) towards healthcare blockchain was proposed by Guo and colleagues (2018) [76–80]. Using this method to sign a message does not attest to the sender's identity, rather it attests to a claim (like an access policy) about the traits that have been assigned to him by an identifiable authority. By distributing secret pseudorandom function (PRF) seeds across the authorities, the system can withstand collision attacks [81].

The encryption keys of popular techniques must be changed regularly to withstand hostile assaults (e.g., statistical attacks). As processing power and storage space become more limited, the cost of retaining previous keys will increase, making it more challenging to decrypt specific historical information in the future [82]. As a result, storage and administrative costs will increase. A simple backup plus effective retrieval key managment technique for BSNs can be utilised, BSNs can minimize the storage expenses associated with secret keys while protecting the confidentiality of data gathered by sensors from the human body. Using fuzzy vault technology, which eliminates the requirement for key storage, blockchain based service networks (BSNs) can decrypt data without storing the encryption key. As the sensor data is encoded using symmetric encoding, an attacker will have difficulty decoding it (i.e.AES or 3DES). Some of the systems we will compare and analyze are shown in (see below). In most systems, encryption technology is used to safeguard healthcare data on the blockchain. However, no type of encryption is impenetrable. On certain computers, encryption imposes a large burden on computing power. The history of a transaction may disclose the fixed account address as well as information about the user's activity and identity. Malicious attackers may be able to decipher the encryption text stored in the public ledger in some manner.

Key management, on the other hand, is a major concern. To ensure complete data security, private keys must not be revealed. The holder loses access to the data it holds if its private key is misplaced. If the attacker gets possession of a private/symmetric key, the whole data could be exposed [83]. To guarantee the security of an EHR system, developers must consider both encryption and key management.

For further protection, they must ensure that only those individuals who have been granted access to private information may do so. Access control mechanisms are the primary security and privacy safeguards used by non-cryptographic techniques. The purpose of access control mechanisms is to identify, authenticate, and provide access to certain individuals and groups. Secure data exchange with minimum danger of data leaking is extensively utilized using this technology.

3.6.1 How to store large healthcare data

There are EHR systems that can upload medical data to the blockchain. A set as well as constrained block size make it hard to store and process huge quantities of information on the blockchain. In addition, this data would be vulnerable to privacy breaches.

For on-chain validation, only particular metadata, as well as pointers/indices (i.e., off-chain databases locations) of the relevant raw information, are stored on the blockchain, whilst enormous volumes of encrypted original information are stored off-chain using trusted third parties (i.e., off-chain database locations, e.g., cloud computing) [84]. Data security and anonymity may be maintained while the blockchain's storage requirements are lowered. To obtain a user's history data at any moment, they may utilize the index of the most recent blockchain block. Wearable gadget data is encrypted and saved often in the cloud for a predetermined length of time. Blockchain transactions may be used to buy health data for machine learning [85]. To decrypt cloud storage data, buyers need access to and control over enough key shares.

Researchers developed an architecture that makes the utilization of an external store to overcome the blockchain's storage limitation as well as offering precise rollbacks in the event of a false warning. Using a database gatekeeper like this is utilized to store off-line medical records. Depending on whether the gatekeeper has been granted authority to process the request, it may be able to provide the requested information. Healthcare data in the cloud is protected by CCAC (CP-ABE-based access control), which was created by researchers [49]. In the cloud, requestors may validate the quality and integrity of requested data by obtaining data that involves an extraction signature. For protecting the privacy and security of patient information, the raw SignedEHR is signed utilizing attribute-based signatures from medical professionals and then kept in a reputable third-party database [86]. Decentralizing signatures must be used by doctors to sign EHRs, and those signed EHRs must then be transmitted to the blockchain network by submitting the corresponding addresses. A user's signature must be verified as genuine before any data can be accessed, and this can only be done if specific attributes are present.

Paper records, text, images, and more may all be used to store healthcare data. Due to blockchain's constrained block size, for high-capacity storage of information in healthcare systems, additional methods must be considered. It is possible to produce unique DICOM UIDs for each imaging study using the improved JAVA UID class. By storing raw image data off-chain utilizing DICOM UIDs (PHI), it is possible to stop the leakage of confidential health data from the blockchain.

A researcher describes an architecture that enables patients to safely provide other people with access to their imaging data to encourage cross-domain medical picture exchange. No raw medical pictures are stored on the blockchain for any research that has been authorized. It has been suggested that ICS might be used to organize diverse forms of personal healthcare data into a single, searchable table, according to research. Using this method, data may be uploaded once and retrieved several times [87, 88]. Multi-level, as well as multi-dimensional (LD-Index) indexes, have been constructed.

Utilizing category and time hash indices, data can be indexed. The leaf node of the B+ tree provides access to every category [89]. For shared healthcare information, cell granularity makes it simple to use ICS. In the preceding sections, many systems have made use of third-party database systems. Customers may improve application quality by using third-party services (e.g., on the far end of cloud computing) to provide data storage and calculation capability, but this comes at a transmission delay [90]. Third-party services with large storage capacities and high-performance processing have grown increasingly widespread. Because it depends so significantly on third-party services, a single failure point is feasible. As a result, some cloud servers may be gathering private patient information without the user's knowledge. The InterPlanetary File System (IPFS), which employs dispersed hash tables (DHTs) for storing data hash values and enables high storage throughput as well as rapid data retrieval, has no single point of negligence.

3.7 Conclusion

In this chapter, blockchain is shown as having the ability to transform the healthcare industry. Many scientific and practical challenges stand in the way of fully integrating blockchain technology into existing EHR systems. A couple of these difficulties will be examined in further depth in this section. Our research then led us to uncover an array of exciting new fields of inquiry to pursue, including but not limited to the IoT, big data, machine learning, or cutting-edge computing. The results should throw light on future EHR technology that will help our (aging) population.

References

[1] Shi S, He D, Li L, Kumar N, Khan M K and Choo K K R 2020 Applications of blockchain in ensuring the security and privacy of electronic health record systems: a survey *Comput. Secur.* **97** 101966

[2] Ahram T, Sargolzaei A, Sargolzaei S, Daniels J and Amaba B 2017 Blockchain technology innovations *2017 IEEE technology & engineering management conf. (TEMSCON)* 137–41

[3] Gentry C 2009 A fully homomorphic encryption scheme *PhD Thesis* Stanford UniversityStanford, CA

[4] Kalam A A E, Baida R E, Balbiani P, Benferhat S, Cuppens F, Deswarte Y, Miege A, Saurel C and Trouessin G 2003 Organization based access control *Proc. POLICY 2003. IEEE 4th Int. Workshop on Policies for Distributed Systems and Networks* pp 120–31

[5] Rouhani S and Deters R 2019 Blockchain based access control systems: state of the art and challenges *IEEE/WIC/ACM Int. Conf. on Web Intelligence* pp 423–8

[6] Daemen J and Rijmen V 2002 *The Design of Rijndael* (Cham: Springer) p 2

[7] Feng Q, He D, Zeadally S, Khan M K and Kumar N 2019 A survey on privacy protection in blockchain system *J. Netw. Comput. Appl.* **126** 45–58

[8] Huang H, Chen X and Wang J 2020 Blockchain-based multiple groups data sharing with anonymity and traceability *Sci. China Inf. Sci.* **63** 1–13

[9] Ahsan M M, Wahab A W B A, Idris M Y I B, Khan S, Bachura E and Choo K K R 2018 Class: cloud log assuring soundness and secrecy scheme for cloud forensics *IEEE Trans. Sustain. Comput.* **6** 184–96

[10] Patel V 2019 A framework for secure and decentralized sharing of medical imaging data via blockchain consensus *Health Inform. J.* **25** 1398–411

[11] Xia Q I, Sifah E B, Asamoah K O, Gao J, Du X and Guizani M 2017 MeDShare: trust-less medical data sharing among cloud service providers via blockchain *IEEE Access* **5** 14757–67

[12] Pham H L, Tran T H and Nakashima Y 2018 A secure remote healthcare system for hospital using blockchain smart contract *2018 IEEE Globecom Workshops (GC Wkshps)* pp 1–6

[13] Ramani V, Kumar T, Bracken A, Liyanage M and Ylianttila M 2018 Secure and efficient data accessibility in blockchain based healthcare systems *2018 IEEE Global Communications Conf. (GLOBECOM)* pp 206–12

[14] Ab Rahman N H, Glisson W B, Yang Y and Choo K K R 2016 Forensic-by-design framework for cyber-physical cloud systems *IEEE Cloud Comput.* **3** 50–9

[15] Zhang P, White J, Schmidt D C, Lenz G and Rosenbloom S T 2018 FHIRChain: applying blockchain to securely and scalably share clinical data *Comput. Struct. Biotechnol. J.* **16** 267–78

[16] Outchakoucht A, Hamza E S and Leroy J P 2017 Dynamic access control policy based on blockchain and machine learning for the Internet of Things *Int. J. Adv. Comput. Sci. Appl.* **8** 417–24

[17] Chen M, Yang J, Zhou J, Hao Y, Zhang J and Youn C H 5G-smart diabetes: toward personalized diabetes diagnosis with healthcare big data clouds *IEEE Commun. Mag.* **56** 16–23

[18] Shae Z and Tsai J J 2017 *IEEE 37th Int. Conf. on Distributed Computing Systems (ICDCS) IEEE; 2017 on the Design of a Blockchain Platform for Clinical Trial and Precision Medicine* pp 1972–80

[19] Yang R, Yu F R, Si P, Yang Z and Zhang Y 2019 Integrated blockchain and edge computing systems: a survey, some research issues and challenges *IEEE Commun. Surv. Tutor.* **21** 1508–32

[20] Azaria A, Ekblaw A, Vieira T and Lippman A 2016 Medrec: using blockchain for medical data access and permission management *2016 2nd Int. Conf. on Open and Big Data (OBD)* pp 25–30

[21] Crameri K A, Maher L, Van Dam P and Prior S 2022 Personal electronic healthcare records: what influences consumers to engage with their clinical data online? A literature review *Health Inf. Manag. J.* **51** 3–12

[22] Benchoufi M and Ravaud P 2017 Blockchain technology for improving clinical research quality *Trials* **18** 1–5

[23] Sivagami S, Revathy D and Nithyabharathi L 2016 Smart health care system implemented using IoT *Int. J. Contemp. Res. Comput. Sci. Technol.* **2** 641–6

[24] Grispos G, Glisson W B and Choo K K R 2017 Medical cyber-physical systems development: a forensics-driven approach *2017 IEEE/ACM Int. Conf. on Connected Health: Applications, Systems and Engineering Technologies (CHASE)* pp 108–13

[25] Dai W, Dai C, Choo K K R, Cui C, Zou D and Jin H 2019 SDTE: a secure blockchain-based data trading ecosystem *IEEE Trans. Inf. Forensics Secur.* **15** 725–37

[26] Fernández-Alemán J L, Señor I C, Lozoya P Á O and Toval A 2013 Security and privacy in electronic health records: a systematic literature review *J. Biomed. Inform.* **46** 541–62

[27] Budida D A M and Mangrulkar R S 2017 Design and implementation of smart HealthCare system using IoT *2017 Int. Conf. on Innovations in Information, Embedded and Communication Systems (ICIIECS)* pp 1–7

[28] Lee S H and Yang C S 2018 Fingernail analysis management system using microscopy sensor and blockchain technology *Int. J. Distrib. Sens. Netw.* **14** 1550147718767044

[29] Nguyen D C, Pathirana P N, Ding M and Seneviratne A 2019 Blockchain for secure ehrs sharing of mobile cloud based e-health systems *IEEE Access* **7** 66792–806

[30] Pussewalage H S G and Oleshchuk V A 2018 Blockchain based delegatable access control scheme for a collaborative e-health environment *2018 IEEE Int. Conf. on Internet of Things (iThings) and IEEE Green Computing and Communications (GreenCom) and IEEE Cyber, Physical and Social Computing (CPSCom) and IEEE Smart Data (SmartData)* pp 1204–11

[31] Tovanich N, Heulot N, Fekete J D and Isenberg P 2019 Visualization of blockchain data: a systematic review *IEEE Trans. Visual Comput. Graphics* **27** 3135–52

[32] Ma S, Deng Y, He D, Zhang J and Xie X 2020 An efficient NIZK scheme for privacy-preserving transactions over account-model blockchain *IEEE Trans. Dependable Secure Comput.* **18** 641–51

[33] Kaur A, Bansal S and Dattana V 2023 Blockchain in healthcare: a systematic review and future perspectives *Deep Learning for Healthcare Decision Making* (Boca Raton, FL: CRC Press) pp 211–43

[34] Zyskind G, Nathan O and Pentland A 2015 Enigma: decentralized computation platform with guaranteed privacy arXiv preprint arXiv:1506.03471

[35] Wang W, Hoang D T, Hu P, Xiong Z, Niyato D, Wang P, Wen Y and Kim D I 2019 A survey on consensus mechanisms and mining strategy management in blockchain networks *IEEE Access* **7** 22328–70

[36] Morelli U, Ranise S, Sartori D, Sciarretta G and Tomasi A 2019 Audit-based access control with a distributed ledger: applications to healthcare organizations *Int. Workshop on Security and Trust Management* pp 19–35

[37] Liu J, Li X, Ye L, Zhang H, Du X and Guizani M 2018 BPDS: a blockchain based privacy-preserving data sharing for electronic medical records *2018 IEEE Global Communications Conf. (GLOBECOM)* pp 1–6

[38] Dey T, Jaiswal S, Sunderkrishnan S and Katre N 2017 HealthSense: a medical use case of Internet of Things and blockchain *2017 Int. Conf. on Intelligent Sustainable Systems (ICISS)* pp 486–91

[39] Al Omar A, Rahman M S, Basu A and Kiyomoto S 2017 Medibchain: a blockchain based privacy preserving platform for healthcare data *Int. Conf. on Security, Privacy, and Anonymity in Computation, Communication, and Storage: SpaCCS 2017 Int. Workshops, 2017, Proc. (Guangzhou, China,* vol 10December 12–15) *pp 534–43*

[40] Esposito C, De Santis A, Tortora G, Chang H and Choo K K R 2018 Blockchain: a panacea for healthcare cloud-based data security and privacy? *IEEE Cloud Comput.* **5** 31–7

[41] Bahga A and Madisetti V K 2013 A cloud-based approach for interoperable electronic health records (EHRs) *IEEE J. Biomed. Health Inform.* **17** 894–906

[42] Zhao H, Zhang Y, Peng Y and Xu R 2017 Lightweight backup and efficient recovery scheme for health blockchain keys *2017 IEEE 13th Int. Symp. on Autonomous Decentralized System (ISADS)* pp 229–34

[43] Juneja A and Marefat M 2018 Leveraging blockchain for retraining deep learning architecture in patient-specific arrhythmia classification *2018 IEEE EMBS Int. Conf. on Biomedical & Health Informatics (BHI)* pp 393–7

[44] Strudwick G and Eyasu T 2015 Electronic health record use by nurses in mental health settings: a literature review *Arch. Psychiatr. Nurs.* **29** 238–41

[45] Dias J P, Reis L, Ferreira H S and Martins Â 2018 Blockchain for access control in e-health scenarios arXiv preprint arXiv:1805.12267

[46] Otero P, Hersh W and Ganesh A J 2014 Big data: are biomedical and health informatics training programs ready? *Yearb. Med. Inform.* **23** 177–81

[47] Yue X, Wang H, Jin D, Li M and Jiang W 2016 Healthcare data gateways: found healthcare intelligence on blockchain with novel privacy risk control *J. Med. Syst.* **40** 1–8

[48] Kim M G, Lee A R, Kwon H J, Kim J W and Kim I K 2018 Sharing medical questionnaires based on blockchain *2018 IEEE Int. Conf. on Bioinformatics and Biomedicine (BIBM)* pp 2767–9

[49] Carvalho J V, Rocha Á and Abreu A 2016 Maturity models of healthcare information systems and technologies: a literature review *J. Med. Syst.* **40** 1–10

[50] Ethereum: Blockchain app platforms https://ethereum.org/

[51] Johnson D, Menezes A and Vanstone S 2001 The elliptic curve digital signature algorithm (ECDSA) *Int. J. Inf. Secur.* **1** 36–63

[52] Zheng X, Mukkamala R R, Vatrapu R and Ordieres-Mere J 2018 Blockchain-based personal health data sharing system using cloud storage *2018 IEEE 20th Int. Conf. on e-Health Networking, Applications and Services (Healthcom)* pp 1–6

[53] Menezes A J, Van Oorschot P C and Vanstone S A 2018 *Handbook of Applied Cryptography* (Boca Raton, FL: CRC Press)

[54] McGhin T, Choo K K R, Liu C Z and He D 2019 Blockchain in healthcare applications: research challenges and opportunities *J. Netw. Comput. Appl.* **135** 62–75

[55] Steinfeld R, Bull L and Zheng Y 2002 Content extraction signatures *Information Security and Cryptology—ICISC 2001: 4th Int. Conf. Proc. (Seoul, Korea, December 6–7, 2001)* vol 4 pp 285–304

[56] Croman K *et al* 2016 On scaling decentralized blockchains *Int. Conf. on Financial Cryptography and Data Security* pp 106–25

[57] Gai K, Wu Y, Zhu L, Xu L and Zhang Y 2019 Permissioned blockchain and edge computing empowered privacy-preserving smart grid networks *IEEE Internet Things J.* **6** 7992–8004

[58] Lamport L, Shostak R and Pease M 2019 The Byzantine generals problem *Concurrency: The Works of Leslie Lamport* (SanRafael, CA: Morgan & Claypool) pp 203–26

[59] Seol K, Kim Y G, Lee E, Seo Y D and Baik D K 2018 Privacy-preserving attribute-based access control model for XML-based electronic health record system *IEEE Access* **6** 9114–28

[60] Begoyan A 2007 *An Overview of Interoperability Standards for Electronic Health Records* (Plano, TX: Society for Design and Process Science)

[61] Ho S Y, Guo X and Vogel D 2019 Opportunities and challenges in healthcare information systems research: caring for patients with chronic conditions *Assoc. Inform. Syst.* **44** 39

[62] Rifi N, Rachkidi E, Agoulmine N and Taher N C 2017 Towards using blockchain technology for eHealth data access management *2017 4th Int. Conf. on Advances in Biomedical Engineering (ICABME)* pp 1–4

[63] Wang S, Zhang Y and Zhang Y 2018 A blockchain-based framework for data sharing with fine-grained access control in decentralized storage systems *IEEE Access* **6** 38437–50

[64] MultiChain: open platform for building blockchains https://multichain.com/

[65] Yaji S, Bangera K and Neelima B 2018 Privacy preserving in blockchain based on partial homomorphic encryption system for AI applications *2018 IEEE 25th Int. Conf. on High Performance Computing Workshops (HiPCW)* (Piscataway, NJ: IEEE) pp 81–5

[66] Mettler M 2016 Blockchain technology in healthcare: the revolution starts here *2016 IEEE 18th Int. Conf. on e-Health Networking, Applications and Services (Healthcom)* pp 1–3

[67] Boonstra A, Versluis A and Vos J F 2014 Implementing electronic health records in hospitals: a systematic literature review *BMC Health Serv. Res.* **14** 1–24

[68] He D, Zhang Y, Wang D and Choo K K R 2018 Secure and efficient two-party signing protocol for the identity-based signature scheme in the IEEE P1363 standard for public key cryptography *IEEE Trans. Dependable Secure Comput.* **17** 1124–32

[69] Kamauu A W, DuVall S L and Avrin D E 2009 Using Java to generate globally unique identifiers for DICOM objects *J. Digit. Imaging* **22** 11–4

[70] Xia Q, Sifah E B, Smahi A, Amofa S and Zhang X 2017 BBDS: blockchain-based data sharing for electronic medical records in cloud environments *Information* **8** 44

[71] Lin C, He D, Huang X, Khan M K and Choo K K R 2020 DCAP: a secure and efficient decentralized conditional anonymous payment system based on blockchain *IEEE Trans. Inf. Forensics Secur.* **15** 2440–52

[72] Hsieh G and Chen R J 2012 Design for a secure interoperable cloud-based Personal Health Record service *4th IEEE Int. Conf. on Cloud Computing Technology and Science Proc.* pp 472–9

[73] Brooks R R, Wang K C, Yu L, Oakley J, Skjellum A, Obeid J S, Lenert L and Worley C 2018 Scrybe: a blockchain ledger for clinical trials *IEEE Blockchain in Clinical Trials Forum: Whiteboard Challenge Winner* 1–2

[74] Liang X, Zhao J, Shetty S, Liu J and Li D 2017 Integrating blockchain for data sharing and collaboration in mobile healthcare applications *2017 IEEE 28th Annual Int. Symp. on Personal, Indoor, and Mobile Radio Communications (PIMRC)* pp 1–5

[75] Yang G and Li C 2018 A design of blockchain-based architecture for the security of electronic health record (EHR) systems *2018 IEEE Int. Conf. on Cloud Computing Technology and Science (CloudCom)* pp 261–5

[76] Blum M, Feldman P and Micali S 2019 Non-interactive zero-knowledge and its applications *Providing Sound Foundations for Cryptography: On the Work of Shafi Goldwasser and Silvio Micali* pp 329–49

[77] Jiang S, Cao J, Wu H, Yang Y, Ma M and He J 2018 Blochie: a blockchain-based platform for healthcare information exchange *2018 IEEE Int. Conf. on Smart Computing (SMARTCOMP)* pp 49–56

[78] Nugent T, Upton D and Cimpoesu M 2016 Improving data transparency in clinical trials using blockchain smart contracts *F1000Research* **5** 2541

[79] Miah S J, Gammack J and Hasan N 2020 Methodologies for designing healthcare analytics solutions: a literature analysis *Health Inform. J.* **26** 2300–14

[80] Sun Y, Zhang R, Wang X, Gao K and Liu L 2018 A decentralizing attribute-based signature for healthcare blockchain *2018 27th Int. Conf. on Computer Communication and Networks (ICCCN)* pp 1–9

[81] GemOS: the blockchain operating system https://enterprise.gem.co/

[82] Guo R, Shi H, Zhao Q and Zheng D 2018 Secure attribute-based signature scheme with multiple authorities for blockchain in electronic health records systems *IEEE Access* **6** 11676–86

[83] Kuo T T, Kim H E and Ohno-Machado L 2017 Blockchain distributed ledger technologies for biomedical and health care applications *J. Am. Med. Inform. Assoc.* **24** 1211–20

[84] Lluch M 2011 Healthcare professionals' organisational barriers to health information technologies—a literature review *Int. J. Med. Inform.* **80** 849–62

[85] Hardjono T and Pentland A 2019 Verifiable anonymous identities and access control in permissioned blockchains arXiv preprint arXiv:1903.04584

[86] Dubovitskaya A, Xu Z, Ryu S, Schumacher M and Wang F 2017 Secure and trustable electronic medical records sharing using blockchain *AMIA Annual Symp. Proc. 2017* p 650

[87] Lloret J, Parra L, Taha M and Tomás J 2017 An architecture and protocol for smart continuous eHealth monitoring using 5G *Comput. Netw.* **129** 340–51

[88] Feng Q, He D, Wang H, Wang D and Huang X 2020 Multi-party key generation protocol for the identity-based signature scheme in the ieee p1363 standard for public key cryptography *IET Inf. Secur.* **14** 724–32

[89] Hyperledger Fabric https://hyperledger.org/

[90] Nakamoto S 2008 Bitcoin: a peer-to-peer electronic cash system *Decentralized Bus. Rev.* **31** 21260

IOP Publishing

Blockchain with Artificial Intelligence for Healthcare
A synergistic approach
Rishabha Malviya, Arun Kumar Singh, Sonali Sundram, Balamurugan Balusamy and Seifedine Kadry

Chapter 4

Challenges in utilizing blockchain for securing health data

Healthcare reform is at the top of the list in today's technologically advanced world. In the case of a natural catastrophe, the existing health database management systems have a single point of failure. The problem of data management in the healthcare sector has quickly been addressed by blockchain technology, which is now at the forefront of the list of viable solutions. In order to keep medical records safe and secure, many individuals are interested in employing blockchain technology. Only a few of today's most important difficulties in healthcare big data management are patients' permissions, data ownership, management, auditing, privacy, security, traceability, and immutability. Many of these issues might be alleviated or even eliminated with the use of blockchain. Only a few studies have examined how blockchain performs in health big data management in light of these potential advantages. This chapter describes how blockchain technology can improve healthcare big data management systems. This chapter examines blockchain's fundamental benefits, available implementation options, and barriers to widespread use for healthcare big data handling.

4.1 Introduction

Rapid digitization in the healthcare sector has produced sensor data that has been digitally processed. Healthcare data researchers and analysts around the world are finding it more difficult to keep up with the massive amounts of data being produced by Internet of Things (IoT) devices as well as other sources. Providers of healthcare data are similarly concerned about protecting patient confidentiality. Consequently, it has become increasingly difficult to deliver specialized services and analyze vast volumes of data. The most important players in healthcare big data are health

doi:10.1088/978-0-7503-5839-2ch4

insurers, providers, payers, and analysts. Those higher up in the chain of command are under a lot of pressure to work together and communicate effectively [1–3]. These four parties are often implicated in breaches of security and privacy. Paper medical records or wearable technology may be used to collect data, but it is the patients themselves who generate it [1]. Those who help patients financially by paying the price of their medical care are known as 'payers' (e.g., insurance companies as well as private sources, etc). They consist of hospitals, clinics, blood banks, and other organizations that receive and hold medical records. These are the people who use the information provided by these resources to conduct their investigations.

This makes it more difficult to keep medical data safe since they are spread out across a variety of organizations [4]. Many current healthcare systems that depend on centralization seem to be susceptible to cyber assaults. The loss of patient privacy and confidentiality may have far-reaching consequences for healthcare providers and the people they serve [5]. Existing healthcare systems lack security, immutability, reliable traceability, auditability, plus transparency when it comes to the management of patient data. Blockchain technology appears to be able to overcome these challenges in today's medical systems [6–9].

The healthcare sector could be completely transformed by blockchain technology. The analysis of healthcare big data will gain from the standardization and regulation of access to data contracts, as well as from an increase in data efficiency and trust [10–15]. Because of these characteristics and the widespread usage of the blockchain in healthcare, it is ideal for handling vast amounts of data and cutting down on administrative costs [16, 17]. To eliminate the need for a middleman in the healthcare network, all parties must agree on a set of terms and conditions. Working with medical records may be a challenge because of the unique data storage and retrieval methods used. Every operation in the blockchain includes a time stamp as well as an associated identification, and copies are sent to all participating network nodes [18, 19]. Therefore, any modifications or updates made to a node are sent to every other node as well as being accessible from anywhere on the planet. The usage of blockchain technology ensures data integrity across endpoints without the need for human intervention.

Few researchers have looked at how blockchain technology might be used to manage huge quantities of healthcare big data, even though there have been many studies on the application of blockchain technology to healthcare [6, 20–25]. It will be an important addition to the body of knowledge because it will focus on key aspects of the blockchain for managing massive amounts of healthcare data, including its fundamental features, implementation opportunities, and challenges, as well as adoption concerns in the healthcare sector. The next section will contain:

- Outline of the blockchain's most noteworthy features and qualities, as well as the healthcare industry's potential advantages.
- Discussion of how this technology may be utilized to alleviate some of the healthcare industry's problems.

- Use of this technology in various healthcare settings, involving hospitals, clinics, as well as nursing homes.
- Determining of the main challenges that this technology's utilization in the healthcare industry faces and the suggested solutions to these challenges.

4.2 Health big data and blockchain technology

4.2.1 Healthcare big data

This huge amount of structured data, with a range of features, is examined by computers to discover patterns associated with it [3]. If you're dealing with a huge and complicated dataset, the term 'big data' is used to characterize the problem. Nearly all of the elements of the healthcare business are now producing enormous quantities of healthcare data as a result of the new digital advancements in healthcare. Medical records can include, for example, x-ray and ultrasound images, MRI (magnetic resonance imaging), patient dialogues with doctors, similar information in text, clinical images, and more [4]. Sensor data from a variety of healthcare devices as well as electronic medical records (EMRs) are the two primary big data directions in healthcare presently accessible. Big data as well as healthcare data mining have a lot in common when it comes to foreseeing future illness. Throughout a patient's care, medical institutions gather data that is used to create EMRs. The IoT is a vast collection of devices that have the potential to gather data. These devices collect information to track the health of various organs or functions in patients. Health data may also be at risk from medical signal processing as well as interchange alongside physical data breaches [13]. Therefore, conducting context-aware analysis of big data as well as carefully evaluating each type of data before processing it is crucial [14].

4.2.2 Blockchain technology

Cryptographic hashing protects the blockchain, a decentralized database of all transactions and related data, on a variety of levels. The three pillars of blockchain are peer-to-peer networks, consensus techniques as well as public-key cryptography [26]. Peer-to-peer networks may manage a distributed ledger by confirming new blocks according to a protocol. Permission management determines if a blockchain is open, private, or part of a consortium [27]. Participation in the consensus procedure on a public blockchain is open to anybody with an Internet connection. In the public blockchain reward system and encrypted digit authentication, two kinds of consensus procedures are employed: the decentralized mechanism of the blockchain safeguards the identity of each participant. When it comes to public and private blockchains, each is under the jurisdiction of a single corporation. The blockchain is in desperate need of a trustworthy middleman because of this. Blockchain consortiums incorporate the greatest elements of both private and public blockchains. Below, you'll see some of the healthcare industry's potential benefits of blockchain technology, as shown in table 4.1.

Table 4.1. Features of blockchain technology.

Features	Description
Decentralization	Decentralization helps healthcare systems become more robust by distributing power away from a centralized or central authority [28]. Due to the decentralization of data storage, several copies of the information are preserved in many places. The data stored on the blockchain is only accessible to those who have the creator's permission to read it. As a further benefit of the blockchain, each user may keep a copy of the transaction log for their records. With no central government or third-party participation, this system is more transparent [29].
Transparency	The network is validated every 10 minutes to reconcile transactions as well as record any data changes, and everyone on the blockchain network receives a comprehensive as well as auditable record of all transactions. A reliable and auditable transaction ledger will be possible thanks to the transparency of health data [30]. Blockchain technology gives healthcare organizations complete visibility over the ingredients utilized in pharmaceutical development, production conditions, and stakeholder workflow through encryption and management systems [31].
Immutability	Any attempt to alter or delete any data from the blockchain ledger is ruled out because of the ledger's immutability. Additional security is provided by the inability to modify data after it has been written to a particular block of memory [28]. It is possible to alter the auditing procedure using cryptographic hashing plus the blockchain's immutability [15]. Health data exchange may be made more secure and trustworthy by using this technique.
Access control for data owners	Owners of data can grant or remove access to their data using blockchain transactions. Significantly, data owners can assign several data categories with varying levels of access protection. Some start-ups can keep confidential medical data private, while others may choose to share it with only a few organizations or even sell it [2]. The blockchain provides a viable means of enforcing meta-consent.
Assessing data quality and certifying data sources	To maintain a high level of trust in medical information, medical contexts must include all information necessary for the creation, access, as well as transmission of health data [31]. The blockchain offers a method for users to trace any changes made to the data to maintain its integrity. Anti-tampering of healthcare systems using blockchain technology may be possible.

Distributed ledger and consensus	The combination of distributed ledgers and consensus methods provides some advantages for the blockchain. Reduced operational inefficiencies result in decreased administrative expenses as a result of DLT (distributed ledger technology). Consistent data and file synchronization are assured by the self-updating nature of blockchains. Consensus algorithms, on the other hand, are in charge of authorizing chain transactions. A single source of truth is now feasible for all healthcare stakeholders. Consensus nodes verify that all valid transactions have been recorded in a consistent ledger that is relayed to consensus nodes through the time-stamping process [32].
Anonymity	For instance, the Secure Hash Algorithm (SHA-256) addresses trust difficulties and enhances anonymity by creating an anonymous user address using a hash value instead of the user's real identity. Anonymity ensures that the sender's and recipient's identities in transactions are kept secret. Smart contracts, which are self-executing programs based on agreements between consumers and suppliers, can be used to control the execution of traceable yet irreversible transactions. Transactions and agreements may be carried out without the need for a third party or an external compliance procedure [33].

4.3 Notable benefits of blockchain to healthcare big data management

Figure 4.1 illustrates the significant advantages of blockchain in dealing with the issues of massive data management in healthcare. These advantages are examined in depth in the following subsections.

4.3.1 Data privacy and security

In the previous decade, healthcare practitioners and organizations have been the victims of needless cybersecurity epidemics [33]. Healthcare data breaches cost USD 380 per second, but data from industry breaches only cost USD 141 per second, according to IBM and Ponemon. Cybersecurity in the healthcare industry may be reduced by using the security architecture of the blockchain [34]. The immutability of data and the usage of hash algorithms make blockchain a safe system.

According to cryptographic principles that underlie blockchain, there is no chance of data theft or mistreatment [35, 36]. Any contract, decision, transaction, or information may be stored in this tamper-proof technology. There is not a single point of failure because the data is distributed throughout the system. Natural disasters and the loss of medical facilities will not have an impact on the health data

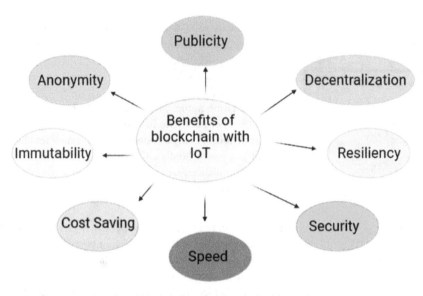

Figure 4.1. Benefits of blockchain technology in healthcare data management.

recorded on the blockchain. The risk of data manipulation is decreased via decentralized data storage. By fusing the physical and digital worlds using block-chain technology, it may be possible to increase trust between healthcare big data suppliers. The three pillars of safety are identification and traceability. Three sorts of digital trust may be provided by blockchain technology [37].

4.3.2 Data interoperability and global data sharing

The cornerstone of research as well as development is the interchange of data between healthcare organizations and academic institutes. Patients' test results, prescription status, and data from other organizations are all examples of data that might potentially be transferred over the IoT. The present condition of interoperability plus connection in medical records is crucial. Clinical technologies, technical specifications, and capabilities are the major factors for most EMR devices [38, 39]. Information cannot be generated and transmitted simultaneously because of these disparities. Another reason why the same-architecture EMRs cannot work together is that each healthcare institution has its own set of unique needs and preferences. An interoperability barrier can be removed and healthcare large data can be managed on the blockchain. At its core, it is a distributed ledger that makes digital assets and transactions visible in real time to all parties involved. It is capable of facilitating basic interoperability between network members. All stakeholders may agree on the same platform, thanks to the consensus-based nature of blockchain technology, which assures data reliability, quality, and consistency [40, 41]. A patient's medical records may be easily accessed and used by any healthcare provider because of the usage of a standardized data code.

4.3.3 Data accuracy

In most cases, patients' medical records are dispersed throughout different hospitals, clinics, as well as insurance providers [42]. To get a precise picture of an individual's medical history, every one of these pieces of information must be put together automatically. When medical records are kept on the blockchain, they may be traced and interfered [43]. This is how it is done. This allows healthcare professionals to provide patients with timely, effective, plus appropriate therapy. Patients' medical histories may be made visible, unchangeable, traceable, and secure for medical suppliers via blockchain technology [26].

4.3.4 Data processing costs

In today's healthcare systems, accessing and exchanging patient data may be prohibitively costly. Many healthcare facilities get the patient's medical records over a long period [44]. From manual or disorganized systems of hospital records, it consumes a lot of time as well as money to get the patient's complete medical data. The usage of blockchain technology may help to cut third-party expenditure in the present healthcare system. With the system's adoption, patients' medical records, which are gathered and preserved from various sources such as patient records, personal wearables as well as mobile devices [45, 46], would have more flexible access. This means that medical firms might save money by having access to all of their patients' medical records without having to commute to various locations where they were previously maintained.

4.3.5 Enhanced data auditing

To ensure that healthcare providers are following established procedures, protocols, regulations, legislation, and laws made by healthcare organizations, audits are carried out [47]. To determine if a healthcare compliance program is working as intended, an auditing approach uses systematic and objective evaluations. The majority of healthcare systems in use today are entirely manual and lack intelligent guidance or integration. As a consequence, auditing is hampered, and the results are inaccurate. To demonstrate the dependability of medical data kept in blockchains, healthcare companies may employ the technology in a certified, tamper-proof, and regular way [48]. Auditors will have an easier time checking transactions on blockchain networks as a result of this. In addition to ensuring that healthcare businesses are adhering to crucial legal standards and laws, blockchain auditing of healthcare data may improve the quality of patient treatment. It may also help to reduce the amount of duplicate data.

4.4 Prominent healthcare areas in which blockchain is useful

Blockchain technology could be utilized for addressing some of the biggest difficulties in healthcare. In the following sections, we'll look at how blockchain may be used in several healthcare sectors.

4.4.1 Patient record management (PRM)

PRM is a common utilization of blockchain in the sector of healthcare. To categorize a patient's medical history, insurance departments often segregate patients' medical histories, making it simpler to do so. It takes a long time and is prone to error due to clumsiness on the part of the user. As a result of this, patients may access their medical records openly and transparently by putting them on the blockchain [49]. When all of a patient's medical records are housed in one place, it makes things simpler for both the patient and the doctor. For the most part, it is impossible to apply the same treatment plan to all patients because of their unique characteristics. As a consequence, delivering personal care necessitates having access to all medical records. It is also important to note that the majority of healthcare systems nowadays do not guarantee the encryption or security of patients' health-related information.

Medical records have become a major issue in the medical community [50]. Data in patient health records may be changed or deleted by patients, thus they cannot claim ownership of them. Medical examinations sometimes need to be repeated when patients move to a new medical institution. As a result, there will be increased cost. The data in a dispersed peer-to-peer network could only be acquired via smart contracts, which is where blockchain comes in to solve the problems listed above. It is safe to transport this data from one hospital to another since it cannot be abused. Because it helps new doctors learn about previous patients' histories, they can better comprehend an illness and address it correctly. Since diagnostic tests previously performed on the patient do not need to be repeated, blockchain lowers the overall cost. The medical records of every patient are replicated and kept on several nodes in the blockchain network, which ensures its security and that it cannot be manipulated [51].

4.4.2 Drug supply chain

The healthcare sector is grappling with a growing problem of prescription fraud and subpar quality. It is believed that abundance of individuals die per year as a consequence of the utilization of illegally sourced medications. The annual worth of the fake medication business is estimated at $200 billion [52]. Health research funding agencies estimate that 10%–30% of the world's pharmaceuticals are fake. One in every 10 medical items sold in low- as well as middle-income nations, is either defective or fraudulent, according to a survey by *The Guardian* [53]. That the pharmaceutical sector is particularly susceptible to the production of phoney pharmaceuticals is shown by this example. There is always a possible risk of forging drugs entering this supply chain [54, 55]. From production stock through wholesale distributors to retail distributors, a drug's supply chain cycle begins when the process of manufacturing is completed. The chain of supply for pharmaceuticals may be tracked by utilizing blockchain technology. Monitoring everything from manufacturing through end-user feedback may help maintain medical standards. Blockchain enables complete visibility into the medical supply chain when the medicine is updated or modified while in transit. There are fewer instances of counterfeiting because medicine recalls are simpler to implement [52]. Transactions on the blockchain are incorruptible since they are recorded and timestamped. The blockchain records every move a medication makes as it travels from one area to the next. As a result, drug tracing is improved, and the likelihood of counterfeit pharmaceuticals is reduced. Anyone in the medical supply chain is free to examine the transaction. Any part of a contract may be verified using this technology, also if one of those characteristics is absent, the contract could be canceled at any moment.

4.4.3 Research and development

Countless swathes of medical records, market research data, and genetic information are regularly mined for information. In research and clinical trials, blockchain has the potential to revolutionize healthcare. Collaboration across several locations and stakeholders, as well as cautious management of vast amounts of personal data, is essential for successful research and clinical trials. Clinical trial data collecting may be made more reliable by using blockchain technology. By utilizing blockchain technology, data integrity can be ensured and errors in data reporting may be corrected [48]. Transparency and accuracy in clinical trial data analytics are both improved as a result. Clinical supply chain tracking and checking, restoring the legitimacy of trial data, patient recruiting, and reducing trial duration may all be helped by using blockchain in clinical research. Genomic and health-related data accuracy may also be checked using blockchain technology, which is a major benefit of this technology. Scientific research is being skewed and misrepresented due to the manipulation of biological and physiological data. Collaborative research might draw greater attention if stakeholders can ensure the data's quality. Genomic data is often shared on the blockchain platform. Preventing genetic disorders and illnesses is a goal of genomic sequencing management in precision medicine.

4.4.4 Ensuring permissions consistency

Healthcare contributors must have the ability to immediately access data of patients in the case of an emergency. Patients' lives may be placed at risk owing to a lack of access to medical records in an emergency [50]. Blockchain technology may be utilized in two ways to securely and effectively handle rights. It is possible to provide accessibility based on predefined rules agreed upon by all parties engaged in a contract using blockchain-based smart contracts. Patients may manage who has access to medical records by using cryptographic keys. Patients will be given a master key to access their medical records. The patient can make a copy of the report available to healthcare professionals and institutions if required. Read as well as write access may be added to smart contracts. The use of smart contacts as well as cryptographic keys based on blockchain may assist to reduce human error.

4.4.5 Telehealthcare systems

Despite its vulnerability to cyber-attacks, telehealth networks offer the potential to break through geographical boundaries in healthcare. A therapist–patient virtual link might put confidential patient information at risk [49]. When designing a telemedicine system, safety, and privacy must be top priorities. In telehealth systems, blockchain can provide essential trust, security, and privacy protection. When data is provided directly rather than via a middleman, telemedicine systems may benefit from improved customer trust. Practitioners also profit from the decentralized, immutable, accessible, and traceable storage of accurate patient data, records, and reports.

4.5 Health insurance

Insurers are now employing a centralized structure for data storage and processing. Third parties or intermediaries are often engaged in the contracting process for health insurance. As a result, the insurance business is plagued with a lengthy and time-consuming data-sharing procedure that is inefficient. Blockchain technology delivers an unmatched level of transparency since it registers every transaction in a decentralized, tamper-proof, traceable, permanent, and dependable way. Another problem facing the insurance business that blockchain may address is interoperability. Automated gathering of agreement papers, transactions, and other data may enhance administrative operations via the use of smart contracts. Smart contracts may potentially be used to identify fraudulent or inflated claims for insurance. Physicians can keep an eye on their patients' coverage of health insurance using blockchain technology. Health insurance claims processing may be simplified and provider directories more accurate using blockchain's consensus methods.

As a consequence, the health insurance business would benefit greatly from the use of blockchain technology.

4.6 Healthcare billing systems

These systems have previously been subject to various types of fraud [54]. To top it all off, generating billing data will take longer and use more resources under the new billing system. Unintentional billing mistakes, such as duplicate operations or incorrect files, may be traced back to the technique of medical billing's complicated coding. Medical billing systems may be made more efficient by combining blockchain with computer-assisted coding techniques. Unlike traditional billing techniques, which may take a long time to claim a charge, blockchain technology can make the payment process easier plus more dependable. The present payment mechanisms are used to generate even greater delays in bill payments in the insurance claims instance, to be more precise. Due to blockchain's ability to store data irreversibly, insurance firms will be able to pay claims more quickly while also lowering the need for extra resources, time, and money.

4.7 Challenges

Despite its numerous advantages and potential applications, blockchain technology is not without its drawbacks, some of which are specific to the domain. The following are a few of the significant challenges faced by this technology in healthcare before it can be broadly embraced.

4.8 Storage cost

Health care and medical records are flooded with data generated by patients and wearable IoT devices. On the other hand, on-chain data storage is quite limited in blockchain design. Blockchain's decentralized and hashed design comes with a high cost in terms of data storage.

Blockchain data access, maintenance, and management may be costly if the data is vast. As a consequence, the design of blockchain applications must take this into account.

4.8.1 Scalability

When blockchain is to be adopted in the healthcare industry, scalability is one of the main difficulties. Millions of people visit private practices, healthcare centers, medical centers, health research organizations, and insurance firms. These amenities are also used by patients on a personal level. In all likelihood, none of them will be able to keep the same blockchain-based idea. By using blockchain technology, more energy is needed from network equipment, which in turn demands more computer power [52]. Big data in healthcare must be scaled up before blockchain can be widely used.

4.8.2 Legislation aspects: privacy laws and regulations

In addition, national privacy rules and regulations must be complied with while using blockchain technology. The rules that apply to blockchain technology vary widely depending on where you reside. The adoption of blockchain is also hindered because of the constantly evolving regulatory environment since it is intended to mature [52]. A lot of laws and regulations governing the usage of blockchain technology are yet in the initial stages of development. Companies should be tokenization has become a more complicated subject. Proper terminology is needed to explain the blockchain's distributed storage system, as well as its data ownership and access rights. There should be clear guidelines and recommendations for regulators from healthcare organizations.

4.8.3 Modification

Because of the inability to edit or delete data due to the immutability of blockchain data, data repairs, and alterations are inevitable. To accommodate any modifications, a new chain must be established or every node must concur on a new block.

These two possibilities are each excessively expensive and unworkable. Blockchain applications must thus be built in a way that reduces the need for data changes.

4.8.4 Ensuring data accuracy

There has to be a comprehensive review of all of the patient information before it can be stored on the blockchain. Healthcare providers may utilize a digital register, an old paper registry, or a completely new one employing blockchain-based technologies. Due to insurance competition, human, and administrative mistakes, charge discrimination, plus tax evasion, most recent medical care information registries are inaccurate. The integrity, as well as usefulness of a specified format, are greatly compromised when there is a lack of information.

4.8.5 Integrating with current systems of healthcare

Integrating blockchain into recent systems will be a challenging undertaking. Healthcare organizations must alter their present methods to use blockchain technology. To ensure a seamless transition to blockchain technology in the sector of healthcare, significant changes have to be made to current practices (e.g. time, meticulous planning, financial resources, and human expertise). It is because of this that smart contracts need a multidisciplinary skill set to be used. Both architectural as well as legal knowledge is necessary for smart contracts to work properly. Healthcare providers must also learn the fundamentals of blockchain technology for these solutions to operate correctly. Attention must be made to building interdisciplinarity to benefit from blockchain-enabled solutions.

4.9 Participation adoption

A cultural revolution is required before blockchain can be used in the healthcare business. For both transaction blocks and cryptocurrency creation, blockchain technology demands a network of networked computers.

Participation should be recognized with incentives for providing computer resources. There may also be a push from health groups for blockchain implementation and network participation. As more people become involved, the greater will be the impact of the blockchain.

4.10 Conclusion

There are several ways in which the medical business might profit from blockchain technology. In the same way that the internet transformed healthcare and adopted telemedicine, this technology may enable healthcare services to progress to the next level by reducing the costs of monitoring, configuring, and processing healthcare big data. There is no need to wait for each patient's data to be entered manually, thanks to a distributed ledger's immediate availability. Furthermore, clinicians will not have to be concerned for the patient to provide them with a truthful medical history since they may obtain the original, accurate, as well as quality source-documented information in real time. There is no need for patients to worry about receiving another opinion from another doctor since the data is available to everybody. Stakeholders with similar medical issues will be able to connect with others across the globe through a blockchain network, which will not only improve their health but also motivate them to combat the illness. Also, patients will be able to pick who they share their data with, and they will have complete control over it.

In this chapter, we delved deep into the topic of blockchain integration with healthcare systems. Decentralized, open, accessible, traceable, auditable, trustworthy, and stable data management is made possible by blockchain for healthcare organizations, which ensures that patient records remain unaltered by tampering. To explain how blockchain may be used to manage large data in healthcare, we went through its capabilities and advantages. This chapter discussed how this technology may be used in the healthcare field. To show how this technology has benefited and complimented various healthcare systems, this chapter highlighted numerous prospective areas. Following the discussion of open research challenges that are hampering the extensive deployment of blockchain-based technology in healthcare, we also addressed these issues. Some technical concerns are needed to be addressed prior to the blockchain being fully integrated into healthcare systems.

References

[1] The future of blockchain in health insurance https://the-digitalinsurer.com/future-block-chain-health-insurance/ (accessed 28 October 2022)

[2] Vazirani A A, O'Donoghue O, Brindley D and Meinert E 2020 Blockchain vehicles for efficient medical record management *NPJ Digit. Med.* **3** 1

[3] What if blockchain technology in healthcare: a systematic review offered a way to reconcile privacy with transparency? https://europarl.europa.eu/RegData/etudes/ATAG/2018/624254/ (accessed 28 October 2022)

[4] Blockchain for healthcare data security https://identitymanagementinstitute.org/blockchain-for-healthcare-data-security/ (accessed 28 October 2022)

[5] Al-Zaben N, Onik M M H, Yang J, Lee N Y and Kim C S 2018 General data protection regulation complied blockchain architecture for personally identifiable information management *2018 Int. Conf. on Computing, Electronics and Communications Engineering (iCCECE)* (Piscataway, NJ: IEEE) pp 77–82

[6] Mazlan A A, Daud S M, Sam S M, Abas H, Rasid S Z A and Yusof M F 2020 Scalability challenges in healthcare blockchain system—a systematic review *IEEE Access* **8** 23663–73

[7] Pandey P and Litoriya R 2020 Implementing healthcare services on a large scale: challenges and remedies based on blockchain technology *Health Policy Technol.* **9** 69–78

[8] Kumar T, Ramani V, Ahmad I, Braeken A, Harjula E and Ylianttila M 2018 Blockchain utilization in healthcare: key requirements and challenges *2018 IEEE 20th Int. Conf. on e-Health Networking, Applications and Services (Healthcom)* (Piscataway, NJ: IEEE) pp 1–7

[9] Holotescu C 2018 Understanding blockchain opportunities and challenges *Conf. Proc. eLearning and Software for Education (eLSE)* vol 14 (Bucharest: Carol I National Defence University Publishing House) pp 275–83

[10] Blockchain: tech for healthcare https://avocadoblock.com/en/blog/2019/3/29/uu7n-kiya06lipblg4o22cd7lhjvhav (accessed 28 October 2022)

[11] Kassab M, DeFranco J, Malas T, Laplante P, Destefanis G and Neto V V G 2019 Exploring research in blockchain for healthcare and a roadmap for the future *IEEE Trans. Emerg. Top. Comput.* **9** 1835–52

[12] Blockchain and healthcaredrug traceability and data management https://medium.com/@juraprotocol/blockchain-healthcare-drugtraceability-data-management-traceability-259dd7c79c24 (accessed 28 October 2022)

[13] What are the top 10 benefits of implementing blockchain? https://dragonchain.com/blog/top-blockchain-benefits/ (acessed 28 October 2022)

[14] Shahnaz A, Qamar U and Khalid A 2019 Using blockchain for electronic health records *IEEE Access* **7** 147782–95

[15] Hasselgren A, Kralevska K, Gligoroski D, Pedersen S A and Faxvaag A 2020 Blockchain in healthcare and health sciences—a scoping review *Int. J. Med. Inform.* 134 104040

[16] Sigwart M, Borkowski M, Peise M, Schulte S and Tai S 2019 Blockchain-based data provenance for the Internet of Things *Proc. of the 9th Int. Conf. on the Internet of Things* pp 1–8

[17] Mattila J 2016 The blockchain phenomenon *Berkeley Roundtable of the International Economy* 16

[18] Onik M M H, Miraz M H and Kim C S 2018 A recruitment and human resource management technique using blockchain technology for industry 4.0 *Smart Cities Symp. 2018* (IET) pp 1–6 .

[19] Yue X, Wang H, Jin D, Li M and Jiang W 2016 Healthcare data gateways: found healthcare intelligence on blockchain with novel privacy risk control *J. Med. Syst.* **40** 1–8

[20] Reddy K H K, Das H and Roy D S 2017 A data aware scheme for scheduling big data applications with SAVANNA hadoop *Networks of the Future* (London: Chapman and Hall) pp 377–92

[21] Xia Q I, Sifah E B, Asamoah K O, Gao J, Du X and Guizani M 2017 MeDShare: trust-less medical data sharing among cloud service providers via blockchain *IEEE Access* **5** 14757–67

[22] Tanwar S, Parekh K and Evans R 2020 Blockchain-based electronic healthcare record system for healthcare 4.0 applications *J. Inform. Secur. Appl.* **50** 102407

[23] Lee C, Luo Z, Ngiam K Y, Zhang M, Zheng K, Chen G and Yip W L J 2017 Big healthcare data analytics: challenges and applications *Handbook of Large-Scale Distributed Computing in Smart Healthcare* (Cham: Springer) pp 11–41

[24] Agbo C C, Mahmoud Q H and Eklund J M 2019 Blockchain technology in healthcare: a systematic review *Healthcare* **7** 56

[25] Islam N, Faheem Y, Din I U, Talha M, Guizani M and Khalil M 2019 A blockchain-based fog computing framework for activity recognition as an application to e-Healthcare services *Future Gener. Comput. Syst.* **100** 569–78

[26] Kumar R and Tripathi R 2019 Traceability of counterfeit medicine supply chain through blockchain *2019 11th Int. Conf. on Communication Systems and Networks (COMSNETS)* (Piscataway, NJ: IEEE)) pp 568–70

[27] Exploring decentralization: blockchain technology and complex coordination https://jods.mitpress.mit.edu/pub/7vxemtm3/release/2 (accessed 28 October 2022)

[28] Pandey P and Litoriya R 2021 Securing e-health networks from counterfeit medicine penetration using blockchain *Wirel. Pers. Commun.* **117** 7–25

[29] Salah K, Rehman M H U, Nizamuddin N and Al-Fuqaha A 2019 Blockchain for AI: review and open research challenges *IEEE Access* **7** 10127–49

[30] Blockchain: the benefits of an immutable ledger https://medium.com/luxtag-live-tokenized-assets-on-blockchain/blockchain-thebenefits-of-an-immutable-ledger-3ecb458fed3b (accessed 28 October 2022)

[31] Sahoo M, Singhar S S and Sahoo S S 2020 A blockchain based model to eliminate drug counterfeiting *Machine Learning and Information Processing: Proc. of ICMLIP 2019* (Berlin: Springer) pp 213–22

[32] Cachin C 2016 Architecture of the hyperledger blockchain fabric *Workshop on Distributed Cryptocurrencies and Consensus Ledgers* vol 310 pp 1–4

[33] Omar I A, Jayaraman R, Salah K and Simsekler M C E 2019 Exploiting ethereum smart contracts for clinical trial management *2019 IEEE/ACS 16th Int. Conf. on Computer Systems and Applications (AICCSA)* (Piscataway, NJ: IEEE) pp 1–6

[34] Healthcare Data Breach Costs Highest for 7th Straight Year https://healthitsecurity.com/news/healthcare-databreach-costs-highest-for-7th-straight-year (accessed 28 October 2022)

[35] Esposito C, De Santis A, Tortora G, Chang H and Choo K K R 2018 Blockchain: a panacea for healthcare cloud-based data security and privacy? *IEEE Cloud Comput.* **5** 31–7

[36] Sengupta J, Ruj S and Bit S D 2020 A comprehensive survey on attacks, security issues and blockchain solutions for IoT and IIoT *J. Netw. Comput. Appl.* **149** 102481

[37] Al Omar A, Bhuiyan M Z A, Basu A, Kiyomoto S and Rahman M S 2019 Privacy-friendly platform for healthcare data in cloud based on blockchain environment *Future Gener. Comput. Syst.* **95** 511–21

[38] Gupta S, Malhotra V and Singh S N 2020 Securing IoT-driven remote healthcare data through blockchain *Advances in Data and Information Sciences: Proc. of ICDIS* (Berlin: Springer) pp 47–56

[39] Tao H, Bhuiyan M Z A, Abdalla A N, Hassan M M, Zain J M and Hayajneh T 2018 Secured data collection with hardware-based ciphers for IoT-based healthcare *IEEE Internet Things J.* **6** 410–20

[40] Reisman M 2017 EHRs: the challenge of making electronic data usable and interoperable *P T* **42** 572

[41] Khan W A, Khattak A M, Hussain M, Amin M B, Afzal M, Nugent C and Lee S 2014 An adaptive semantic based mediation system for data interoperability among health information systems *J. Med. Syst.* **38** 1–18

[42] Chen L, Lee W K, Chang C C, Choo K K R and Zhang N 2019 Blockchain based searchable encryption for electronic health record sharing *Future Gener. Comput. Syst.* **95** 420–9

[43] Zheng Z, Xie S, Dai H N, Chen W, Chen X, Weng J and Imran M 2020 An overview on smart contracts: challenges, advances and platforms *Future Gener. Comput. Syst.* **105** 475–91

[44] Blockchain can be the catalyst for a revolution in precision medicine https://medium.com/projectshivom/blockchain-can-be-the-catalystfor-a-revolution-in-precision-medicine-d55e1e8102 (accessed 28 October 2022)

[45] How blockchain will affect medical billing and coding https://www.mdtechreview.com/news/how-will-blockchain-affect-medicalbilling-and-coding–nwid-264.html (accessed 28 October 2022)

[46] Aich S and Kim H C 2018 Auto detection of Parkinson's disease based on objective measurement of gait parameters using wearable sensors *Artif. Intell.* **117** 103–12

[47] Yu G, Zha X, Wang X, Ni W, Yu K, Yu P and Guo Y J 2020 Enabling attribute revocation for fine-grained access control in blockchain-IoT systems *IEEE Trans. Eng. Manage.* **67** 1213–30

[48] McGhin T, Choo K K R, Liu C Z and He D 2019 Blockchain in healthcare applications: Research challenges and opportunities *J. Netw. Comput. Appl.* **135** 62–75

[49] Farouk A, Alahmadi A, Ghose S and Mashatan A 2020 Blockchain platform for industrial healthcare: Vision and future opportunities *Comput. Commun.* **154** 223–35

[50] TSyed T A, Alzahrani A, Jan S, Siddiqui M S, Nadeem A and Alghamdi T 2019 A comparative analysis of blockchain architecture and its applications: Problems and recommendations *IEEE Access* **7** 176838–69

[51] JXie J, Tang H, Huang T, Yu F R, Xie R, Liu J and Liu Y 2019 A survey of blockchain technology applied to smart cities: research issues and challenges *IEEE Commun. Surv. Tutor.* **21** 2794–830

[52] Ali F, El-Sappagh S, Islam S R, Kwak D, Ali A, Imran M and Kwak K S 2020 A smart healthcare monitoring system for heart disease prediction based on ensemble deep learning and feature fusion *Inf. Fusion* **63** 208–22

[53] Guardian (WHO), 10% of Drugs in Poor Countries are Fake, Says WHO https:// theguardian.com/globaldevelopment/2017/nov/28/10-of-drugs-in-poor-countries-are-fake-says-who (accessed 28 October 2022)

[54] Case study: forging the path to consumer-directed health through blockchain technology https://patientory.com/blog/2019/05/20/ (accessed 28 Octobeter 2022)

[55] Tendulkar S, Rodrigues A, Patel K and Dalvi H 2020 System to fight counterfeit drugs *Advanced Computing Technologies and Applications: Proc. of 2nd Int. Conf. on Advanced Computing Technologies and Applications—ICACTA 2020* (Berlin: Springer) pp 465–70

IOP Publishing

Blockchain with Artificial Intelligence for Healthcare
A synergistic approach
Rishabha Malviya, Arun Kumar Singh, Sonali Sundram, Balamurugan Balusamy and
Seifedine Kadry

Chapter 5

Management of disease using blockchain with AI and wearable technology

Nearly a quarter of the world's adult population has at least one chronic health problem, putting an enormous strain on people, families, and the healthcare system. For chronic illness management, cutting-edge technologies have emerged as a response to the 'smart healthcare' revolution. The usage of smart wearable technology, which provides an uninterrupted flow of healthcare information for illness detection as well as treatment, is one of many aspects that contribute to a healthy lifestyle. How to organize plus analyze the data must be addressed immediately if chronic illness treatment is to be improved with patient outcomes, way of living, as well as privacy protection. Wearable sensors may be used to monitor a patient's physiological data, which can then be used to provide intelligent recommendations for illness diagnosis and therapy. Decentralizing data sharing, empowering users, safeguarding privacy, and assuring data veracity are all possible advantages of blockchain for the healthcare sector. Incorporating artificial intelligence (AI), blockchain, as well as wearable technology might improve the current persistent illness management paradigms, shifting the focus from the hospital to the patients. Theoretically presented in this chapter, a patient-focused technological framework based on wearables, blockchain, and AI is investigated further in terms of managing chronic illnesses. Finally, this new paradigm's shortcomings and prospects are discussed.

5.1 Introduction

A rising number of households with two earners and an aging population have made chronic illness management a necessity for home care providers. In the United States, the expense of treating persistent/chronic conditions like cardiovascular disease was $555 billion in 2014; by the year 2035, that cost is expected to rise to $1.1 trillion [1, 2]. The most regular chronic diseases are chronic renal diseases, cardiovascular as well as cerebrovascular disorders, chronic respiratory diseases, hypertension, diabetes, cancer, obesity, degenerative illness of the joints, and neurological disorders [3]. Due to the widespread buildout of wearable technology, blockchain along with AI, these technologies may be utilized for keeping a record of the health of individuals suffering from chronic diseases.

For monitoring, recording, analyzing, regulating, and intervening in patients with long-term illnesses, portable medical electronic technology that can be worn on the body may be beneficial [4, 5]. Wearables, which collect and analyze a variety of health data in real time, make it possible to keep tabs on patients with chronic illnesses at all times of the day. The utilization of high-performance computers and AI may better forecast threats based on these accessible multidimensional clinical as well as biological sets of data [6]. Many AI systems can gather pertinent data so they can learn from new events that have happened in the past and get better. Physicians can create early therapy for every patient suffering from chronic diseases using AI [7–10]. As a result, there is a risk of information asymmetry and opacity, as well as the possibility of data manipulation, on most medical service platforms. The data storage approach may lower the level of automation in AI machine learning as a result of the 'information island phenomenon,' which may therefore prevent effective information exchange between medical units [3, 4, 8, 9]. In the future, a new generation of transactional apps based on blockchain technology will be able to create trust, accountability, and transparency via the use of a distributed ledger. Blockchain integration into AI-based medical service platforms will increase the transparency and reliability of algorithm diagnosis findings. This will allow for more thorough learning and research, as well as the transmission of information and diagnostic models in a safe, unchangeable, and traceable manner by using distributed storage plus multi-center data collection, patients with chronic diseases can lessen their reliance on more complex treatments. This will cut down on the number of hospitalizations, the difficulty of health examinations, as well as the expense of severe attacks. By fusing physiological as well as clinical information in real-time, intelligent algorithms, medical data based on sensors, as well as blockchain storage and retrieval, sharing can enhance the management of chronic diseases [9–11].

5.2 Prevention and treatment for chronic diseases

The core of the conventional chronic illness model of management is diagnosing, treating, and rehabilitation, with a tracking process. The most popular methods for managing chronic diseases now are the persistent/chronic care model, persistent illness self-management, as well as transitional care [1, 3, 8–10]. It is important to note that chronic illness management is now plagued by various connected issues. These include issues such as a limited management radius and reliance on physical labor. Because they did not have a favorable experience or a sense of access, individuals are hesitant in participating in chronic disease management [11].

Additionally, due to a dearth of extended dynamic monitoring data, practitioners sometimes neglect to track patients on time, which leads to missed diagnoses and an out-of-synch treatment approach.

5.2.1 Medical AI-based wearable devices (WDs)

Wearables, video, plus additional human Internet-of-Things (IoT) devices include end intelligence for improving data collection's proactivity, timeliness, as well as consistency. Field programmable gate array capsulation, for example, is used to offer endpoint devices with local intelligence services [4, 5, 12]. As 5G as well as fog-end computing nodes advance, they will be employed closer to patients, minimizing transmission loss. Cloud intelligence is mostly utilized for training enormous datasets, whereas fog plus edge devices are presenting computing power closer to the processor, allowing for model inference [13]. AI-based medical services can produce digital twin models which properly describe a patient's health features as well as quickly assess a patient's present physical health condition to aid in treating chronic disease [14]. Large-scale data mining or rule-based engines, and deep learning are some of the AI-based techniques used for medical diagnostics. By extracting correlations from a vast quantity of information, big data mining could identify health management models in diagnosing chronic illnesses. Using expert knowledge and business rules, a rule engine may make judgments about a patient's health state. There is now more healthcare data available than ever before, and because deep learning, which is a subtype of AI that is now undergoing rapid development, can produce a much more abstract, structured, as well as peak-level depiction of a patient's medical information for diagnosis [15]. It is possible to achieve the impact of an auxiliary diagnostic with limited medical resources thanks to wearable gadgets powered by AI. In chronic illness management, techniques, and equipment for collecting most healthcare data, like blood pressure, heart rate, fasting glucose, as well as pulse [16], are rather mature [17]. The current study on the topic of posture estimation is linked to chronic illnesses such as lung and heart disease diagnosis. Attitude and recognition data are very valuable because of their comprehensiveness. Electromyogram as well as electronic wearable sensors for skin, wearable visual positioning identifiers, along with the techniques of computer bone key placement which is vision based, are the most often used tools for collecting attitude data.

5.2.2 Integration of AI, blockchain, and wearable technology for the chronic diseases

Managing chronic diseases presently entails both passive treatments plus active monitoring of the health status. Many cutting-edge technologies, including AI, wearable technology, and blockchain, have sparked fresh ideas for chronic illness monitoring in real time [15]. Physiological data were previously inspected using hospital-based methods. Patients with chronic illnesses must be monitored, assessed, and given advice on how to improve their health. Decentralized wearables, digital equipment, and mobile apps have made it easier than ever before to gather personal physical and health data regularly. A combination of wearable technology as well as

AI could be used to improve healthcare delivery [16, 17]. AI will revolutionize the healthcare sector by combining the knowledge of physicians, pharmacists, as well as nutritionists for providing comprehensive, ongoing, along with active management for individuals having chronic diseases. This will result in a scientific way of management mode encouraging the establishment of a healthy state, slowing disease progression, and reducing disability [18].

A complex and nonlinear link of the human body with sicknesses that could not be easily expressed by an equation may be developed by the intelligent medical unit with the usage of machine learning, improving the precision of the results [19]. It will be possible to offer better care for patients by combining AI with wearable technologies. The most crucial issue for chronic illnesses is the timely collection and analysis of a patient's physiological elements of healthcare data while maintaining patient privacy [20]. Privacy and data security concerns might limit the ability of medical units to exchange personal health information. Many published deep learning systems and models lack transparency and testing validation. By serving as a segregated, encrypted, as well as trustworthy shared ledger for the management of the data, blockchain technology may be able to assist in resolving this problem [20, 21]. The system of blockchain employs smart contracts as well as a unified consensus plugin to regulate the co-chain information of WDs, promote cross-chain information exchange, and transfer value across various blockchain platforms while protecting the privacy of patients [22]. These technologies could be utilized for improving the effectiveness of automating information security and the management of chronic illnesses [23–26]. To continuously improve the appropriate algorithm model, wearable device data may be learned by AI and blockchain as well as uploaded to a cloud platform that is stable or to a customized information management structure unit, as shown in figure 5.1. Most of today's scientific study is focused on chronic prevention and treating illnesses. WDs can safely collect patient data and share it with medical institutions thanks to blockchain privacy protection

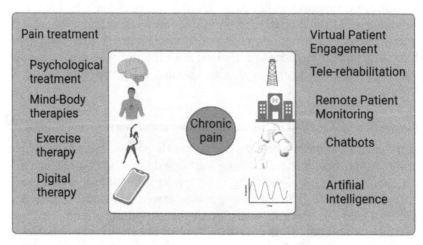

Figure 5.1. The AI and blockchain-based technological method for managing chronic diseases. Created with BioRender.com.

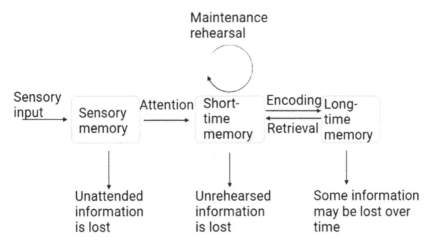

Figure 5.2. The workflow of information processing.

as well as accurate data tracing [27]. Medical institutions may benefit from using AI to manage a sizable amount of data on chronic diseases. Wearables are an essential part of digital health twins because they guarantee the synchronized wireless computation speed of several wearable sensors and successfully address the multipoint detecting health calculation challenge [10–12, 19, 25, 26]. Using an adaptive protocol, they also finish the multimodal calculations of blood glucose, heart rate, blood pressure, oxygenated blood content, temperature, posture as well as respiration. A brief description of the data processing is shown in figure 5.2.

With a focus on the main difficulties in managing most usual chronic diseases, researchers have designed a theoretical system for collecting health data on persistent illnesses utilizing WDs as well as intelligent terminal devices. Researchers have built a system that protects patient privacy while also allowing for the sharing and tracking of healthcare data using blockchain technology. Along with summarizing current theories and approaches, researchers also introduced the subject of ethical dilemmas to the discussion.

5.3 Monitoring and management of chronic diseases

Countries in Europe and North America have extensive expertise in dealing with chronic illness. However, in many poor nations, comprehensive and systematic approaches to chronic illness management are missing. Diabetes, osteoarthritis, osteoporosis, cardiovascular disease, hypertension, as well as cerebrovascular illness are only a few of the chronic ailments that impact the elderly [18]. With the dawn of the information age, new approaches to illness diagnosis and treatment have emerged. Medicine has entered the digital era thanks to advances in big data, AI, blockchain, as well as WDs. The merits of merging multiple technologies are going to be fully realized in this set of digital links. Researchers are investigating cutting-edge methods for managing chronic diseases while utilizing blockchain technology, wearables, plus AI in the state of long-term ongoing collection of health data.

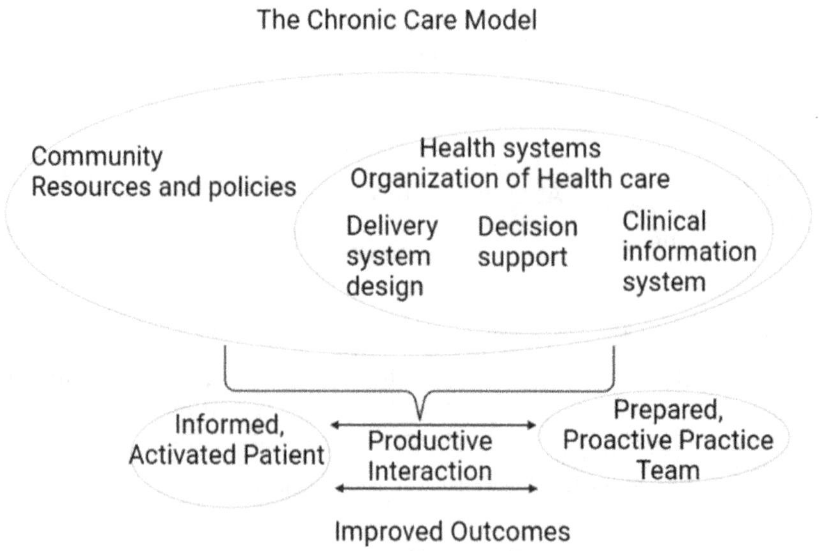

The Chronic Care Model

Figure 5.3. The design of a comprehensive system for the treatment of chronic diseases.

For demonstrating theory as well as structure in-depth, researchers concentrate on the standard treatment of four persistent diseases: diabetes mellitus, cardiovascular disease, lung disease, as well as persistent disorders that require physical rehabilitation.

Our conceptual substructure toward an integrated system in managing chronic diseases is shown in figure 5.3. This chapter discusses wearable technologies, blockchain technology, and the theoretical underpinnings of handling chronic illness data. The use of these technologies in the treatment and prevention of four common chronic illnesses is also shown. Finally, the new paradigm's flaws and future research prospects are highlighted in this chapter.

5.4 Cardiovascular diseases

Cardiovascular disease has grown in recent years into a significant and dangerous issue that impacts human life and threatens world health [27, 28]. If left untreated, heart failure, kidney failure, high blood pressure, stroke, as well as other debilitating conditions are all possible outcomes. Heart disease outcomes may be significantly improved by early detection, effective risk factor reduction, as well as the development of an initial warning model [29].

The utilization of AI in diagnosing as well as treating cardiovascular disease has increased in recent years, which has improved patient care quality, cost-effectiveness, and morbidity in those with a diverse illnesses like coronary artery disease, pulmonary hypertension, heart failure, as well as cardiomyopathy [30]. Whether within their homes or in the hospital setting, patients may manage their health as well as prognosis more effectively by utilizing AI's built-in techniques of care and ongoing real-time monitoring. These techniques can be enhanced and modified on demand. Studies in the past have mostly used naive Bayesian, from the viewpoint of the algorithm's theoretical algorithmic theory, logistic regression as well as supporting vector machine model classification algorithms are employed to construct a corresponding risk model for chronic as well as critical illness occurrences brought on by loss of cardiovascular function. A large portion of 12-lead electrocardiogram (ECG) equipment can analyze and offer an initial diagnosis of myocardial infarction with cardiac arrhythmias, making the AI method for identifying ST elevation generally accessible [27, 28]. Patients might be protected from abrupt cardiac arrest during non-hospitalization by wearable cardioverter-defibrillators incorporating AI technology, research has revealed [27]. A sport-vest polymer consisting of nanofibers covered with an electrically conducting coating was created by researchers [28]. This polymer brought the ECG electrodes near the human body. The linked application may display the ECG as well as collect health data in real time thanks to this signal, which improves comfort and lowers the risk of allergies. Remote monitoring of cardiac disease is made possible by uploading physiological data to the cloud for expert physicians to analyze. The quick advancement as well as the low cost of handheld echocardiography devices have opened new opportunities for community-wide screening plus early diagnosis of valvular heart disease. After images of valvular heart disease have been taken, automated alarms via integrated handheld echocardiography equipment using electronic sensors may be quickly provided to healthcare practitioners via an AI-based system [29, 30]. Clinical therapy may be greatly accelerated by using this handy method of data transmission. According to the recommendations, a multidisciplinary cardiac team should determine which therapy is best for each patient based on their level of independence, comorbidities, age, level of weakness, anatomic issues, preoperative mortality, and preferences [31]. Studies have demonstrated that using computed tomography or echocardiography imaging data, clinical decision support systems which are AI-based can quickly and accurately regulate the ideal size of the valve (and even the type of valve) for interventional therapy [28–31].

Obtaining enough physiological health data may be a problem for machine learning, and this causes delays. The sources of health data that need to be gathered include wearables, portable ECG monitors, biobanking data from social media and activity monitoring as well as current hospital-based e-health records [30]. Using blockchain technology, it is possible to lay out the basis for standardizing the format of medical data for the training of AI, clinical trials, as well as monitoring. Cardiovascular disease detection and therapy may be separated into two components using AI and blockchain technology. In the first step, a distributed storage database is created and data is cleaned up over a certain period using in-depth learning to combine disparate data sources and fully use the data's potential. The second component of the study is to compare and assess the intelligent algorithm model for cardiovascular disease [32]. The ability to track and examine data at the granular level is provided by blockchain technology [25, 30, 31]. Technically speaking, the complementary benefits of combining blockchain and AI can be realized for more individualized cardiovascular treatment, increasing the accessibility of high-quality medical records to support AI training and development while dispersing data from various providers or medical systems, sharing proprietary algorithms for promotion, and incentivizing new approaches with superior performance to those of the competition. The therapy of cardiovascular disease will be easier to use and more effective with the integrated system, and patient comprehension will improve significantly. As a result, it will be easier to take medications and anticoagulants, and the chance of having a heart attack may eventually decrease.

5.5 Pulmonary diseases

Patients with long-term respiratory conditions like COPD and interstitial lung diseases are more likely to suffer from these conditions than those with short-term respiratory conditions like asthma or pneumonia [33–35]. The high mortality and morbidity rates of chronic pulmonary illnesses have made them a significant health concern for the elderly [33]. It is crucial to their disease care to continuously assess the patients' disease progression as well as physical health status. Several wearable sensors could be used for tracking the physical activity of COPD patients. Breath sounds and oxygen saturation levels are continuously monitored using WDs in the home. These devices can also identify pulmonary activity as well as airborne particles linked to lung illness. Wearable technology and a wireless sensor network system were employed by researchers [34] for monitoring patient ECG, blood oxygen saturation, sound, plus the rate of respiration to assess the stepwise effect of treatment.

On the other hand, research into lung disorders has shown considerable potential for the use of AI. A computerized diagnostic model powered by AI can provide a precise assessment of several lung diseases, including COPD, pneumonia, and persistent asthma. For instance, research [35] using an artificial neural network for predicting self-management in COPD sufferers who understand as well as report their symptoms revealed an accuracy of 93.8%. Like this, Rodriguez-León et al [36] investigated how well deep neural networks performed when modeling an amalgamation of symptoms, physical signs, plus objective tests utilizing a total of 22 factors for predicting the starting diagnosis of adult asthma. Tan [37] employed a deep-learning model for segmenting 7927 lung nodules from the National Lung Screening Trial cohort in the United States as an illustration of how AI can be used to detect, categorize, and monitor pulmonary nodules. It has been used in managing pulmonary disorders. Res-App [38] is an applet for mobile phones that measures breathing with the aid of a microphone and offers a tailored assessment for diseases associated with the lower respiratory tract, asthma, bronchiolitis, and pneumonia. According to Fernández-Caramés et al [39], who contrasted four models based on machine learning in handling chronic pulmonary diseases in children, there is proof that the AI model is capable of rapidly recognizing children with asthma as well as ensuring that they receive timely treatment in the event of an emergency [39]. The management of obstructive snoring, a lung condition usually brought on by obesity and concomitant with arrhythmias, hypertension, stroke, and coronary heart disease, is a third instance [40]. Everyday actions such as utilizing a smartphone or wearing a connected wearable gadget are passively gathered to provide data for the blockchain and AI systems. The wireless network can be used to collect a variety of physiological signals generated when using home settings, and cloud-based machine learning algorithms can then process that information [41]. Big data analysis and AI are needed to enable techniques like multimodal remote monitoring plus telemedicine, smartphone engagement tools, and web-based management systems [38–41]. Decentralized multimodal information and algorithms would be beneficial for patients having obstructive sleep apnea because they would enable caregivers to make prompt adjustments and provide personalized care.

5.6 Diabetes mellitus

As the economy grows and people's diets change, diabetes prevalence is rising globally [42]. A hazardous, persistent illness known as diabetes is characterized by elevated blood sugar levels and faulty carbohydrate metabolism regulation [43]. Blood glucose levels in diabetics can fluctuate significantly throughout the day if they do not receive proper care, which may result in serious health issues like kidney failure, atherosclerosis, diabetic retinopathy, and high blood pressure. You must monitor your blood sugar levels closely if you have diabetes. To reduce morbidity and mortality, diabetic patients should be able to keep track of their blood sugar levels more accurately. Finger-prick blood samples are an invasive and cumbersome method of monitoring blood glucose levels, and they are tested with a biochemical analyzer.

The rapid advancement of wireless communication and biosensor technologies has led to the development of an entirely novel type of noninvasive wearable blood glucose monitoring device. A flexible core device serving as the brain and three wedges have recently been created for a wearable artificial pancreas for monitoring glucose levels and their management. Another wearable device that was designed for measuring the blood sugar levels in people suffering from diabetes is a pair of smart contact lenses made by Google/Life Sciences (USA) and Novartis (Basel, Switzerland). The wearable technology powered by AI can monitor a patient's blood glucose levels in real time as well as autonomously control their blood glucose levels by regulating their insulin pumps. AI can assist diabetics in managing their disease more successfully in a variety of ways, including developing a customized diet plan, spotting frequent problems early on, plus offering technical support for insulin injections. To accomplish self-management of glucose levels in the blood, Wu et al [42] developed a system to enhance continual glucose monitoring by including wearable elements to permit remote monitoring as well as warning the patients regarding potential crises. Additional incentives were created, such as the GlucoCoin blockchain-based reward system. A common side effect of diabetes is diabetic retinopathy, which can cause total blindness. If discovered and treated early, diabetic retinopathy may significantly affect a patient's prognosis as well as quality of life. According to a study by Hao and colleagues [14], the implementation of AI increased the rate of screening for diabetic retinopathy in an outpatient clinic from 28.4% to 81.3%. In conclusion, by controlling the glucose levels of blood, AI as well as wearable technology may dramatically delay the onset of diabetes complications like retinopathy plus diabetic foot problems [25, 26, 44]. Using information integration systems that utilize AI as well as blockchain technology, an assessment of risk as well as prompt warnings for hypoglycemia, diabetic ketoacidosis, as well as hyperglycemic hyperosmolar syndrome may be made [42, 45]. Patients having diabetes mellitus would be safer as a result of this.

5.7 Chronic diseases requiring sports rehabilitation

Gait, balance, as well as coordination, are essential in the recovery process from chronic motor system disorders, but they are challenging to assess properly [46, 47].

Wearables may physiologically track the positioning of bones to collect extensive patient data for distance recovery. Wearable systems that utilize blockchain, as well as AI, can monitor posture for patients with persistently abnormal posture as well as provide real-time feedback notifications, reducing the overall time spent in a poor posture state. This technology has tremendous potential for use in physical recovery [48]. This technology incorporates machine learning, AI, three-dimensional reconstruction, wearable posture analysis, and medical rehabilitation theory. It guarantees remote follow-up therapy and provides data support. Utilizing the tracking devices the patient is wearing, AI may be able to generate a three-dimensional image of the patient. The system could pair a warning for health with an improper assessment of heart rate, respiration, pulse, and stride frequency, following the rehabilitation movement. Changes in gait may result from compression myelopathy. The focus of lower limb rehabilitation is now gait training [49–51]. Real-time gait tracking may be possible using wearable technology or shoe sensors. With the advancement of myelopathy, those suffering from cervical stenosis or ossification of a posterior longitudinal ligament could be identified quickly. To categorize individuals who have neurological illnesses and help with the choice of rehabilitative exercise regimens, researchers' study of gait traits in patients having neurological illnesses [47] made use of multiple wearable sensors. AI might be utilized to create a wearable monitoring system that can help individuals with spinal illnesses see the initial indications of paralysis or myelopathy [48]. Kalid et al [51] have established the implementation of machine learning to forecast results following surgery for degenerative cervical myelopathy. Wearables that can control spinal posture are presently commercially available, and patients having scoliosis or persistent injuries need to manage their posture. The physiological curvature, as well as the posture of patients suffering from chronic diseases of the motor system, can now be continually investigated utilizing wearable technology. During spine surgery, it is frequently necessary to place implants into patients for achieving a good reset effect. Examples of these implants include pedicle screws, Kirschner wires, plus artificial intervertebral discs [49, 50].

Shortly, it will become possible to install sensors and technology inside the human body to continuously monitor physiological parameters. Via a prompt IoT information transmission mechanism, wearable sensors can generate quantifiable data and significantly improve the home monitoring of patients. One example is the examination of surface electromyogram data gathered during muscle function.

Several useful experimental platforms have been set up in rehabilitation training to avoid certain mishaps and to boost efficacy [52]. To prevent a patient from falling while undergoing rehabilitation, Pilozzi and Huang [53] developed a technological platform that enables every essential variable to be focused in a secure database. The effectiveness of machine learning which is a network-based, upper limb home rehabilitation system was also examined by Tsukada [54]. They suggested that a machine learning model could contribute to family training, enhance functional Wolf Motor Function Test results, and expand shoulder flexion and internal rotation ranges of motion while receiving treatment. In addition to aiding in the recovery of patients following a sports injury, the utilization of wearable technology and the integration of VR, AR, and MR will make training more entertaining as well as enhance patient compliance [36, 55]. Our firm belief is that a cutting-edge system of sports rehabilitation using wearable technology and blockchain technology is an absolute requirement to avoid the need for more complicated procedures and the subsequent risk of secondary trauma in patients [55, 56].

5.8 Discussion

There are many advantages to combining AI, blockchain technology, sensors, and WDs to keep track of one's physical activity as well as various environments and geographic locations. There is a lot of commercial as well as medical potential for this technology [57, 58]. To fully utilize such distributed real-time multidimensional data for high-performance data calculations, organized and intelligent multidisciplinary integration, and iteration and development in machine learning as well as artificial intelligence, are necessary [54]. A digital managing chronic illnesses platform that uses AI, blockchain, as well as wearable technology can remind patients to take their medications on time, process monitoring the data in real-time, and alert patients as well as doctors when data is not normal, enabling remote treatment monitoring [38]. The therapy of chronic illnesses for elderly patients in rural areas, when they are far away from major hospitals, or at a time when it is challenging to utilize medical facilities, like the time of a pandemic, has displayed substantial utility using distant telemedicine [58]. The expansion of wireless networks for communication, blockchain, wearable sensors, as well as AI technologies is anticipated to increase the variety and precision of the medical IoT [59].

A clinician's ideas and imagination may translate the inherent potential of these technologies into therapeutic and societal utility. As a result of their use in the medical industry, these technologies have enhanced the lives of many people, but they also have the potential to raise ethical questions [58, 59]. First and foremost, there is a risk that the security and precision of the AI algorithm utilized to diagnose illness would be compromised, endangering the patient's health. AI's capacity to be understood by patients may be at odds with their fundamental right to privacy. In addition, the public interest may be harmed if AI diagnoses are priced fairly. AI replicates the human brain's decision-making process, although it lacks actual human intelligence. The patient data are obtained following the specifications of the algorithm's design, whereas the algorithm as well as its rules are provided by humans. This means that present AI approaches remain tools, and the central figure in any discussion of ethical considerations is still the person who developed the technology. There are also significant problems with anti-interference and security risks from transmission technologies in the healthcare IoT. WDs must compete with other Wi-Fi-connected devices and not use a frequency identical to those devices to prevent network outages and problems with alert transmission [57, 58, 60].

In addition, there will be concerns with interoperability, efficiency, and security when blockchain is used in this system's structure. To solve an issue that calls for collaboration, blockchain-based service providers and consumers must be able to interact effortlessly. However, the standards used by various institutions are not united as they should be. The adoption of a common standard for blockchain would speed up industry consensus on the technology and aid in developing a large-scale social blockchain ecosystem. As the amount of data increases dramatically, more suitable frameworks must be created to reduce blockchain efficiency problems across businesses [59]. According to a recent study, 51 percent of harmful attempts are related to security vulnerabilities. Finally, it is necessary to address the question of linked regulatory policies. The stability of these technologies depends on the implementation of appropriate regulations. As a result, all relevant policies must be implemented as quickly as feasible.

5.9 Limitation

Multiple flaws in the study's design need care when interpreting its findings. The conclusions drawn here are not relevant to other disciplines like finance and marketing and are primarily applicable to medical conditions and their associated units. This is due to a few things. Another drawback is that since the material is derived from the fields of medicine, informatics, AI, as well as computer science, professional perspectives may be limited to people working in these fields only. Is it permissible to research policy and ethics? There may have been research omitted from this study because it was not published in English, or because it was published in other subjects or languages. Lastly, the medical applications of AI based on blockchain as well as WDs are wide-ranging, and we did not cover all elements of its concepts and structure in depth.

5.10 Conclusion

This chapter describes the innovative applications of wearable technology based on blockchain as well as AI for the treatment of chronic illnesses. Techniques for keeping an eye on patients were discussed. When debating and making recommendations for prospective digital solutions, the flaws of this integrated system were also exposed. In addition, this chapter discussed the many problems and difficulties associated with the day-to-day clinical and administrative treatment of chronic illnesses. A medical management system for chronic illnesses that prioritizes the utilization of vast amounts of patient data may be developed using blockchain technology. To make it simpler to administer the proper emergency help during an acute exacerbation, other features like real-time positioning, meteorological conditions (visual and acoustic), and sensors built inside the device are also required. The incorporation of WDs, blockchain, and AI will significantly improve the handling of chronic illnesses, and it would be interesting to see how this technology will support patients as well as physicians in routine healthcare.

References

[1] Katwa U and Rivera E 2018 Asthma management in the era of smart-medicine: devices, gadgets, apps and telemedicine *Indian J. Pediatr.* **85** 757–62

[2] Bauer U E, Briss P A, Goodman R A and Bowman B A 2014 Prevention of chronic disease in the 21st century: elimination of the leading preventable causes of premature death and disability in the USA *Lancet* **384** 45–52

[3] Subramanian M, Wojtusciszyn A, Favre L, Boughorbel S, Shan J, Letaief K B, Pitteloud N and Chouchane L 2020 Precision medicine in the era of artificial intelligence: implications in chronic disease management *J. Transl. Med.* **18** 1–12

[4] Hamine S, Gerth-Guyette E, Faulx D, Green B B and Ginsburg A S 2015 Impact of mHealth chronic disease management on treatment adherence and patient outcomes: a systematic review *J. Med. Internet Res.* **17** e52

[5] Allegrante J P, Wells M T and Peterson J C 2019 Interventions to support behavioral self-management of chronic diseases *Annu. Rev. Public Health* **40** 127–46

[6] Lin L F, Lin Y J, Lin Z H, Chuang L Y, Hsu W C and Lin Y H 2017 Feasibility and efficacy of wearable devices for upper limb rehabilitation in patients with chronic stroke: a randomized controlled pilot study *Eur. J. Phys. Rehabil. Med.* **54** 388–96

[7] Guo Y, Liu X, Peng S, Jiang X, Xu K, Chen C, Wang Z, Dai C and Chen W 2021 A review of wearable and unobtrusive sensing technologies for chronic disease management *Comput. Biol. Med.* **129** 104163

[9] Silva P, Jacobs D, Kriak J, Abu-Baker A, Udeani G, Neal G and Ramos K 2021 Implementation of pharmacogenomics and artificial intelligence tools for chronic disease management in primary care setting *J. Pers. Med.* **11** 443

[8] Frederico M B, Oetom A, Sahu K S, Kuang A, Fadrique L X, Velmovitsky P E, Nobrega R M and Morita P P 2019 Disruptive technologies for environment and health research: an overview of artificial intelligence, blockchain, and internet of things *Int. J. Environ. Res. Public Health* **16** 3847

[10] Lu L, Zhang J, Xie Y, Gao F, Xu S, Wu X and Ye Z 2020 Wearable health devices in health care: narrative systematic review *JMIR mHealth uHealth* **8** e18907

[11] Zheng X, Sun S, Mukkamala R R, Vatrapu R and Ordieres-Meré J 2019 Accelerating health data sharing: a solution based on the internet of things and distributed ledger technologies *J. Med. Internet Res.* **21** e13583

[12] Abe Y, Ito M, Tanaka C, Ito K, Naruko T, Itoh A, Haze K, Muro T, Yoshiyama M and Yoshikawa J 2013 A novel and simple method using pocket-sized echocardiography to screen for aortic stenosis *J. Am. Soc. Echocardiogr.* **26** 589–96

[13] Porter P *et al* 2019 A prospective multicentre study testing the diagnostic accuracy of an automated cough sound centred analytic system for the identification of common respiratory disorders in children *Respir. Res.* **20** 1–10

[14] Hao Z, Cui S, Zhu Y, Shao H, Huang X, Jiang X, Xu R, Chang B and Li H 2020 Application of non-mydriatic fundus examination and artificial intelligence to promote the screening of diabetic retinopathy in the endocrine clinic: an observational study of T2DM patients in Tianjin, China *Ther. Adv. Chronic Dis.* **11** 2040622320942415

[15] Chomiak T, Xian W, Pei Z and Hu B 2019 A novel single-sensor-based method for the detection of gait-cycle breakdown and freezing of gait in Parkinson's disease *J. Neural Transm.* **126** 1029–36

[16] Golabchi F N, Sapienza S, Severini G, Reaston P, Tomecek F, Demarchi D, Reaston M and Bonato P 2019 Assessing aberrant muscle activity patterns via the analysis of surface EMG data collected during a functional evaluation *BMC Musculoskelet. Disord.* **20** 1–15

[17] Zhang Y, Yu H, Dong R, Ji X and Li F 2021 Application prospect of artificial intelligence in rehabilitation and management of myasthenia gravis *BioMed Res. Int.* **2021** 1–6

[18] Pareja-Galeano H, Garatachea N and Lucia A 2015 Exercise as a polypill for chronic diseases *Prog. Mol. Biol. Transl. Sci.* **135** 497–526

[19] Kiran M S, Rajalakshmi P, Bharadwaj K and Acharyya A 2014 Adaptive rule engine based IoT enabled remote health care data acquisition and smart transmission system *2014 IEEE World Forum on Internet of Things (WF-IoT)* pp 253–8

[20] Araújo F, Nogueira M N, Silva J and Rego S 2021 A technological-based platform for risk assessment, detection, and prevention of falls among home-dwelling older adults: protocol for a quasi-experimental study *JMIR Res. Protoc.* **10** e25781

[21] Jourdan T, Debs N and Frindel C 2021 The contribution of machine learning in the validation of commercial wearable sensors for gait monitoring in patients: a systematic review *Sensors* **21** 4808

[22] Mendes-Soares H *et al* 2019 Assessment of a personalized approach to predicting postprandial glycemic responses to food among individuals without diabetes *JAMA Netw. Open* **2** e188102–e2

[23] Hsu W C, Sugiarto T, Lin Y J, Yang F C, Lin Z Y, Sun C T, Hsu C L and Chou K N 2018 Multiple-wearable-sensor-based gait classification and analysis in patients with neurological disorders *Sensors* **18** 3397

[24] Tropea P *et al* 2019 Rehabilitation, the great absentee of virtual coaching in medical care: scoping review *J. Med. Internet Res.* **21** e12805

[25] Bashshur R L *et al* 2014 The empirical foundations of telemedicine interventions for chronic disease management *Telemed. e-Health* **20** 769–800

[26] Peyvandi A, Majidi B, Peyvandi S and Patra J 2021 Computer-aided-diagnosis as a service on decentralized medical cloud for efficient and rapid emergency response intelligence *New Gener. Comput.* **39** 677–700

[27] Mekov E, Miravitlles M and Petkov R 2020 Artificial intelligence and machine learning in respiratory medicine *Expert Rev. Respir. Med.* **14** 559–64

[28] Buekers J, Theunis J, De Boever P, Vaes A W, Koopman M, Janssen E V, Wouters E F, Spruit M A and Aerts J M 2019 Wearable finger pulse oximetry for continuous oxygen saturation measurements during daily home routines of patients with chronic obstructive pulmonary disease (COPD) over one week: observational study *JMIR mHealth uHealth* **7** e12866

[29] Contreras I and Vehi J 2018 Artificial intelligence for diabetes management and decision support: literature review *J. Med. Internet Res.* **20** e10775

[30] Dwivedi A D, Srivastava G, Dhar S and Singh R 2019 A decentralized privacy-preserving healthcare blockchain for IoT *Sensors* **19** 326

[31] Xie Y, Zhang J, Wang H, Liu P, Liu S, Huo T, Duan Y Y, Dong Z, Lu L and Ye Z 2021 Applications of blockchain in the medical field: Narrative review *J. Med. Internet Res.* **23** e28613

[32] Barrett M *et al* 2019 Artificial intelligence supported patient self-care in chronic heart failure: a paradigm shift from reactive to predictive, preventive and personalised care *EPMA J.* **10** 445–64

[33] Kaplan A *et al* 2021 Artificial intelligence/machine learning in respiratory medicine and potential role in asthma and COPD diagnosis *J. Allergy Clin. Immunol. Pract.* **9** 2255–61

[34] Colantonio S, Govoni L, Dellacà R L, Martinelli M, Salvetti O and Vitacca M 2015 Decision making concepts for the remote, personalized evaluation of COPD patients' health status *Methods Inf. Med.* **54** 240–7

[35] Ather S, Kadir T and Gleeson F 2020 Artificial intelligence and radiomics in pulmonary nodule management: current status and future applications *Clin. Radiol.* **75** 13–9

[36] Rodriguez-León C, Villalonga C, Munoz-Torres M, Ruiz J R and Banos O 2021 Mobile and wearable technology for the monitoring of diabetes-related parameters: systematic review *JMIR mHealth uHealth* **9** e25138

[37] Tan T E *et al* 2021 Retinal photograph-based deep learning algorithms for myopia and a blockchain platform to facilitate artificial intelligence medical research: a retrospective multicohort study *Lancet Digit. Health* **3** e317–29

[38] Study: Smartphone app that listens to breathing, determines respiratory diseases is 89 percent accurate. https://www.mobihealthnews.com/content/study-smartphone-app-listens-breath-ing-determines-respiratory-diseases-89-percent-accurate (accessed on February 2023)

[39] Fernández-Caramés T M, Froiz-Míguez I, Blanco-Novoa O and Fraga-Lamas P 2019 Enabling the internet of mobile crowdsourcing health things: a mobile fog computing, blockchain and IoT based continuous glucose monitoring system for diabetes mellitus research and care *Sensors* **19** 3319

[40] Fan X, Yao Q, Cai Y, Miao F, Sun F and Li Y 2018 Multiscaled fusion of deep convolutional neural networks for screening atrial fibrillation from single lead short ECG recordings *IEEE J. Biomed. Health Inform.* **22** 1744–53

[41] Bugajski A, Lengerich A, Koerner R and Szalacha L 2021 Utilizing an artificial neural network to predict self-management in patients with chronic obstructive pulmonary disease: an exploratory analysis *J. Nurs. Scholarsh.* **53** 16–24

[42] Wu C T, Li G H, Huang C T, Cheng Y C, Chen C H, Chien J Y, Kuo P H, Kuo L C and Lai F 2021 Acute exacerbation of a chronic obstructive pulmonary disease prediction system using wearable device data, machine learning, and deep learning: development and cohort study *JMIR mHealth uHealth* **9** e22591

[43] Pépin J L, Bailly S and Tamisier R 2020 Big data in sleep apnoea: opportunities and challenges *Respirology* **25** 486–94

[44] Cheung C C, Krahn A D and Andrade J G 2018 The emerging role of wearable technologies in detection of arrhythmia *Can. J. Cardiol.* **34** 1083–7

[45] Song Y, Min J and Gao W 2019 Wearable and implantable electronics: moving toward precision therapy *ACS Nano* **13** 12280–6

[46] Qadri Y A, Nauman A, Zikria Y B, Vasilakos A V and Kim S W 2020 The future of healthcare internet of things: a survey of emerging technologies *IEEE Commun. Surv. Tutor.* **22** 1121–67

[47] Williamson J R, Telfer B, Mullany R and Friedl K E 2021 Detecting Parkinson's disease from wrist-worn accelerometry in the UK Biobank *Sensors* **21** 2047

[48] Nam K H, Kim D H, Choi B K and Han I H 2019 Internet of things, digital biomarker, and artificial intelligence in spine: current and future perspectives *Neurospine* **16** 705

[49] Zhang H, Song C, Rathore A S, Huang M C, Zhang Y and Xu W 2020 mHealth technologies towards Parkinson's disease detection and monitoring in daily life: a comprehensive review *IEEE Rev. Biomed. Eng.* **14** 71–81

[50] Thoenes M, Agarwal A, Grundmann D, Ferrero C, McDonald A, Bramlage P and Steeds R P 2021 Narrative review of the role of artificial intelligence to improve aortic valve disease management *J. Thorac. Dis.* **13** 396

[51] Kalid N, Zaidan A A, Zaidan B B, Salman O H, Hashim M and Muzammil H J J O M S 2018 Based real time remote health monitoring systems: a review on patients prioritization and related 'big data' using body sensors information and communication technology *J. Med. Syst.* **42** 1–30

[52] Jiang W, Majumder S, Kumar S, Subramaniam S, Li X, Khedri R, Mondal T, Abolghasemian M, Satia I and Deen M J 2021 A wearable tele-health system towards monitoring COVID-19 and chronic diseases *IEEE Rev. Biomed. Eng.* **15** 61–84

[53] Pilozzi A and Huang X 2020 Overcoming Alzheimer's disease stigma by leveraging artificial intelligence and blockchain technologies *Brain Sci.* **10** 183

[54] Tsukada Y T *et al* 2019 Validation of wearable textile electrodes for ECG monitoring *Heart Vessels* **34** 1203–11

[55] Merali Z G, Witiw C D, Badhiwala J H, Wilson J R and Fehlings M G 2019 Using a machine learning approach to predict outcome after surgery for degenerative cervical myelopathy *PLoS One* **14** e0215133

[56] Koydemir H C and Ozcan A 2018 Wearable and implantable sensors for biomedical applications *Annu. Rev. Anal. Chem.* **11** 127–46

[57] Yu G *et al* 2020 The role of artificial intelligence in identifying asthma in pediatric inpatient setting *Ann. Transl. Med.* **8** 1367

[58] Tomita K, Nagao R, Touge H, Ikeuchi T, Sano H, Yamasaki A and Tohda Y 2019 Deep learning facilitates the diagnosis of adult asthma *Allergol. Int.* **68** 456–61

[59] Kaspar G, Sanam K, Gholkar G, Bianco N R, Szymkiewicz S and Shah D 2018 Long-term use of the wearable cardioverter defibrillator in patients with explanted ICD *Int. J. Cardiol.* **272** 179–84

[60] Kuo T T, Gabriel R A, Cidambi K R and Ohno-Machado L 2020 EXpectation Propagation LOgistic REgRession on permissioned blockCHAIN (ExplorerChain): decentralized online healthcare/genomics predictive model learning *J. Am. Med. Inform. Assoc.* **27** 747–56

IOP Publishing

Blockchain with Artificial Intelligence for Healthcare
A synergistic approach
Rishabha Malviya, Arun Kumar Singh, Sonali Sundram, Balamurugan Balusamy and Seifedine Kadry

Chapter 6

Leveraging blockchain technology in remote healthcare services

The demand for patient care and health services has increased due to recent challenges and the global spread of COVID-19. Telemedicine and telehealth systems can be utilized to minimize the transmission of COVID-19 when delivering healthcare services. COVID-19 patients impose a substantial impact on healthcare systems, making them potentially valuable in the use of limited healthcare resources. Current telemedicine systems are often posing challenges for researchers in detecting fraudulent activity related to patient insurance claims and the verification of medical providers' credentials. This chapter has covered the potential benefits of integrating blockchain technology in telehealth and telemedicine businesses, as well as the problems that are associated with implementing it. The significance of blockchain technology in safeguarding personal data, ensuring operational transparency, maintaining the integrity of medical records, and detecting fraudulent activities related to patient insurance claims and physician credentials has been widely acknowledged.

6.1 Introduction

Patient care and health services must display transparency, flexibility, and security [1, 2] in light of the global spread of the COVID-19 coronavirus. As a preventative step that reduces the risk of diseases being passed from person to person, virtual communication channels have become increasingly popular as a result of the COVID-19 pandemic. As a direct result of this, there has been an increase in the utilization of telehealth as well as telemedicine technology. As a result of the need to prevent the spread of the COVID-19 virus, there has lately been an increase in demand for telehealth and telemedicine services across a variety of platforms and companies [3–6]. Some examples of these include JD Health, Teladoc Health, and Rush University Medical Centre (RUMC). Access to medical care can be expanded through the use of telemedicine and remote consultations, which also leads to better patient outcomes. The current state of telehealth and telemedicine systems provides a big challenge because they are centralized, which emphasizes the possibility of errors or difficulties occurring in a single area. Telemedicine and e-health systems face potential risks to their credibility and efficiency due to public and private data breaches [7, 8]. This latest technology, blockchain, has the potential to provide solutions to these important problems. The shared ledger of health data in the blockchain is validated and synchronized across all nodes connected to the block-chain [9, 10]. The technology of blockchain has the potential to solve a variety of difficult problems, some of which include tracing the travel routes of diseased patients, securing the records of remote clinical counseling, tracing the location of medication and medical testing kits in supply chains, and verifying the validity of substandard healthcare test kits.

Telemedicine allows medical practitioners the ability to remotely monitor, assess, and treat patients while taking advantage of cost-effective services. This enhances healthcare access, workforce efficiency, and technological capacity, and minimizes the risk of COVID-19 transmission among physicians, staff, and patients. Telehealth, facilitated by digital information and communication technology, can empower patients to improve self-care and access knowledge and assistance [11, 12]. Digital health services have been effective in reducing the spread of environmental infections, as demonstrated in figure 6.1.

Integrating blockchain technology into newly developed healthcare systems is a possibility for the safe digitalization of medical records, which is one of the technology's many advantages. This includes ensuring the authenticity of medical information, verifying the credibility of users accessing patient records, managing the identity of devices used for remote patient care, and protecting patient confidentiality. Blockchain technology possesses several key characteristics, includ-ing accessibility, traceability, data integrity, and confidentiality for user information (figure 6.2).

The decentralization feature in current healthcare systems prevents unauthorized hacking and deletions of information in the patient's EHR [13–15]. The mechanisms of the blockchain create trust among participants in the telemedicine and blockchain ecosystem [10]. To ensure the immutability of health data, all transactions in the ledger must undergo digital signing before confirmation and recording. Table 6.1 presents the benefits and unique features of utilizing blockchain technology in the digitalization of healthcare and telemedicine. Blockchain technology offers numer-ous advantages to the healthcare industry, including rapid and secure sharing of EHRs, efficient processing of client data, cost-effectiveness, high reliability, effective data protection, confidentiality, and enhanced accessibility. Health records can also be transparently authenticated using this method [16–18]. The implementation of secure log data in interactive medical techniques such as 'Doctor in the Loop' could enhance their safety by mitigating potential risks of database manipulation [19]. Contracts and blockchain technology enhance the effectiveness as well as security of

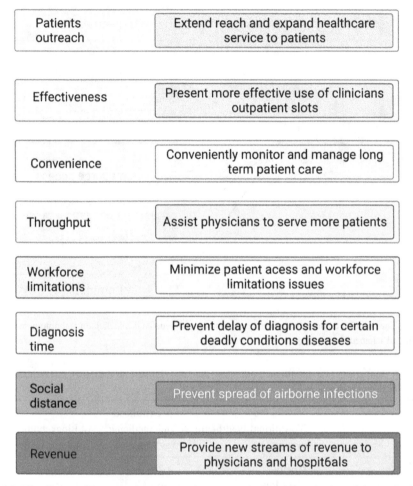

Figure 6.1. The diagram illustrates the various advantages of telehealth and telemedicine technologies in comparison to conventional medical care.

e-health along with telecommunication services. A smart contract is an application of blockchain-based software that can carry out its instructions. Traditional healthcare systems necessitate the presence of a facilitator to carry out various business activities. Pre-existing regulations are converted into smart contract features to build trust among participating organizations [20].

Automated systems are being proposed to replace the widespread use of agreements in current healthcare systems [21]. Previous research has focused mostly on investigating the following topics: the confidentiality of patients' EHR [22], the COVID-19 outbreak's trackability [23–25], the management of the drug supply chain [26–28], and the digitization of the telemedicine industry [29, 30]. The telemedicine system discussed in research [31] utilized decentralized storage of InterPlanetary File System (IPFS) hashes for electronic health records (EHRs) within an Ethereum-based framework. A study by researchers [32] suggests that

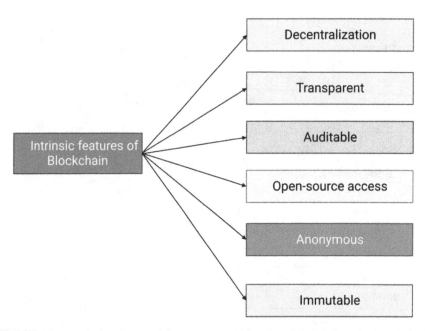

Figure 6.2. The diagram depicts the essential components and benefits of blockchain technology in the field of telehealth and telemedicine applications.

Table 6.1. A comparison of conventional, centralized, and decentralized telehealth and telemedicine systems based on blockchain technology.

Parameters	Traditional healthcare system	Centralized telemedicine system	Blockchain supported telemedicine
Cost	Costly	Cheap	Cheap
Patient waiting time	Very long	Short	Short
Requirement for in-person visit	Required	Not required	Not required
Data provenance	Not required	Not required	Required
Health record manipulation	Can be done	Can be done	Cannot be done
Documentation	Yes	No	No
System administration	Centralized	Centralized	Decentralized

utilizing AI and blockchain technology can be an alternative method for protecting patient health data. Individuals may receive financial compensation for sharing their patient data through smart contracts in a blockchain-based solution [33]. The Ethereum-based system demonstrated in the research enables time-based tracking of the health of the patients and the recording of dates for medication intake [34]. As stated in a study, the purpose of storing an EHR on the chain is to guarantee the permanent storage of data, preventing any modifications or deletions by network users within the telemedicine system [30]. Patients have the freedom to connect or disconnect the network of their own choice. The role of blockchain-based systems in a variety of healthcare areas has been the subject of investigation by a large number of researchers, who have provided an overview and comparison of the results.

6.2 Blockchain in the area of telemedicine and healthcare

Blockchain technology exhibits various benefits for telehealth and telemedicine, as depicted in figure 6.3. One notable advantage is its capability to build trust among participants in the healthcare sector.

6.2.1 Patient consent management

Comprehensive patient medical records, encompassing past medical histories, prescription medications, diagnoses, and treatment strategies, plays a significant role in optimizing the efficacy of virtual healthcare. Healthcare providers, including hospitals and pharmacies, require secure communication of EHRs to confirm the accuracy of patients' records of medical information [10, 35–43]. Regulations in the field of telemedicine healthcare have given people the power to have control over and management of their clinical data. The sharing of EHRs with specialists can have long learning times. In addition, there is a lack of trust in the servers managed by third parties that are responsible for patient consent management services. In addition, conventional methods of consent management do not make it possible to conduct fair audit tests. By taking away the need for middlemen, distributed ledger technology known as blockchain can make it easier to build trust. Blockchain

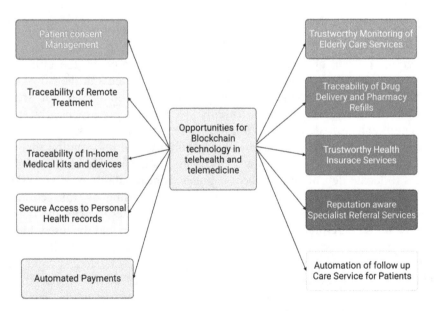

Figure 6.3. The diagram illustrates the various roles that blockchain technology plays in the fields of telehealth and telemedicine.

employs individuals from multiple participating organizations to ensure and uphold consent management [44–46]. Audits and the verification of the application of approval management rules can be carried out with the help of blockchain's ability to maintain consistency, record changes, and be transparent. Multiple entities can access data that has been saved on the blockchain as well as devices used for regional storage.

6.2.2 Traceability of remote treatment

For telehealth as well as telemedicine to achieve success, patients and experts need to engage in an online practice that presents an in-person interaction. Both direct-to-consumer (D2C) and business-to-business (B2B) models can be applied in the field of telehealth services. Patients can electronically connect with physicians for medical consultations and educational services, such as discussing a patient's operation. Guardians of the patients also have the option to engage remotely through systems that provide audio and video conferencing features. Guardians can utilize asynchronous video and image transmission in electronic face-to-face consultations to accurately assess patients' health conditions [5, 47]. Telemedicine systems currently suffer from a lack of data exchange between healthcare companies, resulting in the fragmentation of patients' health records. Blockchain technology provides a single and consistent representation of a patient's EHR for all relevant users. Participating entities can access and view health records to trace the patient's medical history. Blockchain technology can be utilized for conducting investigations of digital information, specifically for determining the identities of visitors and their corresponding activities.

6.2.3 Tracking of in-home medical kits and devices

Self-diagnosis outside of a clinical setting can be facilitated by the utilization of medical equipment and supplies that are accessible to patients in their own homes. The utilization of commercially available test kits and equipment for analyzing specific biochemical reactions can potentially lower healthcare expenses by enabling self-checkups and early detection of illnesses. When it comes to standard centralized telemedicine systems, a lack of openness, accessibility, and information that can be independently verified regarding medical kits makes it hard for both patients and clinicians to locate dependable medical supplies from reputable producers [48, 49]. The use of blockchain technology allows for the recording of transactions on a distributed ledger that is associated with the ownership of testing kits and the results they provide. The results of performance evaluations could be used by smart contracts to help decide popularity ratings given to medical test kits and other devices used for in-home care. Customers, medical professionals, and facility engineers can make use of the data provenance records of in-home medical test kits as well as their quality scores to discover accurate and dependable medical kits produced by reliable producers.

6.2.4 Secure access to personal health records

The personal health record (PHR) refers to a comprehensive record that encompasses a patient's health information, personal details, and other relevant data associated with their medical care. The individual responsible for the data is in charge of creating, updating, and overseeing the PHR [50]. The EHR contains vast health records as it is handled and monitored by healthcare professionals. The provision of virtual healthcare services in the traditional system primarily depends on virtual servers, which are less reliable due to their operation by a single organization. The security of traditional cloud-based systems' health records (PHRs) is also affected. Medical record owners can maintain privacy by utilizing the basic features of decentralized blockchain technology. Patient consent agreements may be utilized to register patients and grant them access to their personal health information, by the policy. Furthermore, it facilitates the sharing and regulation of client data among authorized users, while complying with the data holder's specified provisions [9, 16].

6.2.5 Automated payments

In current healthcare systems, many different groups, including patients, carers, and insurance companies, face the involvement of third-party payment processors. In contrast, centralized payment settlement methods exhibit drawbacks such as slow processing, the risk of hacking, and a lack of accountability. Micropayments need more support from centralized payment settlement systems and are often associated with high costs. The blockchain platform facilitates the use of cryptocurrency tokens for telehealth micropayments. Transferring currency tokens to the network operator's wallet is a reliable and transparent approach for resolving payment settlement issues [51–53]. Digitally authorized payment settlements offer various benefits, including preventing healthcare providers and customers from rejecting future transactions. Blockchain technology can be utilized to implement a cash-on-delivery service, which has the potential to reduce instances of payment fraud. Pharmacies can receive monetary assets when they successfully provide drugs to remote patients, typically through contractual agreements.

6.2.6 Trustworthy monitoring of care services

Because of recent developments in the Internet of Things (IoT), it is now possible to carry out online surveillance of a patient's health by making use of various types of biomedical sensors [54–58]. The monitoring and storing of PHRs on a performance server are made possible by biomedical sensors. This may help medical professionals gain a better knowledge of their patients. There is a possibility that vital signs, such as the rate of the heart and the temperature of the body, have correlations with health-related data. Medical errors can occur due to inaccurate data collected by a malfunctioning device. Blockchain technology enables the use of smart contracts to register and authorize permissions to access biological sensors, and these ledgers can be used for storing EHRs. Smart contracts can notify healthcare providers in case of

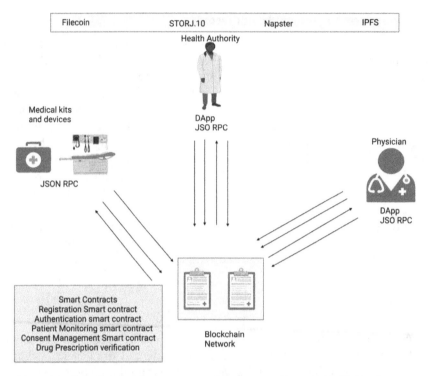

Figure 6.4. Blockchain-based smart contract-based system. Created with BioRender.com.

emergencies. IoT solutions that are powered by blockchain can alert patients when it is time to get more of their medication while they are receiving therapy at home. A smart contract-based solution that uses blockchain technology to continuously monitor a patient's health is depicted in figure 6.4. The system ensures that only individuals who have obtained explicit permission from the patient and possess a duly signed consent form are granted access to their EHR.

6.2.7 Tracking of drug delivery and pharmacy refills

Physicians are required to utilize blockchain technology for the secure exchange of pharmaceutical prescriptions with local pharmacies in the digital online consultation-based healthcare sectors. The utilization of hash functions in blockchain technology can mitigate prescription errors and inhibits unauthorized changes of information [27, 59]. Registered chemists utilize the blockchain to access and process medicine prescriptions, ensuring their accuracy and timely delivery to patients. Consequently, the shipper can utilize blockchain technology to publicly disclose the current location of the shipment, facilitating enhanced monitoring and tracking capabilities for chemists and patients. Patients and healthcare professionals all can use the accessibility and traceability of blockchain transactions to confirm the accuracy of a medicine's data source [23]. When a specific condition is met, a smart contract can initiate an automated prescription refill order with the pharmacy.

The pharmacy can re-validate and verify the prescription. Subsequently, the medication is conveyed to the recipient, leading to modifications in the patient's medical records.

6.2.8 Trustworthy health insurance services

Stringent privacy laws and limited incentives discourage many individuals from sharing their personal medical information with insurance providers. Consequently, patients exhibit a greater tendency to select insurance plans that would reject valid claims. Virtual healthcare law guarantees that patients have the same rights to payment as they do for physical healthcare. Fraud in the insurance industry, such as fraudulent medical claims made to insurance companies, often requires significant time and effort to discover the truth based on the available information. Blockchain technology enables insurance companies to access all the medical records of the patient, aiding in the reduction of insurance fraud through consent-based methods. Patients who provide consent for insurance companies to use their medical data may receive rewards. Furthermore, certain insurance companies promote policyholders with cryptocurrency tokens as a means of promoting a healthy lifestyle, specifically by monitoring their gym attendance [53, 60]. Smart medical devices connected to patients can utilize blockchain technology to establish trust.

6.2.9 Reputation-aware specialist referral services

The involvement of multiple individuals, such as referring healthcare practitioners, patients, and consulting healthcare professionals, is necessary for telemedicine diagnosis and treatment [31, 61]. Healthcare partnerships and blockchain-based contracts enable remote care coordination by facilitating the request for professional advice and opinions. Healthcare providers can store referral papers on an IPFS-based server, that generates an IPFS hash of the information documents. This hash can then be used to place documents on the blockchain, allowing consulting healthcare professionals to access it within a blockchain-based solution. When an IPFS hash is recorded on the blockchain, it enables the verification of any modifications made to a document stored on the IPFS-based server. The consulting healthcare professional may review the patient's health report, which can subsequently be kept on the blockchain ledger by healthcare specialists. Reputation scores on the blockchain can be modified by considering both the overall service duration and customer satisfaction rating of the consulting healthcare practitioner.

6.2.10 Care service digitization for clients

After a patient has finished receiving treatment, follow-up care services can be utilized to continue monitoring the patient's overall health. Patients may be required to send the results of blood and urine tests to their physicians as a part of the follow-up service ahead of joining a conference online [62]. There is the possibility that automated patient follow-up procedures might be carried out using smart contracts, which are an element of blockchain technology. [46, 63] Patients, physicians, and nursing staff can all receive reminders about scheduled follow-up appointments using smart contracts, which can be sent to them. During the patient's last follow-up appointment, the doctor may review the EHR of the patient to verify their current health status. Patients can utilize smart contracts to register and exchange an IPFS hash with their physician to obtain health reports. This is possible when using IPFS servers that are capable of storing medical test results.

6.3 Telehealth and telemedicine blockchain

Blockchain solutions such as Mediledger, CallHealth, and Embleema have facilitated the establishment of confidence and efficiency in health systems. Blockchain-based solutions like WellLinc, MedBlock, and MedRec [64] enable healthcare providers to engage in transparent operations. The following gives an explanation of five innovative medical sets utilizing blockchain technology that have recently been introduced.

6.3.1 MedCredits

MedCredits is a system that is based on Ethereum that facilitates telemedicine for dermatologists, aiding in the diagnosis and treatment of patients. Reputation-based systems are employed to promote honest behavior and discourage dishonest behavior, to protect consumers from malicious entities. A Token-Curated Registry (TCR) service has been implemented to verify doctors' licenses, ensuring that only highly qualified experts can participate in the network [65]. To facilitate secure payments and verify medical claims, MedCredits makes use of two smart contracts that are built on the Ethereum blockchain. Before posting a description of their health issues and relevant photographs, patients are required to deposit escrow into a smart contract wallet. The medical history of a patient can be accessed via the blockchain by physicians, who can then utilize this information to make diagnoses and recommend treatments. Smart contracts are utilized for obtaining a secondary evaluation from another clinician and verifying the authenticity of the case [65, 66].

6.3.2 Medical chain

A healthcare network has developed virtual physician consultation and healthcare information marketplace services using Ethereum and Hyperledger Fabric technologies. Patients can securely provide their medical information to healthcare professionals by pre-established terms and conditions. Patients who have been approved can confidentially develop the terms of an agreement for third-party healthcare practitioners to access and use their EHR data through the EHR marketplace functionality of the Medical chain platform. Medical chains can utilize the pre-approved features of Hyperledger Fabric to create security regulations that serve various types of access control. Medical chain utilized a third-party registration service known as 'Civic's registration service' to manage the keys [53]. The ERC20 token is a piece of software that was designed for the Ethereum network with the goals of promoting open access to digital services, enabling safe payments, and identifying fraudulent activity in insurance companies [67, 68].

6.3.3 HealPoint

HealPoint has made on-demand telemedicine services accessible through the utilization of the Ethereum platform. Virtual health consultation services enable individuals to conveniently communicate their symptoms, medical history, and vital signs to healthcare professionals. HealPoint's Ethereum-based smart contracts, utilizing the Schelling-coin algorithm, facilitate global access to medical advice from various clinical specialists [69]. HealPoint utilizes an artificial intelligence (AI) system to effectively match and recommend doctors to patients based on their specific health symptoms. Upon confirming the individual's identification and credentials, specialists within their network proceed to either grant or reject the physician's membership application. Furthermore, doctors are required to deposit their portion of funds into a wallet associated with a smart contract as a measure to mitigate the risk of fraudulent activities [46]. All communications with individuals are registered for verification purposes before being included in the ledger.

6.3.4 My Health My Data (MHMD)

MHMD is an open biomedical information network that empowers individuals and organizations by granting them access and control over their data. Efforts have begun to modify the existing method of recording sensitive information. Furthermore, this program encourages hospitals to provide open access to patient data for research purposes while ensuring anonymity. Blockchain, flexible authorization, private information profiles, multilayer de-identification technology, smart contracts, and big data analytics are key tools and capabilities. The system utilizes a public blockchain network to store data securely using hash-based encoding. Smart contracts are used to automatically execute transactions based on user-defined parameters. The utilization of a system that is based on blockchain in the presence of various individuals involved facilitates the decentralization of authority, thereby providing robust security measures against fraudulent activities. Storing data in a secure and decentralized manner facilitates transparency, traceability, trackability, verification, security, and data provenance. The blockchain-based solution supports the MHMD's objective by facilitating secure and dependable information exchange among individuals, hospitals, research institutes, and enterprises [70].

6.3.5 Robomed

On the Ethereum blockchain, the operations and management of the Robomed network of clinical organizations are managed via smart contracts. Patients are supposed to receive value-based care, which is another name for high-quality medical treatment, to improve their overall health. Smart contracts on the Ethereum platform enable healthcare companies to utilize Robomed EHR to register, connect, and manage their accounts within the Robomed network. Robomed's EHR module includes fundamental features such as real-time tracking of patient interactions, medical personnel judgment, access privilege management for healthcare employees, and specialized timetable display. Patients now can access telemedicine consultations, make appointments, and comply with the requirements of their authorization agreement for providing their EHR with the clinic where they receive medical care by using the Robomed mobile module. Robomed organizations can utilize smart contracts to monitor and validate patients' health outcomes and adhere to clinical guidelines for value-based healthcare. All Robomed companies are authorized to use RBM, an Ethereum token, for payment purposes. The RBM coin follows the ERC-20 standard that is present on the Ethereum network [71, 72].

6.3.6 Organizational challenges of blockchain

Conventional telemedicine systems commonly use old techniques for storing, maintaining, and safeguarding patients' data. Because of this limitation, the potential for collaboration between multiple stakeholders in healthcare and providers is limited. This potential increase in the expense of the system may have an important impact on the standard of medical attention that is offered to patients. The use of immutable transaction records and medical data makes it possible for blockchain technology to facilitate the safe storage and continuous monitoring of a patient's comprehensive and accurate medical history [73–75]. Blockchain systems have the potential to revolutionize telemedicine. However, their progress is slowed by factors such as limited awareness, platform instability, and inadequate privacy and data standards [76]. It is necessary to conduct additional research to develop detailed standards and regulations before the wider implementation of blockchain technology in the disciplines of telehealth and communications. In addition, it is vital to investigate the financial motives that encourage businesses to make the change to using blockchain technology.

6.3.7 Security vulnerabilities of smart contracts

Smart contracts with bugs or vulnerabilities can compromise the security of patient medical records, leading to potential alteration or destruction [77, 78]. For instance, a smart contract with restricted access can modify a patient's electronic health record or access funds from a legitimate user's account by utilizing a re-entrancy security operation [79]. The researcher provides several diagnostic methods, including SolCover, ZeppelinOS, and Oyente [80]. Smart contract programmers can utilize these tools to identify weaknesses in their contracts that could be exploited by external attacks [17, 77]. The provided approaches are insufficient in addressing all types of smart contract flaws and defects. Smart contracts require thorough testing for vulnerabilities using various test cases and multiple testing tools before deployment.

6.4 Increasing transaction pace and large-scale health data sets

To prevent diagnostic errors in e-health and health services blockchain-based systems, it is crucial to maintain a medical record of the patient in a standardized and daily format [81]. Telehealth services generate a substantial amount of data, necessitating efficient data processing to extract useful information from medical records. The present blockchain platforms are adversely affected by the vast amount of healthcare data, which results in increased transaction fees and prolonged waiting periods for completion [82, 83]. The Ethereum platform can handle twenty transactions in a single second [84]. Furthermore, the storage requirements of distributed ledger technology increase proportionally with the growing number of transactions in telehealth services. The addition of an additional edge- or fog-based layer is one potential improvement that might be made to the frameworks that are currently being utilized for the production of data [85].

6.4.1 Support for bridge connectivity

Healthcare providers and patients seek secure connectivity of referral services on blockchain platforms. Blockchain platforms' compatibility support enables users to connect directly with each other, eliminating the need for intermediaries [26]. Through the utilization of a platform that permits compatibility, medical practitioners are now able to conduct activities on the Ethereum blockchain network using Bitcoin tokens. Interoperability among blockchain systems presents several challenges, such as the divergence in programming languages and consensus mechanisms supported by different platforms [86, 87]. To safeguard the privacy of telehealth consumers, it is imperative to employ interoperable solutions that are efficient, secure, and resilient to errors.

6.5 Conclusion

In the context of investigating remote medical care, this chapter explains why it is critical to implement blockchain technology in a way that is both reliable and trustworthy. This chapter takes a look at some new blockchain-based projects which have improved efficiency so that doctors may provide healthcare services to their patients remotely. Researchers have identified several areas requiring further investigation to improve current blockchain-based systems for enhanced remote health and telemedicine services. In conclusion, we would like to highlight several significant findings and offer our final remarks.

- The use of blockchain technology can protect medical records from being hacked by ensuring strict compliance with the rules that are described in patient authorization forms.
- Continuous remote patient monitoring is essential to reduce the occurrence of medical errors. Developing efficient blockchain technologies can significantly improve the utilization of blockchain in the healthcare sector by reducing transaction processing time.
- The tracing function of blockchain technology can be of assistance to those working in the medical field in the detection of fraud involving the educational qualifications of physicians and diagnostic gadgets that are typically used for home diagnosis.
- Because of the high level of data confidentiality that is provided by both private and cooperative blockchain technology, these technologies are well-suited for the digitalization of telehealth and telemedicine services.

References

[1] Azim A, Islam M N and Spranger P E 2020 Blockchain and novel coronavirus: towards preventing COVID-19 and future pandemics *Iberoam. J. Med.* **2** 215–8

[2] Nguyen D C, Ding M, Pathirana P N and Seneviratne A 2021 Blockchain and AI-based solutions to combat coronavirus (COVID-19)-like epidemics: a survey *IEEE Access* **9** 95730–53

[3] Kumar D, Sood S K and Rawat K S 2023 IoT-enabled technologies for controlling COVID-19 spread: a scientometric analysis using CiteSpace *Internet Things* **23** 100863

[4] Gonçalves R L *et al* 2023 Usability of telehealth systems for noncommunicable diseases in primary care from the COVID-19 pandemic onward: systematic review *J. Med. Internet Res.* **25** e44209

[5] Alarjani M and Alhaider M 2023 A review of challenges of block chain with COVID-19: a review paper *Eur. J. Health Sci.* **8** 32–49

[6] Hollander J E and Carr B G 2020 Virtually perfect? Telemedicine for COVID-19 *New Engl. J. Med.* **382** 1679–81

[7] Jin Z and Chen Y 2015 Telemedicine in the cloud era: prospects and challenges *IEEE Pervasive Comput.* **14** 54–61

[8] Ekeland A G, Bowes A and Flottorp S 2010 Effectiveness of telemedicine: a systematic review of reviews *Int. J. Med. Inform.* **79** 736–71

[9] Mahajan H B, Rashid A S, Junnarkar A A, Uke N, Deshpande S D, Futane P R, Alkhayyat A and Alhayani B 2023 Integration of Healthcare 4.0 and blockchain into secure cloud-based electronic health records systems *Appl. Nanosci.* **13** 2329–42

[10] Murala D K, Panda S K and Sahoo S K 2023 Securing electronic health record system in cloud environment using blockchain technology *Recent Advances in Blockchain Technology: Real-World Applications* (Cham: Springer) pp 89–116

[11] Hopkins B S *et al* 2023 Outpatient telemedicine in neurosurgery: 15,677 consecutive encounters in a comparative analysis of its effectiveness and impact on the surgical conversion rate *J. Neurosurg.* **1** 1–10

[12] Stowe S and Harding S 2010 Telecare, telehealth and telemedicine *Eur. Geriatr. Med.* **1** 193–7

[13] Khatoon A 2020 A blockchain-based smart contract system for healthcare management *Electronics* **9** 94

[14] Bennett B 2017 Using telehealth as a model for blockchain HIT adoption *Telehealth Med. Today* **2** 1–4

[15] Margheri A, Masi M, Miladi A, Sassone V and Rosenzweig J 2020 Decentralised provenance for healthcare data *Int. J. Med. Inform.* **141** 104197

[16] Dagher G G, Mohler J, Milojkovic M and Marella P B 2018 Ancile: privacy-preserving framework for access control and interoperability of electronic health records using blockchain technology *Sustain. Cities Soc.* **39** 283–97

[17] Hu Y C, Lee T T, Chatzopoulos D and Hui P 2020 Analyzing smart contract interactions and contract level state consensus *Concurr. Comput. Pract. Exp.* **32** e5228

[18] Pham H L, Tran T H and Nakashima Y 2019 Practical anti-counterfeit medicine management system based on blockchain technology *2019 4th Technology Innovation Management and Engineering Science Int. Conf. (TIMES-ICON)* pp 1–5

[19] Holzinger A, Weippl E, Tjoa A M and Kieseberg P 2021 Digital transformation for sustainable development goals (SDGS)—a security, safety and privacy perspective on AI *Int. Cross-Domain Conf. for Machine Learning and Knowledge Extraction* pp 1–20

[20] Zheng Z, Xie S, Dai H N, Chen W, Chen X, Weng J and Imran M 2020 An overview on smart contracts: challenges, advances and platforms *Future Gener. Comput. Syst.* **105** 475–91

[21] Hasselgren A, Kralevska K, Gligoroski D, Pedersen S A and Faxvaag A 2020 Blockchain in healthcare and health sciences—a scoping review *Int. J. Med. Inform.* **134** 104040

[22] Chukwu E and Garg L 2020 A systematic review of blockchain in healthcare: frameworks, prototypes, and implementations *IEEE Access* **8** 21196–214

[23] Ting D S W, Carin L, Dzau V and Wong T Y 2020 Digital technology and COVID-19 *Nat. Med.* **26** 459–61

[24] Vaishya R, Haleem A, Vaish A and Javaid M 2020 Emerging technologies to combat the COVID-19 pandemic *J. Clin. Exp. Hepatol.* **10** 409–11

[25] Ahmad R W, Salah K, Jayaraman R, Yaqoob I, Ellahham S and Omar M 2023 Blockchain and COVID-19 pandemic: applications and challenges *Cluster Comput.* **26** 2383–408

[26] Rabah K 2017 Challenges and opportunities for blockchain powered healthcare systems: a review *Mara Res. J. Med. Health Sci.* **1** 45–52

[27] Houtan B, Hafid A S and Makrakis D 2020 A survey on blockchain-based self-sovereign patient identity in healthcare *IEEE Access* **8** 90478–94

[28] De Aguiar E J, Faiçal B S, Krishnamachari B and Ueyama J 2020 A survey of blockchain-based strategies for healthcare *ACM Comput. Surv.* **53** 1–27

[29] Shubbar S 2017 Ultrasound medical imaging systems using telemedicine and blockchain for remote monitoring of responses to neoadjuvant chemotherapy in women's breast cancer: concept and implementation *Doctoral Dissertation* Kent State University

[30] Guo R, Shi H, Zheng D, Jing C, Zhuang C and Wang Z 2019 Flexible and efficient blockchain-based ABE scheme with multi-authority for medical on demand in telemedicine system *IEEE Access* **7** 88012–25

[31] Abugabah A, Nizamuddin N and Alzubi A A 2020 Decentralized telemedicine framework for a smart healthcare ecosystem *IEEE Access* **8** 166575–88

[32] Colón K A 2018 Creating a patient-centered, global, decentralized health system: combining new payment and care delivery models with telemedicine, AI, and blockchain technology *Blockchain Healthc. Today* **1**

[33] Hewa T, Braeken A, Ylianttila M and Liyanage M 2020 Multi-access edge computing and blockchain-based secure telehealth system connected with 5G and IoT *GLOBECOM 2020–2020 IEEE Global Communications Conf.* pp 1–6

[34] Griggs K N, Ossipova O, Kohlios C P, Baccarini A N, Howson E A and Hayajneh T 2018 Healthcare blockchain system using smart contracts for secure automated remote patient monitoring *J. Med. Syst.* **42** 1–7

[35] Agbo C C, Mahmoud Q H and Eklund J M 2019 Blockchain technology in healthcare: a systematic review *Healthcare* **7** 56

[36] McGhin T, Choo K K R, Liu C Z and He D 2019 Blockchain in healthcare applications: research challenges and opportunities *J. Netw. Comput. Appl.* **135** 62–75

[37] Hussien H M, Yasin S M, Udzir S N I, Zaidan A A and Zaidan B B 2019 A systematic review for enabling of develop a blockchain technology in healthcare application: taxonomy, substantially analysis, motivations, challenges, recommendations and future direction *J. Med. Syst.* **43** 1–35

[38] Radanović I and Likić R 2018 Opportunities for use of blockchain technology in medicine *Appl. Health Econ. Health Policy* **16** 583–90

[39] Khezr S, Moniruzzaman M, Yassine A and Benlamri R 2019 Blockchain technology in healthcare: a comprehensive review and directions for future research *Appl. Sci.* **9** 1736

[40] Abu-Elezz I, Hassan A, Nazeemudeen A, Househ M and Abd-Alrazaq A 2020 The benefits and threats of blockchain technology in healthcare: a scoping review *Int. J. Med. Inform.* **142** 104246

[41] Tandon A, Dhir A, Islam A N and Mäntymäki M 2020 Blockchain in healthcare: a systematic literature review, synthesizing framework and future research agenda *Comput. Ind.* **122** 103290

[42] Yaqoob I, Salah K, Jayaraman R and Al-Hammadi Y 2021 Blockchain for healthcare data management: opportunities, challenges, and future recommendations *Neural Comput. Appl.* **35** 11475–90

[43] Vellela S S, Reddy B V, Chaitanya K K and Rao M V 2023 An integrated approach to improve e-healthcare system using dynamic cloud computing platform *2023 5th Int. Conf. on Smart Systems and Inventive Technology (ICSSIT)* pp 776–82

[44] Tagde P, Tagde S, Bhattacharya T, Tagde P, Chopra H, Akter R, Kaushik D and Rahman M H 2021 Blockchain and artificial intelligence technology in e-Health *Environ Sci Pollut Res Int.* **28** 52810–52831

[45] Zhang X, Poslad S and Ma Z 2018 Block-based access control for blockchain-based electronic medical records (EMRs) query in eHealth *2018 IEEE Global Communications Conf. (GLOBECOM) (2018 December)* pp 1–7

[46] Ahmad R W, Salah K, Jayaraman R, Yaqoob I, Ellahham S and Omar M 2021 The role of blockchain technology in telehealth and telemedicine *Int. J. Med. Inform.* **148** 104399

[47] Mannaro K, Baralla G, Pinna A and Ibba S 2018 A blockchain approach applied to a teledermatology platform in the Sardinian region (Italy) *Information* **9** 44

[48] Painuly S, Sharma S and Matta P 2023 Artificial intelligence in e-Healthcare supply chain management system: challenges and future trends *2023 Int. Conf. on Sustainable Computing and Data Communication Systems (ICSCDS)* pp 569–74

[49] Weissman S M, Zellmer K, Gill N and Wham D 2018 Implementing a virtual health telemedicine program in a community setting *J. Genet. Couns.* **27** 323–5

[50] Wang C K 2015 Security and privacy of personal health record, electronic medical record and health information *Probl. Perspect. Manag.* **13** 19–26

[51] Prokofieva M and Miah S J 2019 Blockchain in healthcare *Australas. J. Inf. Syst.* **23**

[52] Halamka J D *et al* 2019 Top 10 blockchain predictions for the (near) future of healthcare *Blockchain Healthc. Today* **2**

[53] MedicalChain 2018 White paper: MedicalChain *MedicalChain self-publication*

[54] Kazmi H S Z, Nazeer F, Mubarak S, Hameed S, Basharat A and Javaid N 2020 Trusted remote patient monitoring using blockchain-based smart contracts *Advances on Broad-Band Wireless Computing, Communication and Applications: Proc. of the 14th Int. Conf. on Broad-Band Wireless Computing, Communication and Applications (BWCCA-2019)* vol 14 pp 765–76

[55] Jayaraman P P and Perera C 2017 The emergence of edge-centric distributed IoT analytics platforms *Internet of Things* (London: Chapman & Hall)

[56] ur Rehman M H, Ahmed E, Yaqoob I, Hashem I A T, Imran M and Ahmad S 2018 Big data analytics in industrial IoT using a concentric computing model *IEEE Commun. Mag.* **56** 37–43

[57] Salah K, Alfalasi A, Alfalasi M, Alharmoudi M, Alzaabi M, Alzyeodi A and Ahmad R W 2020 IoT-enabled shipping container with environmental monitoring and location tracking *2020 IEEE 17th Annual Consumer Communications and Networking Conf. (CCNC)* pp 1–6

[58] Gong L, Alghazzawi D M and Cheng L 2021 BCoT sentry: a blockchain-based identity authentication framework for IoT devices *Information* **12** 203

[59] El-Miedany Y 2017 Telehealth and telemedicine: how the digital era is changing standard health care *Smart Homec. Technol. Telehealth* **4** 43–51

[60] Raikwar M, Mazumdar S, Ruj S, Gupta S S, Chattopadhyay A and Lam K Y 2018 A blockchain framework for insurance processes *2018 9th IFIP Int. Conf. on New Technologies, Mobility and Security (NTMS)* pp 1–4

[61] Lee C K 2019 Blockchain application with health token in medical and health industrials *2nd Int. Conf. on Social Science, Public Health and Education (SSPHE 2018)* pp 233–6

[62] Heath S 2020 Patient engagement strategies for post-discharge follow-up care *TechTarget* https://patientengagementhit.com/features/patient-engagement-strategies-for-post-discharge-follow-up-care (accessed May 2020)

[63] Siyal A A, Junejo A Z, Zawish M, Ahmed K, Khalil A and Soursou G 2019 Applications of blockchain technology in medicine and healthcare: challenges and future perspectives *Cryptography* **3** 3

[64] Kumar A, Krishnamurthi R, Nayyar A, Sharma K, Grover V and Hossain E 2020 A novel smart healthcare design, simulation, and implementation using healthcare 4.0 processes *IEEE Access* **8** 118433–71

[65] Sharma A and Kaur P 2023 Tamper-proof multitenant data storage using blockchain *Peer-to-peer Netw. Appl.* **16** 431–49

[66] Todaro J M 2020 Overview of MedCredits *MedX Protocol* https://medium.com/medxprotocol/introduction-to-medcredits-287f9fac03e6 (accessed June 2020)

[67] Munoz D J, Constantinescu D A, Asenjo R and Fuentes L 2020 Clinicappchain: a low-cost blockchain hyperledger solution for healthcare *Blockchain and Applications: Int. Congress* pp 36–44

[68] Aileni R M and Suciu G 2020 IoMT: a blockchain perspective *Decentralised Internet of Things: A Blockchain Perspective* (Cham: Springer) pp 199–215

[69] Buterin V 2014 Schellingcoin: a minimal-trust universal data feed *Ethereum Blog*

[70] Gabrielli S, Krenn S, Pellegrino D, Pérez Baún J C, Pérez Berganza P, Ramacher S and Vandevelde W 2022 KRAKEN: a secure, trusted, regulatory-compliant, and privacy-preserving data sharing platform *Data Spaces: Design, Deployment and Future Directions* (Cham: Springer) pp 107–30

[71] Robomed Network R 2017 Initial coin offering *White Paper* Robomed Network Inc. Russia

[72] Hang L, Choi E and Kim D H 2019 A novel EMR integrity management based on a medical blockchain platform in hospital *Electronics* **8** 467

[73] Bennett B 2017 Blockchain HIE overview: a framework for healthcare interoperability *Telehealth Med. Today* **2**

[74] Raskin M 2016 The law and legality of smart contracts *Geo. L. Tech. Rev.* **1** 305

[75] Hurley D 2018 Blockchain for patient and HCP data rights management: lessons from an enterprise install *Telehealth Med. Today* https://blockchainhealthcaretoday.com/index.php/journal/article/view/56

[76] Kolan A, Tjoa S and Kieseberg P 2020 Medical blockchains and privacy in Austria-technical and legal aspects *2020 Int. Conf. on Software Security and Assurance (ICSSA)* pp 1–9

[77] Mense A and Flatscher M 2018 Security vulnerabilities in ethereum smart contracts *Proc. of the 20th Int. Conf. on Information Integration and Web-based Applications and Services* pp 375–80

[78] Rehman M H, Salah K, Damiani E and Svetinovic D 2019 Trust in blockchain cryptocurrency ecosystem *IEEE Trans. Eng. Manage.* **67** 1196–212

[79] Khan Z A and Namin A S 2020 Ethereum smart contracts: vulnerabilities and their classifications *2020 IEEE Int. Conf. on Big Data (Big Data)* pp 1–10

[80] Chen H, Pendleton M, Njilla L and Xu S 2020 A survey on ethereum systems security: vulnerabilities, attacks, and defenses *ACM Comput. Surv.* **53** 1–43

[81] Mazlan A A, Daud S M, Sam S M, Abas H, Rasid S Z A and Yusof M F 2020 Scalability challenges in healthcare blockchain system—a systematic review *IEEE Access* **8** 23663–73

[82] Böhme R, Christin N, Edelman B and Moore T 2015 Bitcoin: economics, technology, and governance *J. Econ. Perspect.* **29** 213–38

[83] Malavolta G, Moreno-Sanchez P, Schneidewind C, Kate A and Maffei M 2018 Anonymous multi-hop locks for blockchain scalability and interoperability *Cryptology ePrint Archive*

[84] Wood G 2014 Ethereum: a secure decentralised generalised transaction ledger *Ethereum Project Yellow Paper* **151** 1–32

[85] Debe M, Salah K, Rehman M H U and Svetinovic D 2019 IoT public fog nodes reputation system: a decentralized solution using Ethereum blockchain *IEEE Access* **7** 178082–93

[86] Herlihy M 2018 Atomic cross-chain swaps *Proc. of the 2018 ACM Symp. on Principles of Distributed Computing* pp 245–54

[87] Miraz M H and Donald D C 2019 Atomic cross-chain swaps: development, trajectory and potential of non-monetary digital token swap facilities arXiv preprint arXiv:1902.04471

IOP Publishing

Blockchain with Artificial Intelligence for Healthcare
A synergistic approach
**Rishabha Malviya, Arun Kumar Singh, Sonali Sundram, Balamurugan Balusamy and
Seifedine Kadry**

Chapter 7

Smart contracts: a medical intervention that automates remote patient monitoring

The rise in popularity of sensor nodes and health monitoring technologies has led to an increase in problems related to secure data transmission and recording. To ensure the secure analysis and administration of sensing devices that generate protected health information, several studies have proposed the utilization of smart contracts based on blockchain technology. In a local framework, based on detectors communicating with a device, smart contracts activate and activities are recorded on an Ethereum blockchain system. This method enables immediate alerts for patients and medical professionals, while also maintaining a record of the individuals initiating these actions. Automating notifications for everyone involved can help mitigate security issues associated with remote health monitoring. This chapter explores the use of smart contracts to authorize Internet of Things (IoT) devices and presents a legally compliant and secure approach for utilizing medical sensors. This chapter explores the use of blockchain-based smart contracts for the secure evaluation and administration of medical sensors.

7.1 Introduction

IoT devices and wearable technologies have expanded the possibilities for medical sensors in the field of remote patient monitoring. The IoT healthcare trend includes the use of Wireless Body Area Networks (WBANs) [1–3]. Various wearables or implanted medical devices can be utilized to monitor a patient's vital signs, such as heart rate and plasma glucose level. Additional sensors and actuators can be employed to autonomously offer treatments using the data they collect [4–8]. The patient's WBAN devices transmit data to healthcare professionals, while a control device facilitates an interactive user interface, typically in the form of a mobile phone [9]. Remote monitoring allows patients to engage in their daily activities without the need to deal with long waiting times for doctor appointments [10].

The anticipated spike in the utilization of remote patient monitoring for health tracking is estimated to reach 50.2 million individuals by 2021, a significant rise from the current 7.1 million [11, 12]. To enable real-time monitoring, financial rewards were implemented on January 1, 2018, to encourage the adoption of equipment featuring an 'active feedback loop' [7].

The increasing field of smart health monitoring is also accompanied by growing challenges related to the security and efficiency of healthcare information transfer. Integrated health management involves the collection, organization, and analysis of data from various sensor devices, regardless of their manufacturers. Federal legislation is necessary to ensure the secure transmission of Protected Health Information (PHI) due to the high vulnerability of healthcare information systems to attempts at hacking. To safeguard patient privacy, electronic health records (EHRs) need to be easily maintained and transmitted. Accurate documentation of commands given to transducer nodes in smart nodes is necessary to assess the quality of patient care and the sequence of incidents. This serves as both a treatment for the patient and as proof of approval. The integration of smart contracts on the blockchain should be used to create an immutable record of transactions between WBAN devices and healthcare providers. The utilization of medical devices will provide patients with a greater sense of security due to the system's digital ledger and regular safety updates. Secure remote monitoring enables medical practitioners to receive real-time updates on their patients, thereby facilitating precise treatment [13]. The integration of new medical technology into the healthcare system using smart contracts is an innovative technique that automates the notification of health data from various devices. Figure 7.1 illustrates the fundamental structure of the system. The blockchain technology developed by Satoshi Nakamoto is the underlying infrastructure for smart contracts. The decentralized shared ledger serves the purpose of tracking transactions [14].

There are three primary classifications of blockchains: open, corporate, and consortium-based. The primary objective of a public blockchain is to decentralize networks and ensure the secure and transparent transmission of information. Private and consortium blockchains are favored when higher control and privacy are required. This system utilizes a consortium blockchain due to its cost-effectiveness and enhanced security measures for safeguarding personal health information (PHI). Blockchain operates on the principle that no individual is authorized to add transactions to the blockchain, which functions as a comprehensive ledger for all operations.

Numerous industries have experienced advantages through the adoption of blockchain technology. A permanent record can be maintained to document the entire process of a product or subject from the beginning to its conclusion. This technology has applications in verifying the current state of information, confirming the authenticity of the artwork, and establishing ownership of the system. Blockchains can be used to create smart contracts, which are programmable code segments that can be executed when specific conditions are met. This system utilizes

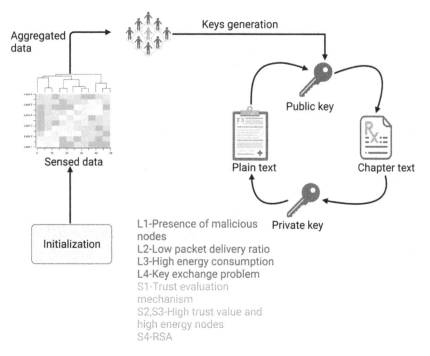

Sensed data

Aggregated data

Keys generation

Public key

Plain text

Chapter text

Private key

Initialization

L1-Presence of malicious nodes
L2-Low packet delivery ratio
L3-High energy consumption
L4-Key exchange problem
S1-Trust evaluation mechanism
S2,S3-High trust value and high energy nodes
S4-RSA

Figure 7.1. The image illustrates how the nodes on the blockchain receive and process raw sensor data before transmitting it to the shared ledger through the network interface.

WBAN devices to generate health data, which can be utilized to activate alarms when specific threshold levels are reached for individual patients. This blockchain enables the tracking of data collected and treatment orders issued by WBAN nodes.

Managing PHI requires a complete dedication to confidentiality and authenticity. This blockchain system ensures validity, verifiability, and user privacy using anonymized accounts and permissioned consortium management. A corporate blockchain, unlike a public blockchain like Bitcoin, can only be accessed and validated by authorized individuals. An anonymous account will be created for each authorized user. Consequently, patients will gain increased autonomy in managing their medical records.

Despite the existence of publications addressing possible applications of blockchain in healthcare, there is currently no evidence of this recommended technique being utilized in similar research or publicly accessible software. IBM's Hyperledger project has promoted the adoption of blockchain technology in healthcare and IoT [15]. However, this operational model lacks references in academic papers [16]. Currently, research on remote patient monitoring (RPM) primarily highlights the use of wireless network sensing devices [10], rather than integrating blockchain technology into RPM operations. Out-of-band methods can also be employed for the authentication of IoT devices. The focus has been on achieving interoperability between EHRs and blockchain technology. MIT has developed a blockchain-based prototype called Medrec, which allows for the exchange of medical records across electronic EHRs [9]. There is interest in developing a blockchain-based EHR system that would consolidate all EHR data into a single block. One example of an Initial Coin Offering (ICO) is the implementation of a blockchain-based EHR system. This system allows patients to have direct control and oversight of their PHI, as compared to being dependent on multiple doctors and medical organizations [13]. Patients are becoming more engaged in their treatment in the current healthcare landscape [17]. Researchers proposed a provision utilizing blockchain technology to allow patients to grant authorization to designated individuals for accessing their clinical information recorded on the blockchain. This technology enables a patient-centric application of the IoT. The blocks within the range of 13–18 are excessively large, leading to a problem. Blockchain blocks serve as records of documents that store brief explanations of data. Storing a patient's complete medical information on a blockchain would necessitate significant storage capacity for each node. This healthcare blockchain application is distinct, although there are several comparable concepts in utilization. Therefore, it can be assured that this blockchain-based healthcare system would exhibit high levels of adaptability.

7.2 System design

The operation of the system is described in this manner. Two medical devices commonly employed for remote patient monitoring include an insulin pump as well as a blood pressure monitoring device. To collect and organize data, an application transfers it to a 'smart device,' such as a smartphone or tablet. The smart contract promptly receives and processes the formatted data, along with specified limits (figure 7.1).

The 'Oracle' serves as the primary information provider for smart contracts within the Ethereum protocol. The Oracle device establishes a direct connection with smart contracts. The smart contract can automatically generate a treatment plan for actuator nodes by utilizing data from both the patient and the medical expert (figure 7.2).

HIPAA regulations prohibit the preservation of medical data on a blockchain or in digital assets. Blockchain technology is utilized as a decentralized and permanent ledger for recording and monitoring things. After the data transmission is finished, a smart contract will be shown to the blockchain to signify its completion. APIs for EHRs facilitate the process of transferring data to an EHR. Additionally, blockchain activity will be implemented to document the treatment instructions provided by both the smart contract and the healthcare practitioner. To ensure the integrity and accuracy of individuals' medical records, it is possible to establish a connection between blockchain transactions and the EHR. Authentication can lead to intentional or accidental modifications of a patient's EHR. This system will utilize a secure and global network blockchain to analyze blocks, perform smart contracts, and validate new blocks. Access to this blockchain will be restricted to authorized entities only. The authentication procedure will limit access to patient data to authorized individuals, including physicians, medical device manufacturers, and patients. For a node to be considered valid, it must receive confirmation from a

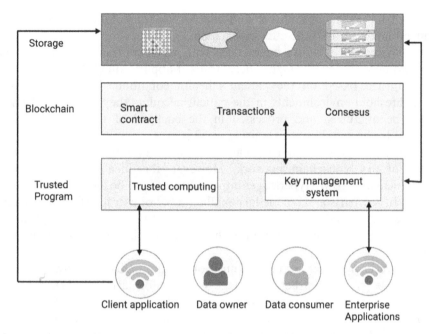

Figure 7.2. This diagram illustrates the process of utilizing preset settings and data obtained from a smart device. The data is then formatted for transmission to a smart contract. Adapted from [18]. CC BY 4.0. © 2020 Shrestha, Vassileva and Deters.

minimum of three members belonging to the pre-approved list of nodes, specifically 10 out of 15. Multiple healthcare organizations could participate in the system while maintaining a certain level of decentralization. Pre-approved verification nodes will replace proof-of-work fees. Rogue nodes are unable to work together and control the blockchain by coordinating the insertion of fraudulent transactions. Practical Byzantine Fault Tolerance (PBFT) may be utilized as a method for obtaining consent and should be thoroughly examined.

Each smart contract may adapt to the specific needs of a patient and its variety of devices. All parent units will invoke a single initial private blockchain. This blockchain will then communicate with the relevant sub-contract for each patient's device, providing the necessary inputs and specific limit settings for each patient. The construction will be divided into tiers. Individual contracts transmit warnings or treatment orders based on data analysis following threshold levels. The device's contract can only be terminated and replaced with a new one after installation, allowing for upgrades without impacting other units.

7.3 Implementation

The Solidity programming language was specifically designed for Ethereum to develop smart contracts as a proof of idea. These operations and smart contracts are not being conducted on Ethereum's public blockchain. Instead, a private chain that is constructed based on Ethereum's architecture was used. This eliminates the requirement for Ether expenditure and enables experimentation beyond the pre-determined limits of the Ethereum blockchain.

Smart devices will establish interactions with smart contracts on the blockchain and uphold user profiles through a decentralized application (DApp). The profiles can be adjusted based on the patient's health condition. Doctors can modify tracking threshold environments in the patient accounts they manage. The sensor data will be organized and processed in the backend of the DApp, and then transmitted to the smart contracts using web3.js.

Remix is utlized, a software tool that incorporates a programmer to evaluate the efficiency of the blockchain network. However, this idea extends beyond the Ethereum network. IBM Hyperledger implementation can be tested using the online system [4]. In comparison, Hyperledger exhibits superior user interface and customer service when compared to Ethereum. Furthermore, a monthly fee is applicable for membership. Efficient administration of the Ethereum platform necessitates a team of experts.

The smart device will establish Bluetooth communication with the Health Contract Caller smart contract to manage system information. A distinct contract will be established for every device that receives data. The Health Contract Caller is notified immediately upon receiving heart rate data from a smart device.

The Health Contract Caller will be utilized to evaluate the heart rate monitor. The computing device will send the information and minimum-level values as variables. The heart rate monitor object will be created as a parameter for the analysis method. The primary purpose of the two distinct subcontracts is to independently analyze and respond to data, rather than giving up control to the main contract. The main contract serves as a 'directory' to enhance modularity and facilitate maintenance. If the analysis yields an unfavorable result, indicating failure, this transaction will be logged on the blockchain. Sending identical code to the computing device can trigger various responses, including user notification, alerting authorities, or initiating specific actions such as administering insulin or high blood pressure medication.

The three sample contracts have been combined into a single GitHub storage [11] to enhance accessibility. A viable alternative to conventional contracts involves utilizing blockchain technology to create separate files containing information details, which can subsequently be accessed and mentioned through their corresponding blockchain addresses.

7.4 System analysis

7.4.1 Comparison to traditional systems

This approach depends on the utilization of blockchain technology, which is an emerging technology. This proposed blockchain solution incorporates cloud computing and database systems to facilitate a comparative analysis with an established remote patient monitoring system. Table 7.1 presents a comparison between the conventional system and the one that has been proposed.

Table 7.1. Comparison table between conventional and suggested system.

Parameters	Traditional systems	Existing system
Confidentiality	End-to-end encryption is employed to securely transfer data to a designated database.	The equivalent level of protection.
Availability	To ensure uninterrupted service during system failures, duplication and effective human management of database backups are necessary.	The presence of a complete blockchain on all nodes enhances resilience to failure and service availability. PBFT algorithms can be employed to address node failures.
Immutability	Databases can be compromised either unintentionally or with malicious intentions.	Verified blocks are permanent and resistant to any attempts at modification, rendering them resistant to all forms of manipulation.
Traceability	Alterations with medical records and logs can occur, making detection undetermined.	Verifiers authenticate transactions to guarantee their consistency and tracking from their origin.
Speed	The rate of transactions is determined by the network's limitations.	The waiting time can be minimized depending on the duration required for block validation.
Privacy	The encryption of communications ensures the protection of end-users personal information from unauthorized access.	The anonymity of patient addresses prevents the linkage of patient information to their identities.
Transparency	Patient information is inaccessible and cannot be linked to their respective records.	Remote monitoring allows patients to closely monitor their health information while maintaining privacy and liberty.

7.4.2 Security analysis

To keep things simple, it is assumed that all cloud and IP protocols are encrypted. Healthcare providers can modify patient thresholds in smart contracts, while patients can only access their data through smart devices [19]. The smart device should include authentication by users' capabilities. To establish the authenticity of a block, it is necessary to have most of the authorization from members of the consortium on the proposed consortium blockchain. Access to the blockchain is restricted to authorized individuals, such as patients and carers, who have been granted permission. It is crucial to ensure that the blockchain does not contain any sensitive patient data. The blockchain ledger enhances safety for healthcare professionals and patients during conflicts or treatment tracking. HIPAA's privacy requirement applies to electronic data transmission. Data that cannot be linked to a specific patient does not receive protection under HIPAA. The blockchain data solely comprises transactional details and does not contain any sensitive PHI.

The practice of using patient account addresses, which can make it difficult to identify individuals, is permitted under the HIPAA standards.

The Privacy Rule generally prohibits the disclosure of personal data, unless authorized by law or in response to a request from an individual or HHS (Health and Human Services). In addition, it provides HHS with authenticated and immutable monitoring records for dispute resolution and investigation. This system implements multiple measures to ensure HIPAA compliance and protect PHI.

7.4.3 Limitations

The primary challenge in a widely dispersed system is to ensure the safety of every individual node. The patient's smart device data is being transmitted to blockchain nodes through a potentially unsecured channel, namely the patient's local wifi, using conventional channel encryption methods. Managing keys can be challenging when multiple intelligent technologies transmit their information to different nodes, causing delays in the validation of the next block. A large-scale key control system could potentially resolve this issue. The effective functioning of a healthcare system depends on the timely acquisition and examination of real-time data. Even with changes to block verification times, there will still be some delay. The smart gadget would gather and combine sensor data periodically and transmit it to the user, instead of presenting information in short intervals. The obstacle can only be resolved through precise adjustment of the transmission time. The severity of the illness and the type of sensor being utilized need a case-by-case assessment. The response team should avoid relying on the current limitations of this technology, as doing so could potentially lead to an increase in the time it takes to respond. Before adding a new node to the blockchain network, personal authentication is necessary, involving the utilization of consensus mechanisms such as PBFT. To prevent the occurrence of unauthorized miners, this measure is implemented. Insufficient online presence of individuals may prevent the establishment of a consensus mechanism by impeding the attainment of the necessary number of valid authorizations and compromising the integrity of the system. In a PBFT system consisting of N nodes, the maximum number of faulty nodes that can be tolerated is $(N - 1)/3$ [5]. It is important to note that this field of study is still changing and therefore, some of these concerns may be addressed in the future.

7.5 Conclusion

Using blockchain-based smart contracts can provide benefits for ensuring the security of data transfer and getting into IoT healthcare. This system utilizes a blockchain-based smart contract architecture to analyze data obtained from a patient's IoT healthcare device. This analysis is conducted according to user-configurable thresholds. Relevant individuals, including the patient and healthcare professionals, would receive the necessary information, while the transaction would be recorded in the blockchain for EHR verification. Smart contracts in Solidity serve as prototypes to illustrate the movement of data within a system. Blockchain technology can enhance the security and HIPAA-compliant notification delivery of remote patient monitoring systems. Healthcare can effectively utilize big data by integrating organized and new data into EHRs and health data lakes. This integration will enhance the reliability of information and lead to more significant outcomes. The subsequent phase involves examining Hyperledger implementation alternatives and incorporating anonymizers to enhance the complexity of linking transactions within a chain.

References

[1] Almashaqbeh G, Hayajneh T, Vasilakos A V and Mohd B J 2014 QoS-aware health monitoring system using cloud-based WBANs *J. Med. Syst.* **38** 1–20

[2] Paterick T E 2023 Why the HIPAA privacy rules are important for physicians to know: Ignore these at your own risk *Podiatry Manage.* 113–7

[3] Paternò L and Lorenzon L 2023 Soft robotics in wearable and implantable medical applications: translational challenges and future outlooks *Front. Robot. AI* **10** 1075634

[4] Sheeraz M M, Mozumder M A I, Khan M O, Abid M U, Joo M I and Kim H C 2023 Blockchain system for trustless healthcare data sharing with hyperledger fabric in action *25th Int. Conf. on Advanced Communication Technology (ICACT)* pp 437–40

[5] Tran T, Nawab F, Alvaro P and Arden O 2023 Unstick yourself: recoverable Byzantine fault tolerant services *2023 IEEE International Conference on Blockchain and Cryptocurrency (ICBC) (Dubai)* 1–9

[6] Griggs K N, Ossipova O, Kohlios C P, Baccarini A N, Howson E A and Hayajneh T 2018 Healthcare blockchain system using smart contracts for secure automated remote patient monitoring *J. Med. Syst.* **42** 1–7

[7] Miranda R, Oliveira M D, Nicola P, Baptista F M and Albuquerque I 2023 Towards a framework for implementing remote patient monitoring from an integrated care perspective: a scoping review *Int. J. Health Policy Manag.* **12** 1–13

[8] Dubovitskaya A, Xu Z, Ryu S, Schumacher M and Wang F 2017 Secure and trustable electronic medical records sharing using blockchain *AMIA Annual Symp. Proc.* **2017** 650

[9] Kaur G, Choudhary P, Sahore L, Gupta S and Kaur V 2023 Healthcare: in the era of blockchain *AI and Blockchain in Healthcare* (Singapore: Springer) pp 45–55

[10] Hayajneh T, Mohd B J, Imran M, Almashaqbeh G and Vasilakos A V 2016 Secure authentication for remote patient monitoring with wireless medical sensor networks *Sensors* **16** 424

[11] Cheikhrouhou O, Mershad K, Jamil F, Mahmud R, Koubaa A and Moosavi S R 2023 A lightweight blockchain and fog-enabled secure remote patient monitoring system *Internet Things* **22** 100691

[12] Boikanyo K, Zungeru A M, Sigweni B, Yahya A and Lebekwe C 2023 Remote patient monitoring systems: applications, architecture, and challenges *Sci. Afr.* **20** e01638

[13] Khwaji A, Alsahafi Y and Hussain F K 2023 A roadmap to blockchain technology adoption in Saudi public hospitals *Int. Conf. on Advanced Information Networking and Applications* 452–60

[14] Nakamoto S 2008 Bitcoin: a peer-to-peer electronic cash system *Decentralized Bus. Rev.*

[15] Abdollahi A, Sadeghvaziri F and Rejeb A 2023 Exploring the role of blockchain technology in value creation: a multiple case study approach *Qual. Quant.* **57** 427–51

[16] Noah B *et al* 2018 Impact of remote patient monitoring on clinical outcomes: an updated meta-analysis of randomized controlled trials *NPJ Digit. Med.* **1** 20172

[17] Apriani D, Devana V T, Sagala A P, Sunarya P A, Rahardja U and Harahap E P 2023 Security using blockchain-based OTP with the concept of IoT publish/subscribe *AIP Conf. Proc.* **2808** 050001

[18] Shrestha A K, Vassileva J and Deters R 2020 A blockchain platform for user data sharing ensuring user control and incentives *Front. Blockchain* **3** 497985

[19] Yue X, Wang H, Jin D, Li M and Jiang W 2016 Healthcare data gateways: found healthcare intelligence on blockchain with novel privacy risk control *J. Med. Syst.* **40** 1–8

IOP Publishing

Blockchain with Artificial Intelligence for Healthcare

A synergistic approach

**Rishabha Malviya, Arun Kumar Singh, Sonali Sundram, Balamurugan Balusamy and
Seifedine Kadry**

Chapter 8

Boosting biomedical research with the integration of blockchain and AI

Patients, researchers, service providers, and regulators are just some of the groups who will face opportunities and problems brought on by the expanding availability of data and advances in artificial intelligence. The use of deep learning and transfer learning technologies can turn ordinary videos and still photos of faces into rich sources of data for predictive analytics. Patients are unable to view their medical records, thus they are not aware of the significance of the information that they hold. This chapter provides an overview of biomedical research, focusing on the topics of artificial intelligence (AI) and blockchain technology. Efforts are being made to enhance biomedical research by exploring novel methods for managing patient data and introducing benefits for continuous health monitoring. This chapter discusses novel approaches to analyzing personal records, including data integration, immediate considerations, and the significance of relationships. Decentralized health data networks powered by blockchain will facilitate advancements in medical discovery, biomarker generation, and preventative healthcare provision. Individuals may be able to regain control of their data, particularly medical information if a global personal data marketplace is created that is both secure and transparent. It might be made possible by technologies such as blockchain and deep learning.

8.1 Introduction

A change has been made to the standard operating procedure of the healthcare sector as a result of the digital revolution in the medical field. The deployment of electronic medical records and the improvement of having access to medical information through digital healthcare systems would be of tremendous benefit to both patients and the professionals who provide healthcare for them. Electronic medical records, and more specifically OpenNotes, have been shown to have the potential to improve both the quality and efficiency of medical care [1, 2]. Biomedical data can be obtained from diverse sources such as medical imaging, routine laboratory testing, and omics data. When compared to the total amount of data generated by social networks and online video-sharing platforms, it is anticipated that the genomics industry will generate a volume of data that is a significant amount of additional information. Multiple national healthcare programs, such as the UK Biobank make use of biobanks in various capacities. The increasing scale and complexity of data in healthcare present both opportunities and challenges. On the one hand, they offer new and interesting perspectives. On the other hand, they can pose obstacles in data analysis and interpretation, as well as raise concerns about patient privacy and security [3–5]. Due to the enormous demand for treating and preventing chronic illnesses, particularly in older people, there is an urgent need for new worldwide integrated healthcare systems. This need has become increasingly urgent in recent years. Recent studies have extensively utilized various types of data, such as genomic, transcriptomic, microRNA, proteomic, antigen, DNA, imaging, metagenomic, mitochondrial, metabolic, and physiologic data, to personalize treatment for cancer and other disorders [6–13]. These strategies lack population-level integration and fail to compare the perception and usefulness of different formats in biology and medicine. Despite some attempts to evaluate the therapeutic efficacy of various methods and use multiple datasets to assess individual health status [14–19]. The integration of blockchain and AI has the potential to accelerate progress in healthcare sciences, leading to improved efficiency and effectiveness in healthcare systems [20–23]. This chapter will discuss deep learning, a recent advancement in next-generation AI [24]. The subsequent section examines the utility of Health and Demographic Surveillance Systems (HDSSs) as a viable approach for data archiving. It then proceeds with an overview of Exonum, an open-source blockchain platform. In the final step of this process, a study is carried out to investigate the potential uses of blockchain-based technology in the healthcare sector. This chapter covers the introduction of the half-life period of analytical importance, as well as data value models for individual and group users, as well as the cost of purchasing data for biomedical applications [25]. Patients are given the potential to gain advantages from their information by obtaining crypto tokens as a reward for providing information or for exhibiting healthy behavior on a platform that is based on blockchain technology [26]. Patients are also allowed to contribute to the growth of biomedical research by giving their data to a platform that is based on blockchain technology. Governments can enhance public engagement in preventing disease and potentially provide a universal basic income to residents who actively participate in these programs. This approach might reduce the load on healthcare resources. Deep learning, along with other machine learning techniques, can address significant data management problems.

8.2 Advancements in artificial intelligence

Health data is growing increasingly complex, making it challenging to examine globally [27]. Likewise, it is becoming more challenging to analyze large-scale global projects uniformly. The preprocessing and analysis of high-quality biological data often present significant challenges due to their diverse and complex nature. Computational biology methods are utilized extensively in healthcare settings, pharmaceutical industries, and the development of novel medications. Within the realm of computational analysis, the approaches of machine learning are some of the most highly regarded and potentially useful technologies. The phenomenal growth of machine learning has been considerably aided by developments in both the processing power of computers and improvements in algorithmic design. Deep neural networks (DNNs), which are a type of machine learning algorithm, are widely used in a variety of research fields, including the discovery of new drugs and the creation of new biomarkers. Other types of machine learning algorithms include reinforcement learning and supervised learning. These algorithms can record significant correlations in healthcare data [28–32]. Recent studies have demonstrated the successful use of feedforward DNNs for predicting pharmacological effects and toxicity [33, 34]. DNNs have also significantly contributed to the creation of biomarkers, which involve identifying distinguishing characteristics of healthy and diseased conditions [35]. Putin *et al* utilized the blood test profiles of patients to train a collection of neural networks, enabling accurate estimation of their ages and genders [36]. Convolutional neural networks (CNNs) were trained using the immune histochemistry of tumor tissue to categorize cancer patients [37]. The FDA authorised Arterys Cardio DL, the first neural network-based platform, in early 2017. It is currently being used in clinical settings. When handling a small dataset, it is advisable to select significant features before training the deep model. This allows DNNs to autonomously extract features from the data [38]. DNNs typically exhibit superior performance in feature extraction compared to alternative machine learning methods. In the discipline of bioinformatics, cluster analysis and other methods of clustering are utilized often [39]. The biological perspective may find it challenging to comprehend the data generated by these primary algorithms. A novel alternative to 'black box' DNNs is available in the form of guided knowledge-based procedures. These techniques include network or route analysis. These techniques allow for the reduction of input components while maintaining biological significance, which is crucial for addressing the interpretability challenges associated with 'black box' methods. Reducing the complexity of drug-induced gene expression patterns can be accomplished through the use of signaling circuit analyses and DNN-based prediction [33]. Pathway activation scores were correlated with expression variations in over 1000 hallmark genes that are widely prevalent. The DNN trained on route scores achieved superior performance compared to the DNN trained on the significant gene set. It exhibited an average calculated accuracy of 0.701 and demonstrated good memory across all three drug pharmacological classes. When compared to the training set, the accuracy of predictions made by classifiers that were trained on gene expression profiles was shown to be much lower. However, the use of signaling pathways for dimensionality reduction resulted in improved performance and increased consistency. Several machine learning systems, such as recursive cortical networks, capsule networks, and symbolic learning, are currently utilized due to recent advancements. Neuronal networks, transfer learning, and generative adversarial networks are getting importance in medical applications and have the potential to benefit personal data markets.

8.2.1 Generative adversarial networks (GANs)

The development of GANs is an extremely encouraging step forward for the science of deep learning. The GAN architecture was presented for the first time in 2014 by Goodfellow [40], and it has shown some encouraging results in the generation of visuals and text. Various researchers employed similar methods. A technique known as adversarial autoencoding (AAE) was trained using this approach. After generating fingerprints, they were employed for the identification of substances possessing the desired properties. Further, novel research was conducted and indicated that the recently synthesized chemicals exhibited chemical patterns resembling anthracycline. [41, 42] The researchers proposed an improved design that incorporated new molecular characteristics such as solubility and the capacity to synthesize a broader range of chemical compounds. The latest training and synthesis procedures of the new model demonstrate the significant potential of drug discovery.

8.2.2 Neural networks with recursion

The clinical history of patients can be compiled using electronic health data, which can then be used to assess the patient's likelihood of developing cardiovascular disease, diabetes, or any number of other long-term health disorders [43]. RNNs (recurrent neural networks) are a highly favorable methodology for analyzing text or time series data. RNNs are widely employed in healthcare for the analysis of electronic medical records, offering significant advantages in this field. RNNs have previously been utilized for predicting the probability of heart failure. The subject with a clinical history of 12 months exhibited an AUC (area under the curve) of 0.883 when tested after 6 months. Analyses of scenarios where predictions were incorrect suggest that patient histories of cardiac disorders, particularly hypertension, are often associated with the development of heart failure in network models. Heart failure is frequently misdiagnosed as an acute condition in cases where there is a lack of or minimal appearance of symptoms [44]. RNNs demonstrated the ability to predict blood glucose levels for individuals with Type I diabetes using data from continuous glucose monitoring devices, for up to one hour. The proposed system may include devices for automated blood glucose and insulin level monitoring. The utilization of RNNs in conjunction with wearable sensors for predicting human activity is a promising development in the field of mobile health. The Deep ConvLSTM model, which utilizes on-body sensor recordings, was employed to predict movements and gestures. This model combines convolutional and recurrent networks with a long short-term memory (LSTM) architecture. Technologies like remote monitoring can greatly benefit the management of chronic conditions like Parkinson's and cardiovascular disease [45, 46].

8.2.3 Transfer learning

The approaches of deep learning demand a significant amount of data to properly train and evaluate the model. Transfer learning has been employed to solve this problem. Individuals should possess the ability to apply the knowledge acquired in one field or dataset to another. Transfer learning is commonly employed in image recognition tasks when there is a lack of sufficient large-scale datasets to train DNN with increased accuracy [47, 48]. A neural network that has been trained on a particular dataset can easily be transformed into a network configuration that is unique because of the architectural design of CNNs, which helps this process. Comparing a network's performance to larger non-biological image datasets such as ImageNet can enhance its performance through further modification. A CNN was trained on ImageNet and subsequently acquired knowledge of the heart's structure through the analysis of MRI data [49]. An average F1 score of 97.66% was reached by the suggested model, which allowed it to accomplish state-of-the-art recognition of cardiac structures. A brain tumor prediction was made using CNNs that were predicted with ImageNet [50].

8.2.4 One- and zero-shot learning

One-shot and zero-shot learning techniques are capable of achieving acceptable results with limited datasets. One-shot learning is a technique that can be employed to learn new data points from a limited amount of examples within the training sets, particularly when the information is limited. In contrast, the goal of zero-shot learning is to learn a new activity without any prior exposure to it in the form of training data. Learning techniques known as one-shot learning and zero-shot learning are both included in transfer learning. Researchers developed a one-shot approach to predict the dangerous effects of medicinal compounds [51]. To create and assess their models, the scientists made use of a graph representation of chemicals related to labels taken from the Tox21 and SIDER databases. The study compared the random forest model with 100 trees to item response theory (IRT), long short-term memories (LSTMs) with attention, and graph convolutional neural networks (GCNs). In most cases, iterative refinement LSTMs demonstrated superior performance compared to Tox21 and the SIDER side effect. Tox21-trained networks were utilized to explore the possibility of employing a single-dose approach in clinical trials for human therapeutics. These endeavors proved unsuccessful, highlighting the challenges associated with translating data obtained from high-risk *in vitro* studies to human clinical trials.

8.3 A system of large-scale storage distance

The increasing volume of data being generated and the growing demand for data storage have prompted the need for the creation of novel data storage solutions. Enhancements to reliability, availability, scalability, and affordability of data storage systems are among the key objectives that need to be achieved. HDSS has demonstrated significant benefits and efficiency in enhancing these needs, despite the presence of different factors. The use of HDSS has gained importance due to the exponential growth of data and computational power in recent decades, although it has been in existence for a considerable period. HDSS utilizes multiple nodes, such as databases or host computers, for data storage. The use of HDSS enables efficient and rapid data access from numerous duplicated or duplicate nodes. When referring to a system in which users store data on numerous peer nodes, the phrase 'distributed database' or 'computer network' is frequently used. The significance of system stability has increased due to the increasing importance of storage failures as a concern in data handling. In recent years, the use of HDSS, a technology that allows data to be replicated across multiple nodes or storage devices, has become increasingly prevalent.

8.3.1 Advances in HDSS

Over the years, HDSS has made significant progress in both its applications and utilization. When it comes to ensuring cost-effectiveness and safeguarding the integrity of data across numerous storage nodes, HDSS applications encounter some issues. HDSS technologies, such as distributed non-relational databases and peer network node data stores, have been utilized to find a solution to this problem. This is a specific example of a blockchain-based implementation for storing data in a peer-to-peer network.

The blockchain can be understood as a decentralized database for tracking a continuously growing dataset. Records are organized into blocks and then encrypted using cryptographic techniques to ensure data integrity. A consensus among a network of users is typically established to determine the criteria for accepting new blocks, thereby ensuring the ongoing maintenance of blockchains. A timestamp or signature, in addition to a link to the prior block in the chain, is attached to each item that makes up a block. The blockchain is specifically designed with a primary focus on ensuring the permanent integrity of data. Modifying previously collected data is not possible without altering subsequent blocks and obtaining consensus from the network as a whole. Blockchain enables the creation of a distributed, open ledger that efficiently and permanently records activity among various individuals and networked database systems. This is achieved through its inherent integrity and consistency. Smart contracts enable the implementation of various business logic functions, such as data processing, verification, and access. These functions are controlled centrally and shared among all of the nodes. Blockchain technology is ideally suited for use in sectors like healthcare and others that deal with extremely sensitive data and are subject to strict laws regarding how that data can be utilized.

8.4 Data privacy and regulatory barriers: their significant concerns

8.4.1 Data privacy issues

There remains a significant portion of individuals who lack a comprehensive understanding of the significance of data collection and processing in the contemporary digital environment [52, 53]. Privacy poses significant challenges in the collection and utilization of data. In the context of healthcare, where significant amounts of personal health data are generated, this becomes ever more important. Regulations and norms exist to protect the confidentiality of data by governing its collection, usage, transmission, access, and interchange. In 1948, as part of the Universal Declaration of Human Rights, the United Nations acknowledged the right to privacy as one of the fundamental human rights. However, there is still no global agreement on the exact definition of privacy [54]. Various interpretations of privacy and regulatory concerns have arisen due to the generation and usage of data.

8.4.2 Regulatory barriers

With the advancement of computers and technology, a substantial amount of data containing private information is regularly generated. Regulations designed to guarantee the proper flow and use of this data may seriously affect development [52]. The Health Insurance Portability and Accountability Act (HIPAA) and the Privacy Rule's minimum requirement [55] are significant initiatives that aim to ensure the proper utilization of data following established standards. Developers and researchers encounter various challenges in accessing and utilizing appropriate information [53, 55–57]. Regulatory barriers such as HIPAA can hinder progress when urgent work needs to be completed efficiently, as they ensure the appropriate use of information. HIPAA requires institutional review boards to approve data usage, potentially increasing complexity [56].

Patients are concerned about the handling of their health and medical information, with most individuals believing that this data should be kept private and protected. It is possible that the accessibility of personal health information would expand along with its usage and disclosure when paper medical records are digitized and stored in electronic formats. Healthcare and public health professionals in the United States may have unequal and insufficient protections at various levels, including federal, tribal, state, and local [58]. HIPAA was created to ensure that individuals will continue to have access to health insurance coverage even if they leave their current jobs and to set standards that will make it easier for businesses involved in the healthcare industry to conduct digital transactions. [59, 60] The HIPAA's administrative simplification provisions mandated the Department of Health and Human Services to set national standards for electronic healthcare transactions to make the system more effective and efficient overall. This was done to enhance the system's effectiveness and efficiency. Technological advancements during this period raised Congress' awareness regarding the potential impact on the confidentiality of medical data. As a result of the most recent revision to HIPAA, the federal government is now required to put in place certain privacy protections for certain categories of individually identifiable health information. Standards for the Privacy of Individually Identifiable Healthcare Information are safeguarded by the HIPAA Privacy Rule, which safeguards patient information that can be used to identify a specific person. According to the definition provided by the Privacy Rule, the term 'protected health information' refers to any data that can be used to identify a particular person. Covered entities are organizations that handle this type of information. Protected health information (PHI) [59, 61] encompasses health-related data that has the potential to uniquely identify an individual. Certain educational and professional data may not be classified as PHI [59, 61]. The Privacy Rule encompasses various provisions, including:

- Offers enhanced management of the patient's health information.
- Implementation of regulations to control the individuals authorized to access and utilize personal health information.
- Healthcare providers and other entities must implement suitable measures to protect private health information.
- The legislation enforces legal consequences, both civil and criminal, on individuals who violate patients' privacy rights.

- Public health responsibilities might require the sharing of specific data.
- Assists patients in making accurate decisions by utilizing their personal health information.
- This rule allows patients to learn more about how their data is used and shared.
- Only discloses the essential minimal quantity of information that must be made public to achieve the goals of the disclosure.
- This feature allows individuals to obtain their medical records and request necessary corrections to any errors.
- Persons can control how their private medical data is used and how it is transmitted about them.

The implementation of rules and regulations as a security strategy is an absolute necessity if one is to preserve the confidentiality and safety of sensitive documents. The difficulty and complexity of these obstacles may hold down the advancement of data utilization [56, 58]. To ensure the correct processing and use of data and to facilitate its efficient utilization to attain breakthroughs in health outcomes, novel processes, and systems are required. These must be designed to meet certain criteria.

8.5 The developments in blockchain

Hash linkages in blockchain ensure the integrity and manipulation resistance of the information. The blockchain is a decentralized database that stores information through the use of state-machine replication. Bitcoin introduced the concept of blockchain, a decentralized electronic currency [62, 63]. The assumptions regarding the decentralization and security of blockchain are based on the susceptibility of certain network contributors, known as 'maintainers,' to failures such as Byzantine fault tolerance.

The following are key elements of both public and private blockchains [64, 65]:

- The linked timestamping of blockchain usage makes it possible to create evidence that is generally acceptable of the presence or absence of certain data or a change in state in the blockchain database. This is made possible by the fact that blockchain usage can be timestamped. This evidence cannot be manipulated by other individuals as long as the core cryptographic primitives (hash functions and signing systems) are safe. Proof of work or anchoring procedures can prevent the maintainers, including themselves, from fabricating evidence and ensure not being changed in the long term. Only mathematically impersonal information is required for a small portion of the data that has been gathered.
- The consensus process employed by blockchain ensures that all unchanged copies of the database have comparable information on its current state [63–68]. Consensus ensures that all unaltered nodes receive an identical set of activity information and that those changes are distributed to all nodes within the system.
- Decentralization of information authentication and authorization within a network can be achieved through the utilization of cryptographic algorithms [69].

As a result, since activities are conducted outside of the blockchain, the effects of a node hack may be reduced.

Blockchain users can be categorized into three groups based on their respective work:

- This type involves individuals who are responsible for both managing the infrastructure and establishing the operational rules of the blockchain. In other words, the maintainers of the blockchain possess unrestricted read and write access over its entire dataset. They also engage in the consensus mechanism, granting them complete authority over information processing.
- External auditors, such as non-governmental organizations and law enforcement agencies, monitor the integrity of blockchain operations by conducting real-time or retrospective checks on the entire transaction processing. Conducting thorough audits necessitates the utilization of an audit replica or, at the very least, read-only rights to a logically complete portion of the blockchain data, as assumed by auditors. Auditors, unlike maintainers, do not engage in active consensus participation. However, they do replicate the entire transaction log, similar to maintainers.
- Clients are individuals who utilize the services provided by maintainers. Clients can verify the integrity of the data they have access to on the blockchain by utilizing cryptographic proofs provided by maintainers and auditors.

In this analogy, miners and pool software can be compared to maintainers and auditors within the Bitcoin system. On the other hand, clients can be likened to non-mining full nodes, simplified payment verification wallets, and key management software in a broader sense. The software on a client computer is commonly known as 'client software' because it has complete read access to the entire blockchain. Blockchains can mitigate trust and counterparty risks through the implementation of cryptographic accountability and suitability mechanisms [70].

- Blockchain addresses the issue of a single point of failure in centralized authorization systems by employing cryptographic authorization methods conducted by the appropriate creators of the information. When there is a requirement for key management, the usage of public-key infrastructure (PKI) may link authorization keys to identities that exist in the real world.
- Validation of data performed on the client side can assist in preventing man-in-the-middle attacks, particularly in situations in which the server side of the system has been corrupted, such as when the user-facing side of the system has been hacked. Client-side validation can be improved by including user interface security and key management, such as by employing the Trusted Execution Environment (TEE) capabilities that are available in modern mobile platforms. This can be done through the inclusion of user interface security and key management.
- Cryptographic proofs can be utilized by various parties, allowing them to have trust in the authenticity and reliability of these proofs. For example,

individuals may rely on cryptographic proofs for purposes like tax accounting or as evidence in legal processes. These cryptographic proofs may take the form of electronic receipts that are issued by a blockchain that manages the supply chain. Even in the case that all of the people responsible for maintaining the blockchain become corrupt, the blockchain may be restored to its former state because of cryptographic evidence.

- Real-time and retroactive authorization systems that provide data authenticity guarantees have the potential to reduce auditing and monitoring expenses. Moreover, this could assist counterparties and regulators in analyzing contractual and systemic risks.
- Characterization of blockchains based on the level of access to blockchain data [65].
- Unrestricted access to all of the information that is kept on the ledger is made available to the broader public through permissionless public blockchains. The consensus mechanism, such as the proof of work used in Bitcoin, allows for censorship resistance. This means that participants can freely join or leave the system, resulting in open access to the blockchain's writing capabilities. In permissionless blockchains, maintainers fulfill their responsibilities through economic mechanisms, such as the implementation of a proof-of-work consensus that imposes significant costs on potential attackers.
- In the context of a financial blockchain scenario, only a select few authorized entities, such as a group of banks, the regulatory body, and law enforcement, own the appropriate read and write permissions on a private blockchain. These permissions allow these entities to read and write transactions on the blockchain. Users, including bank customers, do not now have access to the data stored in blockchains. When considering the implications of blockchain technology, this constraint is critical.
- Public-permission blockchains, which are quite similar to private blockchains, are created to be globally auditable and provide extensive read access to end users.

8.6 The exonumia structure for blockchain projects

Exonum is a blockchain framework that is open-source and was created primarily for public blockchain applications that need full access to blockchain data. Exonum employs three architectural components, namely services, clients, and middleware, for the successful implementation of service-oriented architecture (SOA) [71]. The structure of Exonum is illustrated in figure 8.1.

- Blockchain applications utilize services as the primary development point for protecting the application within the framework. Exonum enables the decentralized distribution of services across multiple blockchains, potentially with pre-established configurations. When a service is designed to be logically comprehensive and minimally essential, its interfaces can be reused and integrated, allowing for a significant level of autonomy. Data retrieval from the blockchain can be achieved using GET endpoints for HTTP REST

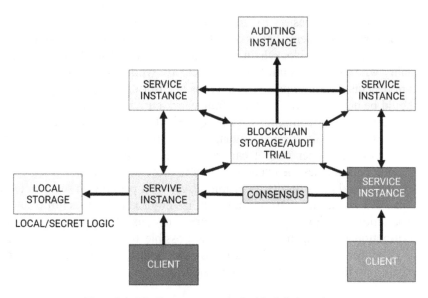

Figure 8.1. The Exonum structure for blockchain projects.

services and POST and PUT requests in blockchain transactions. The blockchain state refers to the current state of the blockchain.

- Customers in a system are responsible for implementing standard SOA functionality. They serve as the main source for activity and read requests. To fulfill this role, customers are equipped with cryptographic key management utilities and tools. These tools enable customers to construct information and verify responses to read requests, including those that require cryptographic verification.

- The use of middleware provides several benefits, including compatibility between clients and services, service replication across network nodes, handling of service lifecycles (including service deployment), data persistence and access control, and support in creating responses to read requests. The computational complexity of a system can be made simpler for service developers by utilizing middleware.

Comparing Exonum to other permissions frameworks, the following are the biggest benefits:

- Exonum's data storage structures are designed to ensure audibility, allowing customers and auditors, including those with limited read access to data, to conduct real-time and retrospective audits of the system [72, 73]. Furthermore, the roster of auditors may be initially undisclosed before the commencement of blockchain operations and may undergo subsequent modifications, either by expansion or reduction, as time progresses.

- The service-oriented framework of Exonum allows for the reuse of services developed for other applications, as well as the addition of new services and modification of existing ones. Utilizing widely adopted protocols like REST and

JSON makes it easier to incorporate third-party applications into the Marketplace ecosystem. This is one of the many benefits of using such protocols. The Exonum-based blockchain platform offers the potential for free interoperability with other Exonum-based blockchains. Middleware can provide significant benefits to service providers in terms of ensuring compatibility. However, it should be noted that the Exonum framework currently does not fully recognize this capability. In comparison to encrypted blockchains and frameworks that make use of domain-specific language/virtual machine indirection, Exonum has a substantially larger output capacity, which is about 1000 transactions per second. This enables the encoding of more intricate transactional logic.

- Exonum's validator node operation depends on pessimistic security assumptions. The consensus method that is utilized by Exonum does not result in the production of single points of failure (such as specialized orchestration/ transaction ordering nodes) [74]. It is possible to change the total number of validator nodes by either adding new nodes, rotating the keys of the existing nodes, or excluding broken nodes.

8.7 Blockchain storage

Exonum utilizes a determined key-value store (KVS) for storing key and value pairs. The KVS supports byte sequences of varying lengths and provides specific operations for controlling these pairs. Blockchain helps with the following:

- To assign a value to a particular key, which may involve creating the key if it does not already exist in the database.
- The key can be utilized to eliminate the combination of key and value.
- Start with any key and iterate backward through all the keys.
- The transmission format used by Exonum enables the split of the key area of a standard KVS into hierarchical typed collections. These hierarchical typed collections can include lists, sets, and maps. It is possible to serialize each item, or each key-value pair in the case of maps. Data manipulations on these collections are translated into actions on the KVS that supports them. The most advanced levels of the hierarchy are representations of data collections and services that are part of a single service. As a result, the objects that make up top-level service collections are represented at the second level of the hierarchy [75]. Collections can be used as elements within higher-level collections to create additional levels of hierarchy.
- The Merkelization identifier can be applied to a collection. A new operation that is referred to as the hash of the collection is made available to Merkelized collections. In the case of a map, this operation reflects a hash affiliation to all of the key-value pairs in the map, as well as all of the objects that are part of the collection. The construction method described in [76] allows for the creation of compact cryptographic proofs, with a logarithmic size relative to the number of entries in the collection.
- One example of a possible strategy is to link all Merkelized collections of a single service to a single hash digest. This would be accomplished like how it

Table 8.1. Exonum service endpoint features.

Characteristics	Transactions	Read requests
Localness	Global (subject to consensus)	Local
Processing	Asynchronous	Synchronous
Initiation	Client	Client
REST service analogy	POST/PUT HTTP requests	GET HTTP requests
Example of the cryptocurrency service	Cryptocurrency transfer	Balance retrieval

is carried out in a blockchain, with the possibility of employing one or more degrees of indirection. It is possible to use a Merkelized meta-map of collection IDs to create the hash digest [77]. In the same way that it condenses all of the data contained in Merkelized collections into a single hash, a blockchain-level hash summary may be used to aggregate all commitments made at the blockchain level. The resulting hash digest at the blockchain level serves as a commitment to the current state and functionality of the entire blockchain [78]. This one hash value has the potential to act as a trusted foundation for the generation of evidence of existence or absence. Table 8.1 provides a summary of the features of the Exonum service endpoint.

A permissionless blockchain, like Bitcoin, can be utilized to anchor the H state and enhance the proofs provided to clients. This helps to mitigate the potential risks associated with history modifications and ambiguity. For more details, refer to the OpenTimestamps protocol's concept of incomplete proofs. Anchoring allows for secure assertion of claims regarding the status of a blockchain, even in situations where the blockchain is no longer accessible due to factors such as widespread compromise or collusion among blockchain validators.

8.8 Network interactions

- Two types of interactions exist between services and the rest of the world:
  - Transactions are the only method by which the state of the blockchain can be modified. The blockchain's consensus algorithm governs the sequencing of transactions and their resulting outcomes. As a result, all incoming transactions are transmitted to all nodes in the network.
  - A read request may include evidence of information presence or absence retrieved from the blockchain. Read requests can be processed by every node in the blockchain network, provided that each node has proper read access to the key spaces that are relevant to the state of the blockchain.
- **Transport layer:** Clients can connect to a single node to handle all requests because of the universal authenticity of transactions and proofs. A rogue node can both withhold broadcasting transactions received from a client and manipulate proofs of reading requests to delay transaction processing.

To convert service endpoint invocations to local method calls, the middleware layer is charged with the responsibility of abstracting the functionality of the transport layer from the service developers. This makes it possible for the middleware layer to stick to the Exonum standard in a manner that is analogous to the functioning of web services within frameworks such as Java EE and CORBA. At present, Exonum nodes can communicate with clients through RESTful JSON transport. Additionally, full nodes can communicate with each other over TCP using a custom binary format.

- **Authentication and authorization:** When confirming transactions, public-key digital signatures are required. This is done to protect the integrity of the transactions and to ensure that they can be universally verified both in real time and in hindsight. Additional non-repudiation and access control granularity can be incorporated through the utilization of PKI if necessary [79]. Web signatures can be used for authentication and authorization of reading requests. This is especially true for requests that are handled using the HTTP GET method. Authenticating the communication channel is another technique that can be taken. This can be done via client-authenticated TLS or the Noise protocol, for example. Service endpoints can be designated as private to enhance security and prevent unauthorized access. In Web services, private endpoints perform the function of administrative interfaces for processing and managing local storage that is associated with a particular complete node. When the HTTP transport is being utilized, private endpoints are provided with an address that is distinct from that of ordinary endpoints. This arrangement simplifies access management and decreases the potential for attacks. Figure 8.2 illustrates various forms of predictive data.

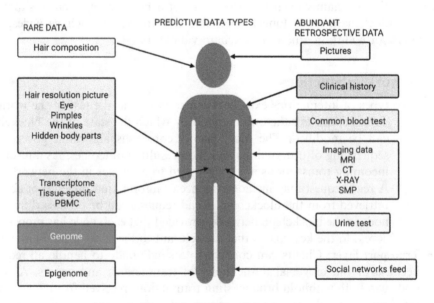

Figure 8.2. Predictive data types.

8.9 Conclusion

Within the context of an AI-facilitated health data exchange on the blockchain, the authors of this chapter carried out an early analysis of the significance of time as well as the aggregate worth of personal data. There is a lot of discussion surrounding the categorization and integration of data, in addition to the temporal significance of both individual data and data combinations. It is projected that a new profession will develop known as 'data economist,' as well as many research institutions that will specialize in the topic of health data economics. Recent advancements in technology have enabled the utilization of selfies, blood tests, and other fundamental data sets to generate highly precise predictions of physiologically relevant attributes, including sex, ethnicity, and age. The significance of various data formats may vary depending on their intended use. Even if the cost of collecting genetic data is much more than the cost of clicking a selfie, the predictive value of the patient's present image may be greater than that of the genome when it comes to determining the patient's age, health status, and death. When multiple kinds of data are combined, their overall usefulness rises above and beyond the sum of their values.

References

[1] Earnest M A, Ross S E, Wittevrongel L, Moore L A and Lin C T 2004 Use of a patient-accessible electronic medical record in a practice for congestive heart failure: patient and physician experiences *J. Am. Med. Inform. Assoc.* **11** 410–7

[2] Leveille S G, Mejilla R, Ngo L, Fossa A, Elmore J G, Darer J, Ralston J D, Delbanco T and Walker J 2016 Do patients who access clinical information on patient internet portals have more primary care visits? *Med. Care* **54** 17–23

[3] Stephens Z D, Lee S Y, Faghri F, Campbell R H, Zhai C, Efron M J, Iyer R, Schatz M C, Sinha S and Robinson G E 2015 Big data: astronomical or genomical *PLoS Biol.* **13** e1002195

[4] Sudlow C *et al* 2015 UK biobank: an open access resource for identifying the causes of a wide range of complex diseases of middle and old age *PLoS Med.* **12** e1001779

[5] Zhavoronkov A and Litovchenko M 2013 Biomedical progress rates as new parameters for models of economic growth in developed countries *Int. J. Environ. Res. Public Health* **10** 5936–52

[6] Gleeson F C *et al* 2017 Assessment of pancreatic neuroendocrine tumor cytologic genotype diversity to guide personalized medicine using a custom gastroenteropancreatic next-generation sequencing panel *Oncotarget* **8** 93464

[7] Kyung H Y, Axtmayer J, Gustin J P, Rajpurohit A and Lauring J 2013 Functional analysis of non-hotspot AKT1 mutants found in human breast cancers identifies novel driver mutations: implications for personalized medicine *Oncotarget* **4** 29

[8] Carpinetti P *et al* 2015 The use of personalized biomarkers and liquid biopsies to monitor treatment response and disease recurrence in locally advanced rectal cancer after neo-adjuvant chemoradiation *Oncotarget* **6** 38360

[9] Bennett C W, Berchem G, Kim Y J and El-Khoury V 2016 Cell-free DNA and next-generation sequencing in the service of personalized medicine for lung cancer *Oncotarget* **7** 71013

[10] Patel S P *et al* 2015 Molecular inimitability amongst tumors: implications for precision cancer medicine in the age of personalized oncology *Oncotarget* **6** 32602

[11] Zhu Q, Izumchenko E, Aliper A M, Makarev E, Paz K, Buzdin A A, Zhavoronkov A A and Sidransky D 2015 Pathway activation strength is a novel independent prognostic biomarker for cetuximab sensitivity in colorectal cancer patients *Hum. Genome Var.* **2** 1–9

[12] Artemov A *et al* 2015 A method for predicting target drug efficiency in cancer based on the analysis of signaling pathway activation *Oncotarget* **6** 29347

[13] Bolotin D A *et al* 2017 Antigen receptor repertoire profiling from RNA-seq data *Nat. Biotechnol.* **35** 908–11

[14] Zabolotneva A A, Zhavoronkov A A, Shegay P V, Gaifullin N M, Alekseev B Y, Roumiantsev S A, Garazha A V, Kovalchuk O, Aravin A and Buzdin A A 2013 A systematic experimental evaluation of microRNA markers of human bladder cancer *Front. Genet.* **4** 247

[15] Di Meo A, Pasic M D and Yousef G M 2016 Proteomics and peptidomics: moving toward precision medicine in urological malignancies *Oncotarget* **7** 52460

[16] Ionov Y 2010 A high throughput method for identifying personalized tumor-associated antigens *Oncotarget* **1** 148

[17] Yin A *et al* 2017 Integrative analysis of novel hypomethylation and gene expression signatures in glioblastomas *Oncotarget* **8** 89607

[18] Lee D, Fontugne J, Gumpeni N, Park K, MacDonald T Y, Robinson B D, Sboner A, Rubin M A, Mosquera J M and Barbieri C E 2017 Molecular alterations in prostate cancer and association with MRI features *Prostate Cancer Prostatic Dis.* **20** 430–5

[19] Niklinski J *et al* 2017 Systematic biobanking, novel imaging techniques, and advanced molecular analysis for precise tumor diagnosis and therapy: the Polish MOBIT project *Adv. Med. Sci.* **62** 405–13

[20] Alexander J L, Wilson I D, Teare J, Marchesi J R, Nicholson J K and Kinross J M 2017 Gut microbiota modulation of chemotherapy efficacy and toxicity *Nat. Rev. Gastroenterol. Hepatol.* **14** 356–65

[21] Sotgia F and Lisanti M P 2017 Mitochondrial biomarkers predict tumor progression and poor overall survival in gastric cancers: companion diagnostics for personalized medicine *Oncotarget* **8** 67117

[22] Nielsen J 2017 Systems biology of metabolism: a driver for developing personalized and precision medicine *Cell Metab.* **25** 572–9

[23] Pretorius E and Bester J 2016 Viscoelasticity as a measurement of clot structure in poorly controlled type 2 diabetes patients: towards a precision and personalized medicine approach *Oncotarget* **7** 50895

[24] Radovich M *et al* 2016 Clinical benefit of a precision medicine based approach for guiding treatment of refractory cancers *Oncotarget* **7** 56491

[25] Zhavoronkov A and Cantor C R 2013 From personalized medicine to personalized science: uniting science and medicine for patient-driven, goal-oriented research *Rejuvenation Res.* **16** 414–8

[26] Chen R *et al* 2012 Personal omics profiling reveals dynamic molecular and medical phenotypes *Cell* **148** 1293–307

[27] Marx V 2013 The big challenges of big data *Nature* **498** 255–60

[28] Libbrecht M W and Noble W S 2015 Machine learning applications in genetics and genomics *Nat. Rev. Genet.* **16** 321–32

[29] Patel L, Shukla T, Huang X, Ussery D W and Wang S 2020 Machine learning methods in drug discovery *Molecules* **25** 5277

[30] Bararardo D G, Newby D, Thornton D, Ghafourian T, de Magalhães J P and Freitas A A 2017 Machine learning for predicting lifespan-extending chemical compounds *Aging (Albany NY)* **9** 1721

[31] Vanhaelen Q, Mamoshina P, Aliper A M, Artemov A, Lezhnina K, Ozerov I, Labat I and Zhavoronkov A 2017 Design of efficient computational workflows for in silico drug repurposing *Drug Discov. Today* **22** 210–22

[32] Polykovskiy D, Zhebrak A, Vetrov D, Ivanenkov Y, Aladinskiy V, Mamoshina P, Bozdaganyan M, Aliper A, Zhavoronkov A and Kadurin A 2018 Entangled conditional adversarial autoencoder for de novo drug discovery *Mol. Pharm.* **15** 4398–405

[33] Aliper A, Plis S, Artemov A, Ulloa A, Mamoshina P and Zhavoronkov A 2016 Deep learning applications for predicting pharmacological properties of drugs and drug repurposing using transcriptomic data *Mol. Pharm.* **13** 2524–30

[34] Wen M, Zhang Z, Niu S, Sha H, Yang R, Yun Y and Lu H 2017 Deep-learning-based drug–target interaction prediction *J. Proteome Res.* **16** 1401–9

[35] Gao M, Igata H, Takeuchi A, Sato K and Ikegaya Y 2017 Machine learning-based prediction of adverse drug effects: an example of seizure-inducing compounds *J. Pharmacol. Sci.* **133** 70–8

[36] Putin E, Mamoshina P, Aliper A, Korzinkin M, Moskalev A, Kolosov A, Ostrovskiy A, Cantor C, Vijg J and Zhavoronkov A 2016 Deep biomarkers of human aging: application of deep neural networks to biomarker development *Aging (Albany NY)* **8** 1021

[37] Vandenberghe M E, Scott M L, Scorer P W, Söderberg M, Balcerzak D and Barker C 2017 Relevance of deep learning to facilitate the diagnosis of HER2 status in breast cancer *Sci. Rep.* **7** 45938

[38] US Department of Health and Human Services Draft guidance for industry and food and drug administration staff? *In Vitro Companion Diagnostic Devices* http://fda.gov/downloads/MedicalDevices/DeviceRegulationandGuidance/GuidanceI)ocuments/UCM262327.pdf

[39] Meng C, Zeleznik O A, Thallinger G G, Kuster B, Gholami A M and Culhane A C 2016 Dimension reduction techniques for the integrative analysis of multi-omics data *Brief. Bioinform.* **17** 628–41

[40] Goodfellow I, Pouget-Abadie J, Mirza M, Xu B, Warde-Farley D, Ozair S, Courville A and Bengio Y 2014 Generative adversarial nets *Adv. Neural Inf. Process. Syst.* **2** 2672–2680

[41] Kadurin A, Aliper A, Kazennov A, Mamoshina P, Vanhaelen Q, Khrabrov K and Zhavoronkov A 2017 The cornucopia of meaningful leads: applying deep adversarial autoencoders for new molecule development in oncology *Oncotarget* **8** 10883

[42] Kadurin A, Nikolenko S, Khrabrov K, Aliper A and Zhavoronkov A 2017 druGAN: an advanced generative adversarial autoencoder model for de novo generation of new molecules with desired molecular properties in silico *Mol. Pharm.* **14** 3098–104

[43] Hivert M F, Grant R W, Shrader P and Meigs J B 2009 Identifying primary care patients at risk for future diabetes and cardiovascular disease using electronic health records *BMC Health Serv. Res.* **9** 1–9

[44] Choi E, Schuetz A, Stewart W F and Sun J 2017 Using recurrent neural network models for early detection of heart failure onset *J. Am. Med. Inform. Assoc.* **24** 361–70

[45] Allam F, Nossai Z, Gomma H, Ibrahim I and Abdelsalam M 2011 A recurrent neural network approach for predicting glucose concentration in type-1 diabetic patients *Int. Conf. on Engineering Applications of Neural Networks* pp 254–9

[46] Ordóñez F J and Roggen D 2016 Deep convolutional and LSTM recurrent neural networks for multimodal wearable activity recognition *Sensors* **16** 115

[47] Pan D, Dhall R, Lieberman A and Petitti D B 2015 A mobile cloud-based Parkinson's disease assessment system for home-based monitoring *JMIR mHealth uHealth* **3** e3956

[48] Piette J D, List J, Rana G K, Townsend W, Striplin D and Heisler M 2015 Mobile health devices as tools for worldwide cardiovascular risk reduction and disease management *Circulation* **132** 2012–27

[49] Margeta J, Criminisi A, Cabrera Lozoya R, Lee D C and Ayache N 2017 Fine-tuned convolutional neural nets for cardiac MRI acquisition plane recognition *Comput. Methods Biomech. Biomed. Eng.: Imaging Vis.* **5** 339–49

[50] Ahmed K B, Hall L O, Goldgof D B, Liu R and Gatenby R A 2017 Fine-tuning convolutional deep features for MRI based brain tumor classification *Medical Imaging 2017: Computer-Aided Diagnosis* 10134 613–9

[51] Altae-Tran H, Ramsundar B, Pappu A S and Pande V 2017 Low data drug discovery with one-shot learning *ACS Cent. Sci.* **3** 283–93

[52] Pandey S, Chaudhary G and Kaushal Mahan V P 2023 Digital public infrastructure for efficient cross-border data flow *T20 Policy Brief* Observer Research Foundation

[53] Boonstra A and Broekhuis M 2010 Barriers to the acceptance of electronic medical records by physicians from systematic review to taxonomy and interventions *BMC Health Serv. Research* **10** 1–17

[54] Kayaalp M 2018 Patient privacy in the era of big data *Balkan Med. J.* **35** 8–17

[55] Evans B J and Jarvik G P 2018 Impact of HIPAA's minimum necessary standard on genomic data sharing *Genet. Med.* **20** 531–5

[56] Locklear T, Lewis R, Calhoun F, Li A, Dickerson K C, McMillan A, Davis L, Dzirasa K, Weinfurt K P and Grambow S C 2023 Advancing workforce diversity by leveraging the Clinical and Translational Science Awards (CTSA) program *J. Clin. Transl. Sci.* **7** e30

[57] Gottlieb L K, Stone E M, Stone D, Dunbrack L A and Calladine J 2005 Regulatory and policy barriers to effective clinical data exchange: lessons learned from MedsInfo-ED *Health Aff.* **24** 1197–204

[58] Yaraghi N and Gopal R D 2018 The role of HIPAA omnibus rules in reducing the frequency of medical data breaches: insights from an empirical study *Milbank Q.* **96** 144–66

[59] Centers for Disease Control and Prevention 2003 HIPAA privacy rule and public health. Guidance from CDC and the US Department of Health and Human Services *Morb. Mortal. Wkly Rep.* **52** 1–17

[60] Hayes E L and Vance K A 2020 Health insurance portability and accountability act of 1996: Health & Public Welfare *Ga. St. Univ. Law Rev.* **37** 153

[61] Rulemaking and Regulations by the Office for Civil Rights. https://www2.ed.gov/policy/rights/reg/ocr/index.html (accessed on April 2023)

[62] Nakamoto S 2008 Bitcoin: a peer-to-peer electronic cash system *Decentralized Bus. Rev.* **31** 21260

[63] Lamport L, Shostak R and Pease M 2019 The Byzantine generals problem *Concurrency: The Works of Leslie Lamport* (San Rafael, CA: Morgan & Claypool) pp 203–26

[64] Swan M 2015 *Blockchain: Blueprint for a New Economy* (O'Reilly Media, Inc)

[65] Strehle E 2020 Public versus private blockchains *BRL Working Paper* (Blockchain Research Lab)

[66] Alshahrani H, Islam N, Syed D, Sulaiman A, Al Reshan M S, Rajab K, Shaikh A, Shuja-Uddin J and Soomro A 2023 Sustainability in blockchain: a systematic literature review on scalability and power consumption issues *Energies* **16** 1510

[67] Korepanova D, Nosyk M, Ostrovsky A and Yanovich Y 2019 Building a private currency service using exonum *2019 IEEE Int. Black Sea Conf. on Communications and Networking (BlackSeaCom) (2019 June)* 1–3

[68] Breitinger C and Gipp B 2017 Virtual patent-enabling the traceability of ideas shared online using decentralized trusted timestamping *Everything Changes, Everything Stays the Same? Understanding Information Spaces. Proceedings 15th International Symposium of Information Science (ISI 2017)* (Glückstadt: Verlag Werner Hülsbusch) pp 89–95

[69] Dwork C, Lynch N and Stockmeyer L 1988 Consensus in the presence of partial synchrony *J. ACM* **35** 288–323

[70] Stallings W 2006 *Cryptography and Network Security, 4/E* (Noida: Pearson Education)

[71] Erl T 1900 *Service-Oriented Architecture: Concepts, Technology, and Design* (Noida: Pearson Education)

[72] Pease M, Shostak R and Lamport L 1980 Reaching agreement in the presence of faults *J. ACM* **27** 228–34

[73] Kwon J 2014 Tendermint: consensus without mining https://tendermint.com/static/docs/tendermint.pdf

[74] Buldas A, Lipmaa H and Schoenmakers B 2000 Optimally efficient accountable timestamping *Proc. of 3rd Int. Workshop on Practice and Theory in Public Key Cryptosystems (PKC2000) (Melbourne, 18–20 January)* pp 293–305

[75] Wu Y, Chen P, Yao Y, Ye X, Xiao Y, Liao L, Wu M and Chen J 2017 Dysphonic voice pattern analysis of patients in Parkinson's disease using minimum interclass probability risk feature selection and bagging ensemble learning methods *Comput. Math. Methods Med.* **2017** 4201984

[76] Asgari M and Shafran I 2010 Predicting severity of Parkinson's disease from speech *2010 Annual Int. Conf. of the IEEE Engineering in Medicine and Biology* pp 5201–4

[77] Jiang F, Huang W, Wang Y, Tian P, Chen X and Liang Z 2016 Nucleic acid amplification testing and sequencing combined with acid-fast staining in needle biopsy lung tissues for the diagnosis of smear-negative pulmonary tuberculosis *PLoS One* **11** e0167342

[78] Yang S N, Li F J, Liao Y H, Chen Y S, Shen W C and Huang T C 2015 Identification of breast cancer using integrated information from MRI and mammography *PLoS One* **10** e0128404

[79] Jirtle R L and Tyson F L (ed) 2013 *Environmental Epigenomics in Health and Disease* (Berlin: Springer)

IOP Publishing

Blockchain with Artificial Intelligence for Healthcare
A synergistic approach
Rishabha Malviya, Arun Kumar Singh, Sonali Sundram, Balamurugan Balusamy and Seifedine Kadry

Chapter 9

Challenges faced in healthcare with blockchain

Blockchain technology has the potential to be widely adopted in various sectors. The adoption of blockchain technologies is enhancing the growing importance of healthcare data management. Blockchain is revolutionizing traditional healthcare methods by providing a more secure platform for exchanging patient data. Blockchain technology could soon be utilized to combine and display a patient's real-time clinical data in a secure healthcare environment. This chapter primarily examines blockchain as a notable healthcare innovation. We investigate the many different applications of blockchain technology as well as the difficulties that arise when attempting to adopt it in the healthcare industry.

9.1 Introduction

Numerous gigabytes of information are created, accessed, and distributed daily in the healthcare sector. It is a vital, but extremely difficult task, to store and communicate massive amounts of data efficiently while maintaining confidentiality and security. In healthcare and clinical applications there is a need for safe, secure, and long-term data exchange, specifically for diagnostics and the sharing of clinical judgements. Efficient transmission of medical evidence to relevant authorities can be facilitated through doctors' implementation of data-sharing practices [1]. Access to current medical records is essential for staff members and general practitioners to effectively provide care to their patients. Clinical data can be transmitted through e-health and tele-medicine to enable healthcare practitioners in different locations to conduct expert reviews [2, 3]. The 'store and forward technology' or other real-time clinical monitoring technologies, such as telemonitoring and telemetry, are utilized in both of these online clinical contexts to facilitate the interchange of patient information. Remote diagnosis and treatment of patients can be facilitated through the utilization of online clinical environments and clinical data interchange. In clinical settings, concerns regarding data privacy, sensitivity, and security are of the utmost importance due to the sensitive nature of patient information. To sustain healthy and productive therapeutic relationships with patients who are located in remote situations, it is vital to have the ability to scale securely, reliably, and in a secure manner data related to communication. It is required to transfer the data in a way that is both secure and efficient [4–6]. This is necessary to receive feedback or confirmation from a panel of clinical specialists. Significant efforts are currently underway to overcome the problem of interoperability in the field. Clinical information exchange between healthcare and research organizations can encounter significant obstacles. The prerequisites for clinical data exchange of this nature encompass transparency, trust, and strong working relationships. Issues such as information agreements, patient matching algorithms, ethical limitations, and legal regulations concerning clinical data may restrict the use of this technology due to its sensitive nature. Several challenges must be resolved before the implementation of clinical data exchange [7].

The Internet of Things (IoT), machine learning, artificial intelligence (AI), and computer vision have the potential to diagnose and treat a variety of chronic illnesses if they are applied in the right context. It is essential to guarantee the confidentiality and safety of healthcare data to maximize its utility in a variety of fields, including biomedical research and the transmission of health data electronically. Consequently, blockchains have gained significant attention in this regard. A blockchain is often implemented after a peer-to-peer (P2P) network has been established. This operating system utilizes cryptography, algorithms, distributed consensus methods, and a multi-field integrated network structure to address the limitations of standard distributed database synchronization. Table 9.1 outlines six

Table 9.1. Essential features of blockchain systems.

Key elements	Descriptive statement of function
Decentralized	Individuals with an Internet connection can access a database system. Multiple systems can access, monitor, store, and update data.
Transparency	The data that is now kept on the blockchain is capable of being updated by prospective users. The immutability of blockchain records makes them more secure by eliminating the possibility of their being stolen or altered.
Immutability	Once a record is saved, altering it requires control over a majority (51% or more) of the node simultaneously.
Autonomy	The blockchain network ensures secure access, transfer, storage, and updating of data by each node, resulting in a reliable and tamper-proof system.
Open source	The blockchain technology's source code may be seen by any user on the network, which ensures that it is readily available to a large number of people. Consequently, the documents are accessible to anyone and can be utilized for the development of novel applications.
Anonymity	The system's enhanced security and reliability come from its ability to transmit data between nodes while preserving the anonymity of the sender.

key attributes of blockchain technology: decentralization, immutability, transparency, anonymity, autonomy, and open source.

Verification is mandatory for all newly initiated transactions within this network. The immutability of a block in a blockchain increases as additional nodes in the network confirm the transactions within that block. Figure 9.1 depicts the sequential progression of events within a blockchain system.

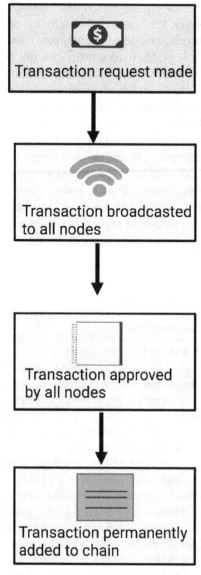

Figure 9.1. A workflow diagram illustrating the overall process of the blockchain.

By incorporating proper clinical data from patients, blockchain technology has the potential to improve the delivery of healthcare in the future. This would be accomplished by developing an efficient and trustworthy healthcare system that would integrate patient data. This study focuses on recent advancements in the utilization of blockchains in healthcare, highlighting various applications in the field. Finally, the subsequent section outlines the organization of the document. Utilizing blockchain technology enables quick summarization of essential information and healthcare activities, thereby offering significant benefits. Blockchain technology (BCT) could potentially benefit the healthcare industry. Concerns have been raised with the utilization of blockchain technology to treat medical and healthcare concerns. The application of blockchain technology has the potential to bring about a dramatic adjustment in the medical field.

9.2 Applications

BCT is gaining popularity in biomedical research, despite its initial development in economics and cryptocurrencies [10]. As illustrated in figure 9.2, BCT can safeguard and protect data that is utilized in a variety of activities that are associated with medicine, telemedicine, genomics, telemonitoring, electronic health, neuroscience, and applications for personalized healthcare.

This section explores several medical fields in which BCT demonstrates significant potential.

9.3 BCT application in electronic health records (EHRs)

In recent years, the desire for an enhanced level of computerization of medical patient information has been pushed mostly by medical practitioners, hospitals, and

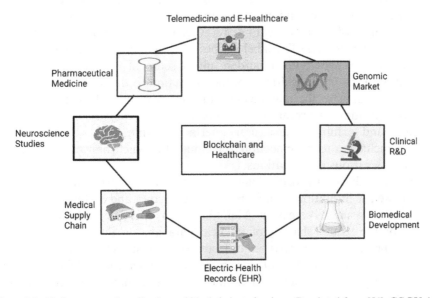

Figure 9.2. Various types of applications of blockchain technology. Reprinted from [54]. CC BY 4.0.

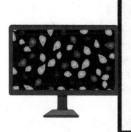

1. More health data from patients via EHR and Mobile application
2. Data encrypted and stored on the Blockchain
3. Encrypted health recomendations relayed back to individuals

Figure 9.3. This image depicts the relationship between EHRs, BCT, mobile health applications, and preventive healthcare.

medical devices. Digitization not only makes data more accessible and facilitates the sharing of that data, but it also lays the groundwork for more precise and rapid decision-making. As can be seen in figure 9.3, the most prevalent use of BCTs in the medical industry right now is in the creation of electronic medical records.

One significant drawback of EHRs is their inability to effectively maintain a comprehensive medical history for patients across multiple healthcare institutions. Patients may lose access to their medical history when they are transferred between doctors due to various circumstances [21–23]. Experts suggest that patients can utilize BCT to access their EHRs.

BCT is utilized by the model known as 'MedRec' to properly manage authentication, data integrity, confidentiality, and data exchange. The decentralized records management system offers patients a comprehensive and unchanging healthcare history, which can be easily accessed by multiple healthcare providers and organizations [24]. Medical records are not stored in the 'MedRec' system, and there is no requirement for an initial adjustment period. The patient's responsibility for the movement of their medical record is recorded on a blockchain, which also guides the transfer process. The label verifies the originality of the obtained record. The patient experiences both a burden and a sense of empowerment when the responsibility for their care shifts from the institution to themselves. Some patients may choose to transfer the management of their personal information to administrative organizations. Current individual patient entrances can be inefficient, time-consuming, and exhibit diverse user interfaces within each organization. The framework includes a user connection to facilitate the synchronization of healthcare records across various organizations.

Challenges with sharing medical data may arise due to restrictions on information control, as well as limitations in information provenance and auditing. Xia *et al* [25] addressed this issue by creating MeDShare, an encrypted blockchain system designed for the secure sharing of medical data among unrelated third parties. When it comes to the transmission and preservation of EHRs between hospitals, cloud service providers, and healthcare research organizations, MeDShare delivers improved data provenance, accurate data management, and increased data security and privacy.

EHRs contain sensitive medical information of the patient that needs to be shared among various healthcare professionals, such as physicians, radiologists, chemists, and researchers, to ensure optimal patient care. Sharing highly-sensitive patient information across multiple organizations may harm patient health and history, posing a significant risk to patient wellbeing and the accuracy of their care records. Because patients with chronic illnesses like cancer and HIV go through various pre- and post-treatment procedures, as well as follow-up and rehabilitation processes, the incidence of risks may be higher in these patients. Chronic illnesses include HIV and cancer. Consequently, there has been a substantial increase in the significance of maintaining an updated medical history for patients. Researchers have proposed using a system that is based on blockchain technology to facilitate the management, maintenance, and sharing of EHRs relating to cancer patients. BCT, which can be accessible, makes it possible to access, manage, and store confidential patient data [26]. BCT could be integrated into clinical practice through the utilization of specific frameworks.

The Estonian medical record blockchain initiative represents a significant real achievement. In 2016, Estonia made a significant announcement regarding the secure storage and accessibility of medical information for medical professionals and insurance companies. This effort established Estonia as a world leader in the application of BCT [27].

The implementation of BCT within the healthcare industry provides patients with a higher level of peace of mind by preserving the honesty and confidentiality of their medical records. The blockchain efficiently detects and classifies every effort to access or modify data. This practice not only enhances patient safety but also aids in the detection of illegal activities, such as identity theft or the manipulation of medical records. Sharing and evaluating records of authorized medical services will be facilitated. Efficient algorithms for patient care enable the seamless integration of errors in medication, hypersensitivities, and drug treatments into blockchain records [28]. The utilization of BCT can enhance treatment accessibility, streamline medical record management, accelerate clinical information verification, enhance security, and optimize care coordination.

9.3.1 Blockchains in clinical research

Clinical trials face various challenges, including privacy, data integrity, and patient enrollment [29]. As the future generation of the internet, blockchain may be able to provide a solution to these problems [30]. Researchers in the healthcare field are utilizing BCT in an attempt to address these issues [31, 32]. In the years to come, BCT, AI, and machine learning will each have a substantial impact on the healthcare sector. Nugent *et al* [31] propose the utilization of an authorized Ethereum blockchain smart contract protocol in combination with clinical data management systems. The problem of getting participants to sign up for the study was the focus of the research [32, 33]. The study's findings indicate that Ethereum transactions are faster than those of Bitcoin. Consequently, it is suggested that utilizing Ethereum smart contracts could enhance the transparency of clinical trial data management systems. Blockchains are currently utilized in clinical research for patient registration. Benchoufi *et al* [34] conducted research and designed a system to securely obtain and store patients' informed consent in a manner that is publicly verifiable and unadulterated. The construction of the system employed BCT.

9.3.2 Blockchains in medical fraud detection

Within the realm of the medical industry, the application of BCT has recently emerged as a potentially significant solution for the administration of supply chains for drugs. The increasing complexity of healthcare requires a greater emphasis on supply management. There is a correlation between disruptions in the healthcare supply chain and adverse effects on the health of patients [35]. Supply chains are highly vulnerable to fraud due to their complex nature and the involvement of numerous entities and components.

Blockchains have the potential to address this problem and potentially mitigate fraud in specific situations by enhancing data transparency and enhancing product traceability. Modifying the blockchain is challenging due to the requirement of smart contracts for the verification and modification of records [36].

9.3.3 Blockchains in neuroscience

Blockchain is gaining significant attention in the field of neurology. Advancements in brain technology have introduced a new model where individuals can control equipment and manipulate data using mental commands, rather than relying on physical interaction with the surrounding infrastructure [37]. Pattern analysis is a method that can be used to determine a person's current mental state. This method involves interpreting the activity patterns produced by a person's brain and then converting those patterns into instructions for external equipment. Neuronal interface devices consist of sensitive sensors, calculation processors, and wireless communication, enabling them to read and interpret brain signals. The control mechanism receives and decodes the brain's electrical impulses. The user wears a head-mounted device to achieve these objectives. The neural interface will utilize complex algorithms and big data for the storage of brain signals. Neurogress has publicly announced its plans to incorporate BCT into its operations. Since 2017, the company has operated in Geneva, Switzerland, and the United States, focusing on neural control technologies for the human operation of drones and robotic arms, AR/VR devices, and smart appliances.

Neurogress has enhanced the precision of its brain-reading capabilities through the utilization of machine learning-based techniques. To achieve this, it must maintain 90% of the information it receives from the brain. The company's whitepaper emphasizes the necessity for a significant number of user cerebral function information by citing as an example the Human Brain Project's require-ment for 'exabytes' of memory. Neurogress says that blockchain is an excellent solution to problems that arise concerning the confidentiality and safety of data storage. This outcome does not come as a surprise. To protect user data from being hacked or otherwise compromised by third parties, a decentralized blockchain is used. The integration of BCT by the Neurogress platform has enhanced its transparency and accessibility. As a result of employing this approach, personal data is safeguarded and kept confidential.

Blockchains are a form of information technology that has the potential to be applied in a variety of different fields, including the monitoring and modeling of cognitive processes as well as brain activity. Blockchain technology is utilized for storage purposes in the digitization of a human brain. A P2P network file system allows for the storage and sharing of files, which are essential parts of personal thought chains. This blockchain-based computational system possesses various characteristics that facilitate the progress of both AI and human capabilities, as well as their potential integration. A computer network can periodically authenticate the source and integrity of a blockchain ledger. By employing this trust mechanism, it is possible to construct a comprehensive understanding of an event by incorporating both its subjective and objective aspects. This approach enables the development of a complete and holistic understanding of the event. Personal thought chains can be utilized on the blockchain to validate individuals and ensure the security of quantified self-data for human beings. One notable advantage of this system is the autonomy it gives in managing privacy and controlling the sharing of personal experiences, without dependence on a centralized authority or third party. Future versions of this technology enable the combination of multiple subjective accounts into a more objective representation of future events at a specific moment. The concept of revisiting past experiences and gaining future perspectives through online platforms is fascinating. Before uploading data related to emotions or sensory experiences in a specific memory to the future blockchain, it is necessary to gain a deeper understanding of the role played by individual mappings, such as sight and smell. Recent technological advancements have made this possible. Soon, wearable technology, biofeedback imaging, brain and nerve implants, and various other sensors could be used to preserve human sensory memories by capturing a multi-factor fingerprint particular to an individual's temporal experience. This research aims to explore the potential applications of these technologies in enhancing decision-making, learning, memory, and rehabilitation.

9.3.4 Blockchain technology and the pharmaceutical sector

The pharmaceutical sector is a rapidly expanding sector within healthcare delivery. The pharmaceutical industry relies on the development of new and valuable medicines to ensure the protection and effectiveness of medical-based products and treatments provided to consumers. The industry's efforts lead to enhanced patient recovery times and improved quality of life [28]. Pharmaceutical companies often face challenges in effectively monitoring their products, which can result in significant risks such as fraud and the spread of fake medications into the market. False pharmaceuticals pose a substantial global health threat. During both the production phase and the research and development (R&D) phase of the process, BCT has the potential to be the most effective option for evaluating, surveillance, and assuring the manufacturing processes of new pharmaceuticals. Hyperledger [38]

Table 9.2. Use cases for blockchain in healthcare.

Applications	Summary
EHR	A digital EHR stored on an authorized blockchain's distributed ledger eliminates the need for human intervention throughout the entire process, from data generation to data retrieval.
Clinical Research	BCT can offer decentralized security for clinical research partnerships involving patient data. This method enables secure data communication among researchers.
Medical fraud detection	The use of BCT prevents information theft and alterations, thereby enhancing fraud detection and ensuring transparent and secure transmission of information.
Neuroscience Research	Brain augmenting, brain re-enactment, and brain thinking are expected to be utilized in upcoming applications based on BCT. The storage of an entire human brain's worth of data digitally necessitates the utilization of a novel technology known as blockchain.
Pharmaceutical industry and research	BCT enables comprehensive tracing throughout each level of the supply chain. The origins, components, and control over medicine are regularly monitored to prevent fraudulent activities and theft.

has developed a counterfeit medicine initiative that utilizes BCT to address the issue of counterfeit medications. There is an urgent requirement to globally monitor, assess, and ensure the entire process of producing and distributing pharmaceuticals using digital technologies. This is particularly important to ensure the reliable and correct supply of drugs to patients. Putting in place a digital drug control system, also known as a DDCS, can assist in preventing the manufacturing and sale of bogus pharmaceuticals [39]. Pfizer, Sanofi, and Amgen collaborated on a study to develop a drug inspection and assessment system using BCT [29]. This technology offers advantages such as improved tracking of counterfeit pharmaceuticals [40], enhanced security for the drug supply chain [41], and increased confidence for customers regarding the quality of drugs they receive [39]. Table 9.2 provides a brief overview of the benefits that can be derived from implementing blockchain technology in the domains of biomedical and healthcare research.

9.4 Challenges

BCT has made significant contributions to various industries [42] and is expected to have even greater influence in the future [43, 44]. On the other hand, many problems haven't been solved yet and need to be worked out before this technology may be utilized successfully (see figure 9.4). This section will explain several significant concerns.

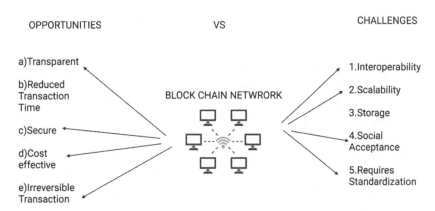

Figure 9.4. Opportunities and challenges of blockchains in healthcare can be represented through a diagram.

9.4.1 The protection of personal information and data

The protection of sensitive information and individual privacy is of the utmost importance and must be addressed [45]. Apps that are built on the blockchain do deal with the requirement of a third party being involved in the storing of information [43]. Blockchain's architecture allows everyone to verify records, instead of relying on a single reliable individual [46]. On the other hand, this greater transparency also exposes the data to possible threats to its privacy and security. When every node can read the data that was sent by a single node, the data's security is put at risk. When a patient does not have a third party authorized to access their medical information, they need to appoint one or more representatives who can act on their behalf in the event of an emergency. This can be done in person or over the phone. This person has the opportunity to reveal patient details to someone else, which could result in severe threats to both the privacy and security of patient data. As a consequence of this, the individuals who are the users of the data will have restricted access to the information because strict safety precautions have been implemented. A security weakness known as a 51 percent attack [47] can potentially make blockchain networks susceptible to attack. This attack is being plotted by a majority group of miners who collectively control more than fifty percent of the blocks on the blockchain network. Miners have control over the network and can prevent new activity from happening without the permission of network leaders [48]. According to Coindesk's reporting, this attack has lately been carried out against five different cryptocurrencies. There is a possibility that patient records contain private information that must not be saved on the blockchain [49].

9.4.2 Managing storage capacity

Storage capacity management is a significant concern in this context. Blockchain was built to handle and process limited data as opposed to maintaining a massive amount of data [50]. This is in contrast to traditional databases, which are meant to store vast amounts of data. The healthcare industry's expansion led to an increased demand for additional storage capacity over time. The healthcare industry regularly manages a significant volume of data. The storage requirements for all photos, including MRI and x-ray scans, that could be acquired by any node on the blockchain in the event of a data breach are significant [51, 52]. The databases utilized in blockchain applications experience rapid development due to their transaction-oriented nature. As the size of databases increases, the process of quickly identifying and retrieving information becomes more challenging, making them inadequate for transactions requiring high speed. Therefore, any blockchain solution must possess scalability and security [29].

9.4.3 Interoperability issues

The problem of interoperability, which refers to the difficulties of merging block-chains from a variety of communication providers and services [45], is one of the challenges that blockchain must overcome. This issue poses challenges to the efficient sharing of data [53].

9.4.4 Standardization challenges

Due to its early stage of development, BCT is expected to encounter standardization challenges when integrated into medical and healthcare domains. International standardization organizations are required to provide authorized and approved standards. Blockchain applications could potentially derive advantages from the implementation of predefined criteria for assessing the information that is trans-mitted within blockchains. These standards must, in addition to analyzing the shared data, also perform the function of safeguards.

9.4.5 Social challenges

The BCT that is now being developed not only has technological obstacles but also societal challenges relating to cultural transformations that it must overcome. Adopting a novel technology that differs from traditional practices is fundamentally challenging. The medical profession has not fully embraced digitalization, especially concerning technologies like blockchain that have not been tested in clinical settings. Convincing physicians to transition from paper forms to electronic ones will require a significant investment of time and effort [29]. The low adoption rate of technology and strategies in the health industry have prevented their widespread acceptance [29, 53]. The available information fails to give validity to the idea that it is a workable and applicable across-the-board solution to all of the problems that exist in the healthcare industry [43]. As can be seen in figure 9.5, a SWOT analysis was carried out to acquire a more in-depth understanding of the threats, opportunities, and weaknesses related to the application of blockchain technology in the healthcare industry and to examine these factors.

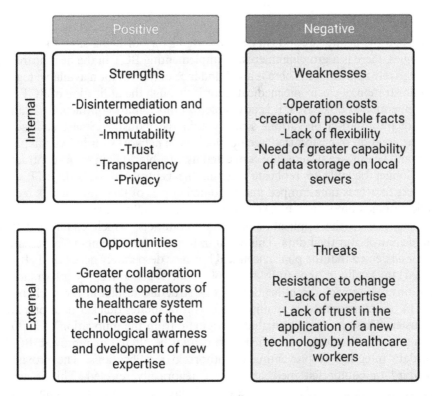

Figure 9.5. A diagram demonstrating the strengths, weaknesses, opportunities, and threats that blockchains present in the healthcare industry.

9.5 Future perspectives

The utilization of BCT in medical factors offers numerous advantages. BCT has the potential to revolutionize medical research by reducing costs associated with monitoring, configuring, maintaining, and operating a central server for information. Additionally, it can minimize the administrative burden of managing medical data. Enrolling patients in clinical trials and ensuring their data is accessible on the public ledger can lead to substantial reductions in processing time.

Physicians can rely on real-time, authentic, and well-documented data to eliminate concerns about patients providing inaccurate medical histories. The transparency of the data eliminates the need for patients to seek a second opinion from another physician, reducing their stress. A blockchain network can facilitate connections among patients worldwide who share similar medical conditions, providing a sense of community and support during their respective treatment with illness. Patients will have full autonomy in determining the recipients of their data, thereby ensuring the preservation of patient confidentiality.

9.6 Conclusion

Even though the healthcare industry has a long history of being slow to accept new technologies, there is a growing interest in implementing BCT in the healthcare sector in the relatively near future. There is an abundance of information available regarding the administration of electronic medical records through the utilization of BCT. Given the aforementioned objectives, it is advisable to utilize smart contracts for managing healthcare information of various scales within the industry. Smart contracts can enable the creation of customized, secure blockchain networks for individual patients. When many healthcare systems are connected using a blockchain smart contract, they will no longer be able to replicate data in the centralized system. BCT enables researchers to access timestamped and validated copies of their findings. A record of scientific results stored on a blockchain might potentially serve as a secure file for researchers due to the application of smart contracts, which enable patients to maintain control over their data. This could be a significant advantage for researchers. It cannot be denied that the pharmaceutical business desperately needs BCT. It can be employed to facilitate the translation of reports generated by pharmaceutical associations. Moreover, the utilization of this structure results in fewer chances for records to be compromised or manipulated, as it facilitates quicker data preparation and transfer. These intriguing attributes originate from the innovation itself. Once a block is placed, it becomes permanent and cannot be altered or removed. BCT will ensure data integrity by preventing unauthorized modifications. The provision of substandard or counterfeit medications is categorically rejected. This is achieved by supervising the entire pharmaceutical supply chain, encompassing manufacturing to distribution. The use of BCT in the area of medical care presents many opportunities—both for individuals and for organizations—that can provide major benefits. It makes it easier to distribute massive amounts of data while simultaneously protecting the confidentiality of every person involved. If BCT can be successfully implemented in healthcare clinical settings, it may open up unique doors for prospects in biological research. Precision medicine relies on the accumulation, exchange, and storage of clinical data on a large scale to develop effective diagnostic and treatment options. Precision medicine has diverse medical applications. It is feasible to utilize a blockchain-based digital brain for neural control systems. Only a few firms have suggested that BCT could be relevant in the field of neuroscience. Many concerns regarding the collection of large-scale data remain pertinent. Empowering individuals to actively participate in their treatment within blockchain-based healthcare systems has the potential to enhance their quality of life.

References

[1] Griebel L, Prokosch H U, Köpcke F, Toddenroth D, Christoph J, Leb I and Sedlmayr M 2015 A scoping review of cloud computing in healthcare *BMC Med. Inf. Decis. Making* **15** 1–16

[2] Houston M S, Myers J D, Levens S P, McEvoy M T, Smith S A, Khandheria B K and Berry D J 1999 Clinical consultations using store-and-forward telemedicine technology *Mayo Clin. Proc.* **74** 764–9

[3] Ciufudean C and Buzduga C 2023 Patient tele-monitoring system *2023 13th Int. Symp. on Advanced Topics in Electrical Engineering (ATEE)* pp 1–6

[4] Casal-Guisande M, Álvarez-Pazó A, Cerqueiro-Pequeño J, Bouza-Rodríguez J B, Peláez-Lourido G and Comesaña-Campos A 2023 Proposal and definition of an intelligent clinical decision support system applied to the screening and early diagnosis of breast cancer *Cancers* **15** 1711

[5] Zhang P, White J, Schmidt D C, Lenz G and Rosenbloom S T 2018 FHIRChain: applying blockchain to securely and scalably share clinical data *Comput. Struct. Biotechnol. J.* **16** 267–78

[6] Berman M and Fenaughty A 2005 Technology and managed care: patient benefits of telemedicine in a rural health care network *Health Econ.* **14** 559–73

[7] Downing N L, Adler-Milstein J, Palma J P, Lane S, Eisenberg M, Sharp C and Longhurst C A 2017 Health information exchange policies of 11 diverse health systems and the associated impact on volume of exchange *J. Am. Med. Inform. Assoc.* **24** 113–22

[8] Azaria A, Ekblaw A, Vieira T and Lippman A 2016 Medrec: using blockchain for medical data access and permission management *2016 2nd Int. Conf. on Open and Big Data (OBD)* pp 25–30

[9] Zhang J, Xue N and Huang X 2016 A secure system for pervasive social network-based healthcare *IEEE Access* **4** 9239–50

[10] Kuo T T, Kim H E and Ohno-Machado L 2017 Blockchain distributed ledger technologies for biomedical and health care applications *J. Am. Med. Inform. Assoc.* **24** 1211–20

[11] Angraal S, Krumholz H M and Schulz W L 2017 Blockchain technology: applications in health care *Circ.: Cardiovasc. Qual. Outcomes* **10** 003800

[12] Yue X, Wang H, Jin D, Li M and Jiang W 2016 Healthcare data gateways: found healthcare intelligence on blockchain with novel privacy risk control *J. Med. Syst.* **40** 1–8

[13] Griggs K N, Ossipova O, Kohlios C P, Baccarini A N, Howson E A and Hayajneh T 2018 Healthcare blockchain system using smart contracts for secure automated remote patient monitoring *J. Med. Syst.* **42** 1–7

[14] Ivan D 2016 Moving toward a blockchain-based method for the secure storage of patient records *ONC/NIST Use of Blockchain for Healthcare and Research Workshop (Gaithersburg, Maryland, United States) ONC/NIST* pp 1–11

[15] Chen Y, Ding S, Xu Z, Zheng H and Yang S 2019 Blockchain-based medical records secure storage and medical service framework *J. Med. Syst.* **43** 1–9

[16] Wang S, Wang J, Wang X, Qiu T, Yuan Y, Ouyang L and Wang F Y 2018 Blockchain-powered parallel healthcare systems based on the ACP approach *IEEE Trans. Comput. Soc. Syst.* **5** 942–50

[17] Jiang S, Cao J, Wu H, Yang Y, Ma M and He J 2018 Blochie: a blockchain-based platform for healthcare information exchange *2018 IEEE Int. Conf. on Smart Computing (SMARTCOMP)* pp 49–56

[18] Cyran M A 2018 Blockchain as a foundation for sharing healthcare data *Blockchain Healthc. Today* **1**

[19] Shubbar S 2017 Ultrasound medical imaging systems using telemedicine and blockchain for remote monitoring of responses to neoadjuvant chemotherapy in women's breast cancer: concept and implementation *Doctoral Dissertation* Kent State University

[20] Ianculescu M, Stanciu A, Bica O and Neagu G 2017 Innovative, adapted online services that can support the active, healthy and independent living of ageing people. A case study *Int. J. Econ. Manag. Syst.* **2** 321–9

[21] Mandl K D, Markwell D, MacDonald R, Szolovits P and Kohane I S 2001 Public standards and patients' control: how to keep electronic medical records accessible but private *Brit. Med. J.* **322** 283–7

[22] Brandon R M, Podhorzer M and Pollak T H 1991 Premiums without benefits: waste and inefficiency in the commercial health insurance industry *Int. J. Health Serv.* **21** 265–83

[23] Toussaint E C 2020 American Fragility: Public Rituals, Human Rights, And The End Of Invisible Man *Colum. Hum. Rts. L. Rev.* **52** 826

[24] Ekblaw A, Azaria A, Halamka J D and Lippman A 2016 A case study for blockchain in healthcare:'MedRec' prototype for electronic health records and medical research data *Proc. of IEEE Open and Big Data Conference* vol 13 pp 13

[25] Xia Q I, Sifah E B, Asamoah K O, Gao J, Du X and Guizani M 2017 MeDShare: trust-less medical data sharing among cloud service providers via blockchain *IEEE access* **5** 14757–67

[26] Dubovitskaya A, Xu Z, Ryu S, Schumacher M and Wang F 2017 Secure and trustable electronic medical records sharing using blockchain *AMIA Annual Symp. Proc.* 650

[27] Wenhua Z, Qamar F, Abdali T A N, Hassan R, Jafri S T A and Nguyen Q N 2023 Blockchain technology: security issues, healthcare applications, challenges and future trends *Electronics* **12** 546

[28] Mettler M 2016 Blockchain technology in healthcare: the revolution starts here *2016 IEEE 18th Int. Conf. on e-Health Networking, Applications and Services (HEALTHCOM)* pp 1–3

[29] Siyal A A, Junejo A Z, Zawish M, Ahmed K, Khalil A and Soursou G 2019 Applications of blockchain technology in medicine and healthcare: challenges and future perspectives *Cryptography* **3** 3

[30] Alsumidaie M 2018 Blockchain concepts emerge in clinical trials *Appl. Clin. Trials* https://www.appliedclinicaltrialsonline.com/view/blockchain-concepts-emerge-clinical-trials

[31] Nugent T, Upton D and Cimpoesu M 2016 Improving data transparency in clinical trials using blockchain smart contracts *F1000Research* **5** 2541

[32] Buterin V 2014 A next-generation smart contract and decentralized application platform *Ethereum White Paper* **3** 1–36

[33] Wood G 2014 Ethereum: A secure decentralised generalised transaction ledger *Ethereum Project Yellow Paper* **151** 1–32

[34] Benchoufi M, Porcher R and Ravaud P 2017 Blockchain protocols in clinical trials: Transparency and traceability of consent *F1000Research* **6** 66

[35] Clauson K A, Breeden E A, Davidson C and Mackey T K 2018 Leveraging blockchain technology to enhance supply chain management in healthcare: an exploration of challenges and opportunities in the health supply chain *Blockchain Healthc. Today* **1**

[36] Badruddoja S, Dantu R, He Y, Upadhayay K and Thompson M 2021 Making smart contracts smarter *2021 IEEE Int. Conf. on Blockchain and Cryptocurrency (ICBC)* pp 1–3

[37] Swan M 2015 Blockchain thinking: the brain as a decentralized autonomous corporation [commentary] *IEEE Technol. Soc. Mag.* **34** 41–52

[38] Liu S, Zhang R, Liu C and Shi D 2023 P-PBFT: an improved blockchain algorithm to support large-scale pharmaceutical traceability *Comput. Biol. Med.* **154** 106590

[39] Plotnikov V and Kuznetsova V 2018 The prospects for the use of digital technology 'blockchain' in the pharmaceutical market *MATEC Web Conf.* **193** 02029

[40] Sylim P, Liu F, Marcelo A and Fontelo P 2018 Blockchain technology for detecting falsified and substandard drugs in distribution: pharmaceutical supply chain intervention *JMIR Res. Protoc.* **7** 10163

[41] Guzman T C G 2018 The role of blockchain in the pharmaceutical industry supply chain as a tool for reducing the flow of counterfeit drugs *Doctoral Dissertation* Dublin Business School

[42] Shae Z and Tsai J J 2017 On the design of a blockchain platform for clinical trial and precision medicine *2017 IEEE 37th Int. Conf. on Distributed Computing Systems (ICDCS)* 1972–80

[43] Alhadhrami Z, Alghfeli S, Alghfeli M, Abedlla J A and Shuaib K 2017 Introducing blockchains for healthcare *2017 Int. Conf. on Electrical and Computing Technologies and Applications (ICECTA)* 1–4

[44] Fernández-Caramés T M and Fraga-Lamas P 2018 A review on the use of blockchain for the Internet of Things *IEEE Access* **6** 32979–3001

[45] Kuo T T and Ohno-Machado L 2018 Modelchain: decentralized privacy-preserving healthcare predictive modeling framework on private blockchain networks *arXiv preprint* arXiv:1802.01746

[46] Zheng Z, Xie S, Dai H, Chen X and Wang H 2017 An overview of blockchain technology: Architecture, consensus, and future trends *2017 IEEE Int. Congress on Big Data (BigData Congress)* 557–64

[47] Radanović I and Likić R 2018 Opportunities for use of blockchain technology in medicine *Appl. Health Econ. Health Policy* **16** 583–90

[48] Huang R, Yang X and Ajay P 2023 Consensus mechanism for software-defined blockchain in internet of things *Internet Things Cyber-Phys. Syst.* **3** 52–60

[49] Linn L A and Koo M B 2016 Blockchain for health data and its potential use in health it and health care related research *ONC/NIST Use of Blockchain for Healthcare and Research Workshop* ONC/NIST *(Gaithersburg, Maryland, United States)* 1–10

[50] Esposito C, De Santis A, Tortora G, Chang H and Choo K K R 2018 Blockchain: a panacea for healthcare cloud-based data security and privacy? *IEEE Cloud Comput.* **5** 31–7

[51] Bennett B 2017 Blockchain HIE overview: a framework for healthcare interoperability *Telehealth Med. Today* **2**

[52] Pirtle C and Ehrenfeld J 2018 Blockchain for healthcare: the next generation of medical records? *J. Med. Syst.* **42** 172

[53] Boulos M N K, Wilson J T and Clauson K A 2018 Geospatial blockchain: promises, challenges, and scenarios in health and healthcare *Int. J. Health Geogr.* **17** 25

[54] Ullah H S, Aslam S and Arjomand N 2020 Blockchain in healthcare and medicine: a contemporary research of applications, challenges, and future perspectives arXiv:2004.06795

IOP Publishing

Blockchain with Artificial Intelligence for Healthcare
A synergistic approach
Rishabha Malviya, Arun Kumar Singh, Sonali Sundram, Balamurugan Balusamy and Seifedine Kadry

Chapter 10

Blockchain and IoT: changing challenges into opportunities

The integration of physical and digital domains is an advanced development in the field of Information Technology (IT). The introduction of IT-based communication between systems and individuals has given rise to a novel structure of intelligence, commonly referred to as 'smartness'. The IoT (Internet of Things) presents a diverse system of applications across various sectors, encompassing intelligent healthcare, intelligent transportation, and intelligent urban centers. Healthcare applications facilitate communication between physicians and patients, particularly in emergencies where patients can be remotely diagnosed using body sensor networks and wearable sensors. The utilization of IoT in the healthcare sector may potentially result in a breach of a patient's confidentiality. Consequently, it is imperative to consider security measures. The topic of blockchain is currently a prominent area of research, with potential applications in various IoT contexts. The implementation of a blockchain-based healthcare system offers numerous benefits, including but not limited to decentralization, immutability, security, privacy, and transparency. The principal objective of this chapter is to enhance the efficacy of healthcare services through the utilization of state-of-the-art computing technologies such as the IoT and blockchain. Consequently, the present chapter commences with a fundamental explanation of the IoT and blockchain. Medication tracking, remote patient monitoring, and health data management are the three key areas of medicine where IoT and blockchain have been explored. The present chapter delves into the implementation of IoT and blockchain technologies in healthcare systems.

10.1 Introduction

Both developing and developed nations must prioritize the healthcare sector as it has a direct impact on individuals' quality of life and overall welfare. The continuous advancement of healthcare investigation and research is essential, as it has the potential to improve the overall quality of life by addressing various health issues and conditions. The healthcare industry has improved in recent years, because of technological advances and discoveries. The incorporation of modern computer technology into the healthcare sector has the potential to improve the presently available capabilities that are currently in existence. The utilization of advanced computer technologies by healthcare practitioners has the potential to facilitate the timely identification of various medical conditions. The implementation of novel computer technologies has the potential to substantially enhance the precision of disease identification during its initial phases. The implementation of novel computer technologies has currently produced favorable outcomes across diverse sectors. The realm of modern technology involves a vast array of revolutionary developments, comprising the IoT, blockchain, natural language processing (NLP), machine learning, image processing, data mining, and cloud computing.

The term IoT refers to the interconnected network of physical devices, vehicles, buildings, and other items that are embedded with sensors, software, and network connectivity, allowing them to collect and exchange data. The term IoT was originally introduced by Kevin Ashton, who is widely recognized as the person responsible for its development [1]. The most prevalent IoT technologies include sensors, wireless technology, cloud computing, and security.

The primary operational procedure of the IoT is comprised of four essential components, namely: (1) the acquisition of data through sensors embedded in devices; (2) the storage of this data in cloud-based platforms for analytical purposes; (3) the transmission of processed data back to the device; and (4) the execution of actions by the device [2]. The potential benefits of the IoT are multiple and may enhance various aspects of everyday life. The primary applications of the IoT encompass intelligent urban and residential environments, intelligent farming, intelligent retail, autonomous vehicles, and healthcare. Security is an essential part of any technology, and IoT networks cannot operate without it. Several measures are currently being undertaken to enhance the security of IoT. These include data encryption and authentication, user privacy, network access control, and trust along with the implementation of security and privacy regulations. The security issue in the IoT arises from inadequate program architecture, resulting in challenges in network security.

If proper initialization is carried out at the physical level in IoT architecture, an unauthorized receiver cannot access an IoT system. The architecture of the IoT comprises various layers, namely the perception, network, application, middleware, and business layers [3]. The objectives and challenges at all levels show unique characteristics. The CIA triad, consisting of confidentiality, integrity, and availability, represents a crucial set of security objectives for the IoT. The classification of

IoT attacks based on risk factors includes four primary categories: 'physical,' 'network,' 'software,' and 'encryption' attacks.

- Node tempering: by manipulating the hacked node, the attacker obtains the encryption key.
- Denial of service (DOS) attacks occur when an IoT system component is physically harmed by an attacker.
- A hacker may get complete control of an IoT system by injecting malicious code.
- The attacker employs noise signals transmitted through radio frequency waves to interfere with RFID communication.
- The attacker employs social engineering techniques to obtain confidential data from the user of an IoT device to accomplish their goals.
- The primary goal of the sleep deprivation assault is to shut down nodes.
- A jammer may be used to disrupt wireless communication in WSNs.

10.1.1 Software attack

- Common forms of cybercrime include phishing attacks. The attacker acquires the user's confidential data using fraudulent websites.
- The utilization of electronic mail attachments and the internet can serve as a means for spreading harmful code, such as a virus, which might cause damage to the system. The self-replicating nature of the virus removes the need for any human intervention.
- The main objective of the attackers is to affect or inhibit the work that is performed by the user.

10.1.2 Network attack

- A traffic analysis attack refers to the intercepting and analysis of communications by an attacker intending to obtain network information.
- The system may be exposed to attacks where an individual mimics RFID signals, modifies the message, and offers the system inaccurate data. The data was altered by the attacker, and the system accepted it.
- Sinkhole attacks are a commonly observed type of attack that is frequently experienced. The primary objective of this attack is to spread inaccurate data on the route to the neighboring nodes within this area.
- A Sybil attack involves mimicking the actions of multiple network nodes by a single rogue node within the network.

10.1.3 Encryption attack

When two devices are interacting with one another, they employ a unique private key to encrypt their communication.

- A side-channel attack refers to a type of attack in which the attacker introduces supplementary information during the transmission of a message between a user and a server or vice versa.
- A cryptanalysis attack transforms a communication from an unreadable format into one that can be read without the attacker having access to the secret key.
- The act of a hacker setting themselves between two nodes to obtain confidential data is commonly referred to as a 'man-in-the-middle attack.'

A wide range of security options are available. The security of IoT networks continues to be a concern due to various weaknesses, including centralization and the presence of a single point of failure. As a result, the IoT may benefit from the addition of blockchain technology, a relatively recent development. IoT security may be improved and made safer by adding the decentralization idea of blockchain technology and eliminating the obstacles and concerns of centralization present in current security solutions. Blockchain can be viewed as a point-to-point distributed network because there is no third party engaged in the transaction or communication. Each transaction is unique and independent of any other transaction. Blockchain technology serves as the foundational framework for the innovative concept of cryptocurrencies. A lot of people assume that cryptocurrency is safe and unbreakable. Security may be improved by using the principles of blockchain in other networks. Everyone has access to a public distributed ledger via the blockchain. A blockchain is a linearly ordered chain of blocks that serves as a decentralized and distributed public ledger for recording and storing data. The storage of transaction data occurs within a block. Each block contains three hashes, namely the hash from the previous block, and the hash generated from the contents of the current block. This part contains both the transaction header and the transaction data. The header of the block contains important information about it. The 'Timestamp' feature is responsible for recording the time when a block is generated. The determination of a block's level of difficulty is based on the mining process. The challenge of determining mathematical work has been resolved through the utilization of the 'Merkle Root,' which serves as a representation of the unique identifiers of all transactions represented within a given block.

The healthcare industry has the potential to remotely monitor patients' health through the utilization of IoT technology. The utilization of IoT sensors that are placed on both the patients' bodies and their surrounding environment enables medical practitioners to conduct remote monitoring. Blockchain technology has the potential to manage drug traceability, medical record management, and other related tasks in the healthcare industry. The IoT is at risk of attacks that compromise its integrity, privacy, confidentiality, and availability (IPVCA) in a networked environment. In other words, exclusive dependence on the IoT for healthcare-related purposes, such as remote patient monitoring, may potentially result in the loss or manipulation of patient data, thereby posing severe and life-threatening consequences. The healthcare industry can potentially enhance its capabilities and safeguard patient data by employing the IoT along with blockchain technology [4].

The implementation of novel and advancing technologies in any given sector may present various challenges. Hence, it is essential especially in the healthcare sector, to identify the challenges that exist. This chapter explores potential healthcare applications that could be created through the utilization of advanced technologies such as blockchain and the IoT. Subsequently, an in-depth examination is presented regarding the challenges that the healthcare industry encounters in the implementation of these two emerging technologies.

10.2 Blockchain technology and related concepts

Blockchain is a novel technological innovation that is currently being implemented across diverse networks to provide an additional level of reliability and safeguarding for networks. The current system for managing patient health records has been substituted with blockchain technology, which is a favored option in numerous record management systems.

The issues with the current patient health record management system are as follows:

- The costs associated with the initial implementation and setup may be high.
- Healthcare providers may experience a period of adjustment to effectively utilize the system.
- The maintenance and updates of the systems may be necessary regularly.
- The systems are susceptible to technical difficulties or periods of inactivity.
- The systems in question may exhibit incompatibility issues with certain devices or software.
- Data security and privacy concerns may arise.
- The complete adoption of electronic records could pose challenges, particularly in cases where certain healthcare providers exhibit resistance to embracing change.
- Electronic record systems may lack user-friendliness.
- The process of accurately and comprehensively transferring all pertinent patient information into the electronic record system may pose a challenge.
- The potential lack of accessibility of the electronic record system for healthcare providers may harm the quality of care provided to patients.

The core technology of blockchain has effectively tackled the challenge of managing vast quantities of health records through its decentralized aspect. The encrypted data is stored within a publicly accessible and decentralized database commonly referred to as a blockchain [5]. The architecture is deemed centralized due to the interconnectivity of each node with the central coordinating system. The central coordinating system is responsible for managing all communication activities among the nodes. In the event of a failure of the central coordinating platform, it would result in the disconnection of all dependent nodes. Consequently, it is essential to make the shift from a centralized to a decentralized system.

A decentralized system comprises multiple coordinators. Decentralized systems lack a central authority. The system operates in a decentralized manner, as it is designed to establish interconnectivity between all nodes without the need for a central coordinator.

Within a blockchain network, each block consists of a set of recently authorized patient records that have been added to the blockchain database. The blockchain indicates blocks consecutively, with each block being securely linked. Within the blockchain's specific framework, every block encompasses patient-related particulars, and a single hash code is produced and retained in a block-by-block manner. Upon the generation and confirmation of the record, this particular block is permanently integrated into the blockchain, thereby contributing to the continuous expansion of the chain.

It is possible to get a better understanding of blockchain technology by studying the way bitcoins operate on the blockchain. In 2009, Santoshi Nakamoto invented Bitcoin, the first decentralized digital money. As a result, the production and administration of Bitcoin are both limited and safe thanks to a variety of encryption and mathematical ideas used by Bitcoin. Regular updates are carried out using algorithmic and cryptographic techniques. The blockchain is an electronic ledger system that is highly secure and is utilized to record Bitcoin transactions. This same system can be employed to manage and protect patients' health records [6].

Decentralization is widely regarded as a fundamental principle in blockchain technology. The preceding hash code is among the aforementioned. The hash code attributed to each block serves as a distinct identifier for the said block. The employed technique for producing this hash is highly intricate. To be incorporated into this particular block, the hash values of all preceding transactions must undergo a process of verification to ensure their accuracy. The hexadecimal value of the Merkle Root, which is located in a block's header, encapsulates data on the corresponding block's record or information.

The blockchain is associated with two additional fundamental concepts, namely the value and proof of labor. To demonstrate the working of the block, presented herein is an example of it.

The utilization of an example can effectively elucidate the operational mechanics of the blockchain. Suppose that individual A intends to transmit medical data information to individual B. Each node within the network is provided with a duplicate of the block that encompasses the communication. A group of miners having the required authority to validate medical data information is in place. The inclusion of medical data information into the blockchain occurs after the validation of the proof of concept by the miners. Ultimately, B acquires the medical data information.

Within the context of a blockchain system, it is imperative to acknowledge that a block holds significant value as it functions as a permanent storage of the latest medical information. The blockchain is comprised of three distinct technologies. The immutability of the blockchain is established through the implementation of private key encryption and a hash function. To ensure most compliance with the principles of the blockchain, a peer-to-peer network is employed [7, 8]. Given that the majority of network users possess the original blockchain, any modifications made to it will be met with rejection.

Blockchains are built using a complex set of protocols and security measures. When it comes to the development of blockchain applications, Solidity is widely regarded as the preferred programming language. Every activity within the production of a new block is thoroughly recorded, reviewed, and subsequently confirmed. Time and date information, as well as a complete set of medical data, are included in this record. Every individual within the blockchain network possesses unrestricted access to the complete ledger. After a miner successfully solves a complex mathematical puzzle, the activity within the blockchain can be verified and documented in the ledger.

10.3 Types of blockchain

To classify the various types of blockchains, it is necessary to consider three distinct categories: open, private, and consortium. Individuals from all over the world have the opportunity to engage in a public blockchain, which bears similarities to the concept of Bitcoin. In the context of the blockchain, miners possess the capability to both access and contribute data to the blockchain.

Nevertheless, a private blockchain is characterized by significant limitations and restrictions. In the majority of instances, an individual possesses the capacity to concurrently authenticate an activity and insert a novel block to the blockchain. The hybrid model represents a collaborative arrangement between public and private blockchains. The process of verifying and adding activities to the database is conducted by a collective team of individuals, as opposed to being entirely dependent on the efforts of a single person. Blockchain is a decentralized and safe from hackers digital ledger that operates without the need for intermediaries.

10.3.1 Decentralized applications

The functionality of the blockchain is dependent upon the utilization of decentralized applications. Centralized systems have encountered a multitude of challenges. Smart contracts, which are integral components of decentralized architectures, are activated by the user. Smart contracts function on the Ethereum platform, which is characterized by its decentralized nature. The initial proposal for the launch of the project was put forth in 2013, and subsequently, its implementation started in 2015. The value token associated with the Ethereum blockchain is commonly known as Ether, which is represented by the abbreviation ETH in various transactions and operations. Through the utilization of a smart contract, a provider of services can provide state data, which subsequently enables the creation of a collection of smart contracts [9]. A smart contract is a computerized system that is utilized to facilitate, verify, or enforce the negotiation or performance of a contract. It operates on a decentralized platform, eliminating the need for intermediaries and enabling direct validation of the contract. The term was introduced by Nick Szabo, an esteemed computer scientist, and cryptographer, in 1996. As per his statement, the utilization of a public ledger could be employed for the implementation of smart contracts.

The following are some of the benefits of decentralized applications:

1. **Autonomy:** The involvement of a broker or attorney may not be necessary, as the individual takes responsibility for signing off on the agreement.
2. **Trust:** Decentralized applications that use blockchain technology employ contemporary encryption methodologies to safeguard documents and data. This data is spread across a decentralized network, which is monitored by a shared ledger. The ledger will refuse to accept any data that has been damaged or altered in any manner.
3. **Backup:** Documents on the blockchain are kept in several places and copied.
4. **Accuracy:** Manual labor is time-consuming and error-prone; smart contracts are quicker and more cost-effective.

10.3.2 The blockchain and its potential uses

A blockchain system, similar to a conventional bank account, functions just like a digital wallet through which data information can be transferred between different entities. This technology enables individuals to acquire, retain, and subsequently disseminate data to others. The aforementioned factors include security measures, efficient data transmission, comprehensive data acquisition, and universal accessibility. Blockchain technology is available in a diverse range of implementations.

10.3.3 Depending on the security of the private key

The private key is securely stored on a cloud-based server within the hot wallet, which is a software application utilizing blockchain technology. In the context of a cold wallet, it is important to note that only the activity hash is disseminated throughout the network. This type of wallet securely stores all transaction data in unencrypted form. A cold wallet is more protected compared to a hot wallet concerning such characteristics.

10.3.4 Based on device and clients

There exists a diverse range of options that individuals can select from within this particular subcategory. These encompass physical wallets, which are material things, and online wallets, which are digital platforms.

In addition to cryptocurrencies, blockchain technology can be applied in various other domains. The aforementioned sectors encompass a range of industries, including but not limited to financial services such as banking and payment processing, healthcare, law enforcement, voting systems, the Internet of Things (IoT), online music platforms, real estate, and numerous others.

10.3.5 Peculiar features of blockchain

Blockchain technology possesses distinct and significant characteristics including decentralization, transparency, open source nature, autonomy, immutability, and anonymity. These qualities make it an effective and exceptional technology for ensuring security and reliability within a healthcare network inspired by the IoT [10].

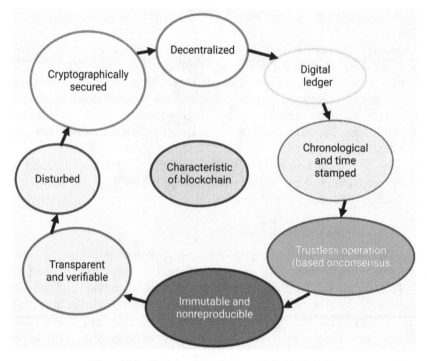

Figure 10.1. The important elements of the blockchain.

The examination of blockchain requires the utilization of various terminologies. The elements depicted in figure 10.1 illustrate several significant components of blockchain technology.

10.3.6 Public distributed ledger

Everyone can access the information on a blockchain. Since the beginning of the blockchain, all participants within the network possess the ability to access and observe the complete historical record of all activities that have occurred. Before any changes are made to blockchain, the user must give his or her consent. Any modifications to the blockchain require approval by the majority of network users [11]. It is essential to acknowledge that this particular segment of the ledger is accessible to the general public. Hyperledger is an open source software framework that enables individuals to construct their blockchain solution. Access to the Hyperledger ledger is limited to those directly involved in the activity, ensuring that only authorized individuals can view and modify its contents.

10.3.7 Hashing encryption

The utilization of hashing encryption is employed as a means to maintain security within the context of the blockchain. The utilization of hash functions plays a crucial role in the implementation of digital encryption within blockchain technology.

The Merkle Root is a representation in hexadecimal format that contains the data. The blockchain incorporates a digital signature as a supplementary protecting measure. Each user is assigned their own set of private and public keys.

10.3.8 Mining

Miners selectively deliver exclusively valid data to other nodes, thereby collecting all information transmitted throughout the network. Each miner creates a new block by combining multiple data information that has been previously collected.

10.4 Decentralization

Blockchain is characterized by its key attribute of decentralization. This suggests that the data is not confined or stored in a singular location. The blockchain, on the other hand, keeps a record of all of the information included within each block. The distribution of data to multiple nodes is not facilitated by a central authority. Each block is accompanied by a digital ledger that undergoes verification. Various research domains, such as cloud computing, IoT, edge computing, and big data, employ blockchain technology as a means of transferring from a centralized model to a decentralized one [12].

10.4.1 Immutable

The term 'immutable' is used to describe something that remains constant and unchanging. To uphold the security of the blockchain, blocks must remain unchangeable and resistant to modification. The concept of proof of work plays a crucial role in achieving the goal of immutability. The primary responsibility of miners is to alter the nonce, a cryptographic value that serves as evidence of computational work. To ensure the uniqueness of a block's hash address, a nonce is employed as a variable value that must be smaller than the target value. The probability of successfully computing proof of work is relatively low. To obtain precise evidence regarding performance, it is necessary to conduct multiple tests. In particular, in situations where the attacker gains control over a majority of the nodes, specifically exceeding 51% of the total nodes, there exists a singular method that is to modify the block [13].

10.4.2 Anonymity

Anonymity refers to the state in which a user's personal information is not present within the blockchain. The anonymity set comprises two distinct components, namely one for the sender and another for the recipient. The transmission of data to other users through this method does not reveal the true identity of the sender. Blockchain addresses are utilized as a means of engaging with other users within the blockchain ecosystem. The true identity of the other user is not disclosed through this method [13, 14].

10.4.3 Enhanced security

To preserve anonymity within the context of the blockchain, it is essential to use hashing encryption, given the public nature of the ledger. The utilization of blockchain technology offers numerous benefits in comparison to conventional systems, particularly enhanced security [15, 16]. The contents of the block play an essential part in recognizing the concept of hashing encryption. A block serves as a storage space for data. The information is specifically divided from the header within this particular block. The Merkle Root is a cryptographic hash value located in the header of a block, which serves as a summary of the data contained within the block. The process of cryptography is carried out through the utilization of the hash function within the context of blockchain technology [17].

10.4.4 Persistency

Mining plays a pivotal role within the conceptual framework of the blockchain. Ensuring the accuracy of the information and instantly rejecting any incorrect data are essential aspects of the field of mining [18]. The miner is the first body to identify the nonce value that meets the predetermined conditions.

10.4.5 Traceability

The capacity to trace a data's origin and flow of events along the supply chain is known as traceability. The Blockchain utilizes the hash key to establish a connection between each block and its adjacent two blocks, thereby forming a sequential chain of interconnected blocks [9].

10.5 IoT and related concepts

10.5.1 IoT architecture

The IoT is built upon the foundation of TCP/IP (Transmission Control Protocol/ Internet Protocol). The design of IoT comprises various critical factors, such as scalability, interoperability, reliability, and quality of service (QoS). The diagram presented in figure 10.2 illustrates the comprehensive structure of the IoT along with its various structured layers:

10.5.1.1 Perception layer
The device layer, also referred to as the perception layer, constitutes the foundational layer. The sensors situated within this particular layer are responsible for gathering data related to the immediate surrounding environment.

10.5.1.2 Transport layer
Various network technologies, including WiFi, 3G, LAN, and RFID, are employed to facilitate the transmission of sensor data across different layers.

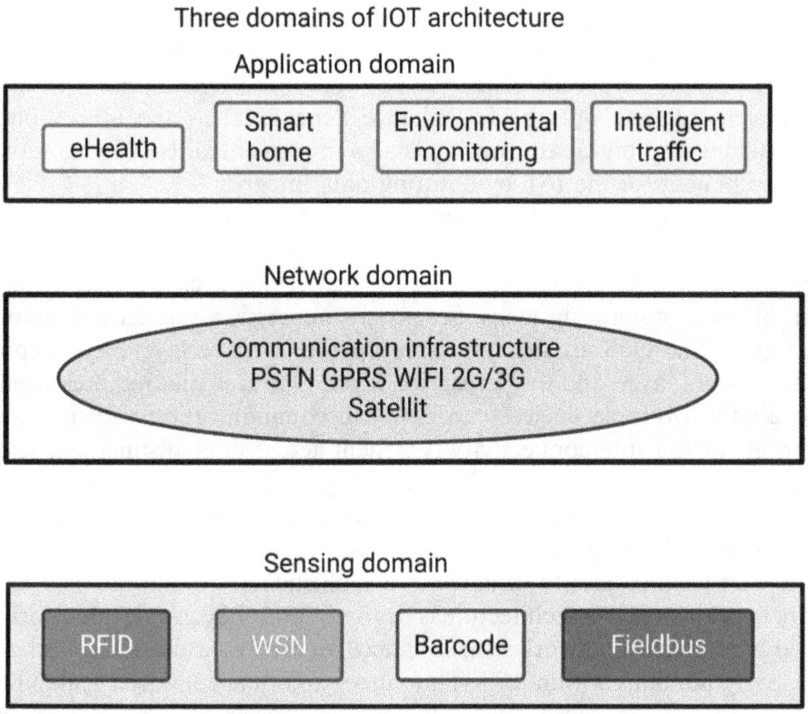

Three domains of IOT architecture

Application domain

Figure 10.2. Domains of IoT architecture.

10.5.1.3 Processing layer
A lot of data is stored and processed at this layer. This layer makes use of modules and ideas such as databases, cloud computing, and large-scale data analysis.

10.5.1.4 Application layer
The delivery of services that are specific to a particular application is facilitated through this layer.

10.5.1.5 Business layer
This layer also encompasses future activities and corporate initiatives, which encompass various aspects such as apps, business and profit structures, and user privacy.

To satisfy the requirements of certain applications, numerous researchers have created additional designs for the IoT. The initial design of Named Data Networking (NDN) was proposed by researchers [19, 20]. At the network layer, NDN provides support for various IoT functionalities, such as data aggregation and security, among others. The IoT encompasses a wide range of applications with varying characteristics and functionalities. NDN exhibits the potential to fulfill various requirements of IoT applications, primarily due to the capability of NDN nodes to enable data availability for diverse consumers, facilitated by their low-power operation. NDN can increase the energy effectiveness of the network. The NDN protocol possesses an extensive number of attributes that can effectively address the primary requirements of the IoT. Additionally, the network offers an energy-efficient caching option. To enhance dependability, the utilization of in-network caching and multipath routing is also implemented. NDN also serves as a security component for the IoT by ensuring data integrity.

The investigation into the significance of QoS within the context of the IoT has been examined in several scholarly articles [21]. The topics of inquiry, control, and monitoring duties are thoroughly examined. Various facilities are required to perform different monitoring tasks. Service awareness is a critical requirement for ensuring QoS. The QoS architecture is composed of three layers: the application layer, the network layer, and the perception layer. One area that requires attention is interoperability. Multiple devices can establish communication with one another. The necessity of IoT interconnectivity is evident across three distinct levels, namely the data model, the message, and the network [22]. This concept encompasses the principal applications of the IoT. In contrast to the existing design, which comprises the concept of delivering messages from start to finish, the proposed structure integrates web technologies to offer a more sophisticated resolution. The software-defined networking (SDN) architecture is beyond the architectural framework that is employed to establish a network with enhanced security measures. The utilization of multiple SDN domains within an IoT architecture offers enhanced scalability [22]. Compatibility was a key component of the previous design, which is still achieved by this one.

10.6 Conclusion

IoT technology is now widely employed across various sectors, including agriculture, healthcare, and smart cities. The healthcare industry can use the IoT in various ways, such as enhancing patients' health and ensuring medicine traceability. The integration of blockchain technology with IoT has the potential to successfully address a wide range of security concerns associated with the IoT. The enhancement of this system's security can be achieved through the utilization of blockchain, a decentralized technology. The integration of blockchain technology in the healthcare sector ensures the safeguarding of critical patient data from unauthorized modification and unauthorized disclosure. This chapter endeavors to identify various applications of IoT and blockchain technology to improve the overall performance and strengthen the existing healthcare industry. This study provides a comprehensive analysis of the potential applications of IoT and blockchain technology within the healthcare sector, with a specific emphasis on the remote monitoring of patient's health, medication tracking, and the management of medical data. It also covers several potential challenges and issues associated with the implementation of two groundbreaking technologies, specifically the IoT and blockchain, within the healthcare sector. Overall it can be concluded that the integration of these two technologies holds significant potential within the healthcare sector, prepared to bring about revolutionary changes.

References

[1] Kizza J M 2020 Internet of Things (IoT): growth, challenges, and security *Guide to Computer Network Security* (Cham: Springer) pp 517–31

[2] Gokhale P, Bhat O and Bhat S 2018 Introduction to IOT *Int. Adv. Res. J. Sci. Eng. Technol.* **5** 41–4

[3] Jabraeil Jamali M A, Bahrami B, Heidari A, Allahverdizadeh P, Norouzi F, Jabraeil Jamali M A, Bahrami B, Heidari A, Allahverdizadeh P and Norouzi F 2020 IoT architecture *Towards the Internet of Things: Architectures, Security, and Applications* (Cham: Springer) pp 9–31

[4] Wang J, Chen W, Wang L, Ren Y and Sherratt R S 2020 Blockchain-based data storage mechanism for industrial internet of things *Intell. Automat. Soft Comput.* **26** 1157–72

[5] Kumar N M and Mallick P K 2018 Blockchain technology for security issues and challenges in IoT *Procedia Comput. Sci.* **132** 1815–23

[6] Hoy M B 2017 An introduction to the blockchain and its implications for libraries and medicine *Med. Ref. Serv. Q.* **36** 273–9

[7] Fernández-Caramés T M and Fraga-Lamas P 2018 A review on the use of blockchain for the Internet of Things *IEEE Access* **31** 32979–3001

[8] Deng Z, Ren Y, Liu Y, Yin X, Shen Z and Kim H J 2019 Blockchain-based trusted electronic records preservation in cloud storage *Comput. Mater. Contin.* **58** 135–51

[9] Reyna A, Martín C, Chen J, Soler E and Díaz M 2018 On blockchain and its integration with IoT. Challenges and opportunities *Future Gener. Comput. Syst.* **88** 173–90

[10] Wang Q, Zhu F, Ji S and Ren Y 2020 Secure provenance of electronic records based on blockchain *Comput. Mater. Contin.* **65** 1753–69

[11] Cheng J, Li J, Xiong N, Chen M, Guo H and Yao X 2020 Lightweight mobile clients privacy protection using trusted execution environments for blockchain *Comput. Mater. Contin.* **65** 2247–62

[12] Puthal D, Malik N, Mohanty S P, Kougianos E and Yang C 2018 The blockchain as a decentralized security framework [future directions] *IEEE Consum. Electron. Mag.* **7** 18–21

[13] Lin I C and Liao T C 2017 A survey of blockchain security issues and challenges *Int. J. Netw. Secur.* **19** 653–9

[14] Zheng Z, Xie S, Dai H, Chen X and Wang H 2017 An overview of blockchain technology: architecture, consensus, and future trends *2017 IEEE Int. Congress on Big Data (BigData Congress)* 6 pp 557–64

[15] Mattila J 2016 The blockchain phenomenon—the disruptive potential of distributed consensus architectures (No. 38) *ETLA Working Papers*

[16] Wang J, Chen W, Wang L, Sherratt R S, Alfarraj O and Tolba A 2020 Data secure storage mechanism of sensor networks based on blockchain *Comput. Mater. Contin.* **65** 2365–84

[17] Ra G J, Roh C H and Lee I Y 2020 A key recovery system based on password-protected secret sharing in a permissioned blockchain *Comput. Mater. Contin.* **65** 153–70

[18] Khan R, Khan S U, Zaheer R and Khan S 2012 Future internet: the internet of things architecture, possible applications and key challenges *2012 10th Int. Conf. on Frontiers of Information Technology* pp 257–60

[19] Jacobson V, Smetters D K, Thornton J D, Plass M F, Briggs N H and Braynard R L 2009 Networking named content *Proc. of the 5th Int. Conf. on Emerging Networking Experiments and Technologies* pp 1–12

[20] Amadeo M, Campolo C, Iera A and Molinaro A 2014 Named data networking for IoT: an architectural perspective *2014 European Conf. on Networks and Communications (EuCNC)* pp 1–5

[21] Jayaraman R, Salah K and King N 2019 Improving opportunities in healthcare supply chain processes via the internet of things and blockchain technology *Int. J. Healthc. Inf. Syst. Inform.* **14** 49–65

[22] Desai P, Sheth A and Anantharam P 2015 Semantic gateway as a service architecture for IoT interoperability *2015 IEEE Int. Conf. on Mobile Services* pp 313–9

IOP Publishing

Blockchain with Artificial Intelligence for Healthcare
A synergistic approach
Rishabha Malviya, Arun Kumar Singh, Sonali Sundram, Balamurugan Balusamy and Seifedine Kadry

Chapter 11

Future prospects for blockchain technology in healthcare

Access, administration, integration, and exchange of health information is a challenge for patients and healthcare practitioners, particularly in the digital era. Medical records should be in the patient's control, and they should be able to share their health information with any doctor they choose safely and privately. In the event of a catastrophic disease epidemic such as COVID-19, the healthcare system is expected to be better equipped to manage public health hazards due to enhanced patient data accessibility and more resilient data-sharing infrastructure. The present healthcare technology falls short of meeting the requirements due to limitations in privacy, security, and compatibility with the ecosystem. This chapter explores the potential utility of blockchain technology for solving some of the most challenging and pressing issues in healthcare. Health-related blockchain goods and important factors are summarized in this chapter, as well as difficulties and potential for using blockchain technology in healthcare.

11.1 Introduction

Healthcare professionals encounter a significant challenge in effectively managing the vast quantities of personal health information that are produced as a result of conducting operations and providing services. Wearables, as well as other healthcare monitoring technology, create enormous volumes of personal health information. It is difficult to acquire, comprehend, utilize, and exchange health data since it is difficult to standardize across systems. Complex IT systems make maintaining and sharing them a difficult undertaking because of the wide range of information they contain [1]. The time and resources needed to request, deliver, receive, and compile patient data are considerable. The creation of comprehensive patient perspectives, better care and treatment, improved communication, and better health outcomes are all made possible by healthcare systems with proper data management and secure retrieval [2].

Furthermore, the healthcare sector is grappling with challenges such as interoperability, unavailability of medical information, inadequate and insecure community health data, and other related issues. In light of recent public health problems, it is clear that the present healthcare system lacks interoperability. Finally, protecting the privacy of patient data presents a significant difficulty for the healthcare industry. The old legacy IT infrastructure of many healthcare companies makes them easy targets for ransomware and other threats [3].

The concept of patient-driven connectivity, in which the patient leads the exchange of health data, has lately gained attention [4]. Nevertheless, infrastructure, computer programs, and strategic approaches for integrating the many forms of data accessible to the healthcare business are still in the early phases of development [5]. Current healthcare data systems have limitations when it comes to patient privacy, data integrity, quality, or accuracy. The healthcare industry is investigating the potential of new technologies for dealing with these problems. There is an urgent need for a new technology that can allow patient-centered interoperability.

Patients may be at the heart of the healthcare ecosystem by using blockchain technology to tackle some of the industry's interoperability issues [6].

There is a lack of research on the application of blockchain technology in healthcare at present. An absence of information about the many solutions that have been developed, tested, and/or implemented can be found in the present body of literature. The potential benefits of incorporating blockchain technology into healthcare systems warrant further investigation to determine its efficacy in improving health outcomes and mitigating the risk of chronic diseases within local populations [7]. Based on the outlined structure, the subsequent sections of this document will be presented in the following manner. The subsequent segment of the material will expound upon the rudimentary principles of blockchain technology and its constituent elements that facilitate its operation. Finally, we look at how blockchains may help the healthcare sector meet these obstacles, as well as the vital responsibilities they'll play in ensuring that patient data is secure and easy to access [8]. Section three covers all of this and more. Among the hurdles of integrating the blockchain-enabled healthcare system are technological, organizational, and behavioral. This section encompasses a variety of healthcare solutions that are based on blockchain technology, with several examples being presented [9].

11.1.1 Blockchain technology

For this century, blockchain technology has been a game-changer in many ways. As well as providing operational and regulatory efficiency, it promotes traceability and visibility across the supply chain of a wide range of businesses. The distributed ledger technology (DLT) known as 'blockchain' has captured the interest and financial resources of the financial services industry. A blockchain is a distributed ledger technology in which each block is connected to the preceding one through a process known as mining, resulting in a chain of interconnected data. A mathematical formula is used to solve the issue of pending transactions. When a block is mined, miners use computer programs to produce hashes, which are unique to that block [10]. Every individual block comprises the cryptographic hash of the preceding block, a timestamp, and transactional data. The network or chain is constructed by storing data from previous blocks and transactions. Modifications to the information within a single block possess the capability to trigger a chain reaction, which could result in the complete cessation of the blockchain. To create a permanent, unchangeable digital record, every machine in a blockchain network locks in at the same moment. Distinct regulations govern the eligibility criteria for adding a new block to the chain in each blockchain system [11]. Blockchain technology offers a distinct array of advantages for the exchange of data and transactions on a decentralized peer-to-peer network that cannot be altered. The utilization of blockchain technology has been widespread in the realm of financial transactions and cryptocurrency [12]. Even though blockchain technology has been implemented in diverse domains such as entertainment, manufacturing, and healthcare, its benefits of enhanced security and privacy have not been disregarded [13].

Using blockchain technology to improve the healthcare industry's interoperability might be a significant step toward putting patients at the center [6]. One of the most important benefits is its capacity to place patients at its center [14]. The medical records of patients can be accessed and shared via mobile applications, remote monitoring, and a data management system based on blockchain technology. This system empowers patients to retain authority over their personal information [7]. This section examines the potential of blockchain technology to address critical challenges faced by the healthcare industry.

11.1.2 Blockchain-based approaches to critical issues

The healthcare industry in the United States is the largest globally, with annual expenses surpassing $1.7 trillion [15]. The United States pays an average annual healthcare expenditure of $10 739, surpassing the collective average of all other nations. Nearly 18 percent of the GDP is spent on healthcare costs (GDP). In 2027, if nothing changes, the healthcare business is expected to account for approximately 20% of the US GDP [16]. Strategies and methods are being used by the healthcare sector to reduce medical and pharmaceutical expenses as well as to increase the standard of services.

The healthcare business is fast evolving in a variety of ways as a result of the problems, concerns, and possibilities that technology presents. Primarily, the current arrangement no longer constitutes a collaboration among major pharmaceutical companies, government entities, and professionals with medical training. Medical and pharmaceutical expenses continue to rise, and IT firms are entering the market intending to impact patient access and treatment quality by implementing strategies and techniques. These firms are putting a lot of money into R&D to improve the health of their customers. Second, the current healthcare system only treats us after we get ill; it does not work to prevent disease in the first place. As we move toward a world where data-driven choices are the norm rather than the exception, COVID-19 may accelerate the trend toward continuous healthcare. Sensors included in smartwatches and other wearable devices from businesses such as Apple, Google, Amazon, and other digital giants constantly track a patient's vitals like blood pressure and temperature of the body as well as their breathing and movement patterns. Devices like this may collect information about your diet, sleep patterns, and more, which can then be used to make informed decisions about your health. Using digital health research, these firms developed software targeted at improving the lives of patients on a broad scale by tracking everyday activities and providing proactive advice. An opt-in contact tracking system that will be launched by Apple and Google is the newest COVID endeavor.

The utilization of mass consumer data, tracking of the amount of active, and accurate interface among monitored users as well as their health data will be used to perform complete contact tracing [17].

To improve healthcare, any technological strategy must take into account the demands of patients, providers, and regulators from a variety of viewpoints, as well as the particular problems that healthcare faces compared to other industries. Patients benefit from improved results, cheaper costs, and more compliance with healthcare regulations thanks to the fervent exploration of blockchain by a variety of interested parties [18]. The utilization of blockchain technology within the health-care industry is increasingly gaining popularity. Many healthcare executives in 18 countries, including more than two-thirds of those who took part in an IBM poll, believe that blockchain would free them from the burdens of bureaucracy and outmoded technology that limit their ability to innovate and adapt [19]. The second-largest healthcare insurance company announced in 2019 that it will store 40 million customers' health data on blockchain technology [20].

Table 11.1 presents a comprehensive summary of the diverse applications of blockchain technology in the healthcare and life sciences sectors [13, 19–23]. The following sections provide an in-depth look at how blockchain may aid in healthcare data management.

11.2 Data collection and storage

Personal health data generated by wearables and other healthcare monitoring technology is enormous. The healthcare system's ability to make data-driven choices relies heavily on the management and safe retrieval of this data. The current healthcare system creates data just by doing business and delivering services. In the course of their lifetimes, patients engage with several healthcare providers, resulting in data being dispersed across the provider's system. Data stewardship is commonly retained by providers, resulting in a disorganized data trail and deteriorating patient access. The high volume, diversity, and rapidity of healthcare data make it unique. The goal of non-uniformity requires utilizing multiple variables and real-time data analysis. A considerable number of datasets are inaccessible due to the lack of

Table 11.1. Potentials of blockchain in healthcare as well as in life science industries.

Categories	Potential application	Major advantages
Patient	Patients empowerment	Patient confidence is bolstered
	Patients can preserve a record of their medical history.	Access to reliable information for patients is made easier.
	A patient's most recent medications are easily accessible online.	Allows for more effective teamwork.
	Patients can safely exchange data with their healthcare professionals.	Transparency is improved. The patient's experience is enhanced and personalized.
		Improves operational efficiency and lowers expenses. Allows people to access their medical records online from anywhere.
		Prescribers may obtain their most recent medications using this service.
Regulation and compliance	Tracking of compliance.	It provides a real-time audit trail that is trustworthy and verifiable.
	Check based on smart contracts	Establishes a framework for automatically enforcing privacy rules.
		While the data itself is not revealed, it is possible to track who has shared it and with whom.
Intercompany process	Money is being transferred.	Smart contracts are used to facilitate instantaneous financial transactions. Facilitates faster processing of payments.
	The supply chain for medical gadgets.	Allows the patient full visibility into all assets across the supply chain.
	Cold chain logistics and other related services.	Facilitates secure and private interactions between healthcare devices and providers.
		Brings together all financial transactions under a single system.
Back offices and the administration	Management of the revenue.	It becomes easier to detect and locate problem spots.
		Administrative expenses are reduced.
		Enhances trustworthiness and transparency.
		Boosts the efficiency of financial transactions
Pharmaceuticals	Verifies the source of the medication.	Pharmaceutics may be tracked and traced.

(*Continued*)

Table 11.1. (*Continued*)

Categories	Potential application	Major advantages
	Consolidates industry-wide information into a single point of access	Counterfeiting tactics need proof of authenticity.
		Aids in the prevention of the transit and sale of fake goods.
		Permits the detection of all side effects associated with medicinal therapy.
Research and development	Making clinical trials attainable.	Stops intellectual property (IP) theft.
		Enables authentication of any document and ensures that its presence can be verified by users.
		The availability of a big, verified, and anonymous patient database.

standardization across various systems, making them difficult to utilize, recognize, and distribute.

11.3 The present state of medical records and history

The present healthcare record-keeping and data-gathering systems include the following features [6, 14, 24]:

- The foundation of this approach is rooted in the relationship between the patient and the physician.
- Despite having access to the data, it consistently fails to use it.
- It makes obtaining healthcare a lengthy and arduous procedure.
- Critical information about patients is dispersed across several platforms.
- Many healthcare systems are unable to offer essential therapy to patients because of a lack of vital data availability.
- It has a detrimental effect on the management system since many participants lack the necessary knowledge to ensure a smooth process.
- It has a low level of security and dependability for healthcare data.

The majority of medical records are currently maintained in hard copy format and distributed across multiple locations within the healthcare industry. Care coordination, quality measurement, and mistake reduction are all impossible with them [15].

There are several places where healthcare data may be gathered digitally. It is critical to get the most out of this healthcare data while keeping things simple. In the healthcare business, the ability to capture and keep information cost-effectively and securely is a major concern [2]. Data portability and consistent interoperability across a variety of platforms are also critical considerations [22].

11.3.1 The potential of blockchain in healthcare records maintenance

Blockchain technology is a suitable solution for electronic data that requires verification and acceptance of its integrity, particularly when various individuals have authorized access to the data. The utilization of blockchain technology has been proposed as a potential solution for the protection of confidential medical records [25]. If blockchain technology is used to monitor transactions in the healthcare industry, it may have a positive impact. Blockchain technology is best utilized in an open consumer transfer pricing environment [26], where the importance of older information is decreasing and the rate of data generation is consistent and reliable. Medical records and important medical history information are all being assessed for security on the blockchain. Patient data will be available on the blockchain for doctors and patients to access from anywhere, anytime in the future [27].

In all stages, a complex protection mechanism and consistent portability are made possible by the blockchain. Healthcare providers may establish an integrated health records system in which the patient is at the center, and owns the private key to their information. Patients are in charge of who has access to and uses their data. The integrated solution powered by blockchain aids in record reconciliation and fraud prevention. There are several benefits to having a system like this, including the ability to view and manage one's medical history from anywhere in the globe, as well as to securely share that information with any healthcare practitioner [2]. A recent study proposed a medical information preservation system based on blockchain technology to ensure the authenticity and accuracy of recorded information, while simultaneously safeguarding the privacy of its users. The proposed data system enables users to store essential information for a long time. If there is any suspicion of data manipulation, it is possible to verify the data's authenticity [28]. A recent scholarly investigation has suggested the adoption of a blockchain-powered framework to facilitate the exchange of personal health data, thereby promoting the development of electronic health systems and safeguarding the confidentiality of users. The potential of blockchain technology to enhance diagnostic accuracy in systems that prioritize confidentiality and privacy is attributed to its consistency [29].

11.3.2 Data sharing and interoperability

The process of patient identification becomes more challenging due to the limitations imposed on the exchange of patient data as well as electronic health information by suboptimal interoperability, resulting in two distinct categories of challenges [5]. The absence of widely recognized patient identities and procedures that prevent access to patient information severely hamper effective healthcare. The current COVID-19 pandemic highlights the importance of compatibility. There is a pressing need for an enhanced data-sharing framework to enhance communication between patients and healthcare providers, as well as to streamline the transfer of information for managing public health emergencies. If a patient sees a doctor who is not their primary care physician, they should have simple access to their medical information. In addition, clinicians might do remote monitoring and telemedicine consultations if the flow of health data was improved. As a result, patients are better able to keep their physicians up to date on any changes to their health status [3]. Providing patients with up-to-date, accurate information on their risk factors, symptoms, and treatment outcomes becomes more important as the number of confirmed instances of the coronavirus rises. The existing system's lack of interoperability is further highlighted by public health issues [3].

11.3.3 Existing data sharing

Sharing medical records is challenging since they are kept in a centralized IT system. It takes a long time and money to request, deliver, receive, and compile patient data. Regulations, mismatched backend systems, and fragmented shared medical information have all slowed medical data management technology development to a crawl. It is difficult to transfer, retrieve, and analyze data since healthcare storage systems do not collaborate or share data. Thus, patients are unable to interact with their medical history since most of the data is housed in silo systems [2].

11.3.4 Blockchain solutions for data sharing

The utilization of blockchain technology holds promise in streamlining the transfer of healthcare information and resolving the longstanding compatibility challenges within the healthcare sector. The hash ID, which will serve as each patient's unique identification in the permission healthcare blockchain, is used to identify them. Because of the hashing, each ID is distinct and the user's data is protected. The responsibility of providing the decryption key for their associated data blocks would lie with the patients, with their healthcare providers. Interoperability and improved security are only some of the benefits of this new technology, which might ultimately benefit patients [14]. Accurate, current, and thorough medical records help patients and doctors alike.

11.3.5 Data security and identity management

Healthcare data breaches are heightening patients' anxieties about privacy and security. Global cybersecurity insurance business Beazley discovered that 45% of malware assaults in 2017 hit healthcare companies [30]. Because of hacking, the number of records that have been compromised is growing. According to the HIPAA journal, there have been over 350 documented breaches within the healthcare business since 2009 [31]. The Department of Health and Human Services reported that in 2018, a total of 13 million healthcare data were compromised due to hacking incidents [32]. In the year 2016, health data breaches exposed the personal information of about 27 million patients [33]. The UnityPoint Health hospital network experienced a security breach in 2018, whereby unauthorized individuals gained access to the medical records of 1.4 million patients. At present, this constitutes the most significant disclosure of medical data within the United States, as of the time of composing this statement. The stolen data includes test results, treatments, patient social security numbers (SSNs), and insurance details.

11.3.6 Existing data security issues

When it comes to storing sensitive patient data, healthcare organizations are particularly vulnerable because of the prevalence of out-of-date legacy IT systems. Healthcare organizations are often the target of sophisticated cyberattacks due to the volume of personal health information they hold. Providers might lose millions of dollars if they cannot access patient data and other critical information. As a preventative measure, healthcare organizations are putting money into cutting-edge security technology such as real-time security monitoring systems, real-time data backups, and enhanced data encryption. As the incidence of cyberattacks has risen and concerns about data security and patient privacy have grown, there is an urgent requirement for enhanced security of IT. Healthcare institutions are allocating resources towards cutting-edge security technology, including but not limited to, improved data backup systems, complicated encryption systems, artificial intelligence (AI), and security platforms that operate in real-time. The aim is to proactively detect and address issues before they escalate into critical situations.

11.4 Blockchain-based identification and data security solutions

Healthcare data security as well as identity management may be improved by using blockchain technology [34]. It can thwart attacks and keep personal information safe from unauthorized access. When data is uploaded to the blockchain, it is encrypted and cannot be deciphered. It uses a private identity key that is exclusively known to the person to authenticate transactions. To put it another way: healthcare providers should have access to the individual's medical records to access them, unlike current healthcare data technologies. Having better data cooperation between healthcare practitioners enhances the possibility of a precise diagnosis as well as the probability of efficient treatment, as well as the capacity to offer cost-effective care. As long as the patient's private information is protected, they may choose which service providers to share it with. Anti-counterfeiting tactics may be guaranteed since it gives verification of medical record ownership [23].

Healthcare may save $100 billion yearly by implementing blockchain technology, according to a new BIS research report. As a consequence of the savings, data breach-related expenditures, operational costs, and information technology costs will be reduced, as will counterfeit fraud and insurance fraud. It is anticipated that healthcare blockchain applications will experience a compound annual growth rate of 64 percent from 2018 to 2025. It'll be valued at more than six billion dollars by the year 2025 [35].

11.4.1 The importance of a social and economic database

The significance of economic and social factors in overall health has been acknowledged by both clinicians and researchers for a considerable period. Personal characteristics alone, according to this school of thinking [36], cannot accurately predict one's health state. The focus of socioeconomic statistics is on the environment, society, and community. This information is of utmost importance for developing health management strategies that are customized according to the distinct requirements of a particular demographic. A greater understanding of illegal drug usage, domestic violence, and economic disparities may be gained by analyzing socioeconomic data [36]. Hence, it is imperative to ensure that socioeconomic data is comprehensive and precise to prevent inequality among various socioeconomic and ethnic groups. This data must be provided for healthcare practitioners to successfully implement community health management initiatives [37]. Claims data is a crucial form of socially based information for professionals in the field of health informatics. This type of data typically includes relevant dates of treatments, diagnostic codes, and associated expenditure. This data may help medical professionals better understand the patients they are caring for and the most important health issues they face. Prescription medicine data gives insight into how patients cope with chronic health disorders and diseases for healthcare providers and policymakers. The establishment of a sophisticated public health infrastructure capable of collecting, storing, analyzing, and preserving data about the overall population is essential for the effective delivery of healthcare services.

11.4.2 Existing socioeconomic data and blockchain solutions

The National Quality Council and the Institute of Medicine, for example, focus primarily on obtaining socioeconomic behavior information directly from patients. For healthcare providers to successfully implement community health management techniques in 2014, electronic health records (EHRs) must incorporate data on socioeconomic determinants of health, both organizations said. Before a primary care practitioner can utilize the information in their EHR in a manner that is useful, accurate, and consistent, a great amount of effort must be made with the use of blockchain, privacy agreements, and data sharing, the maintenance of the integrity of the data along with quality, as well as the transfer of significant socioeconomic and behavioral health data into EHRs, which must all be made simpler.

11.4.3 Financial and record-keeping systems based on the blockchain

The medical bill-filing procedure may contain errors and omissions. The utilization of blockchain technology presents a viable solution to address the aforementioned challenge by streamlining payment execution and mitigating the risk of fraudulent conduct.

The utilization of smart contracts is facilitated by the implementation of blockchain technology. The utilization of decentralized distributed ledger technology, commonly referred to as blockchain, is employed to document the specifics of the agreement established between the purchaser and vendor [38]. The term 'smart contract' refers to a contract that is implemented without the need for human intervention. The blockchain address of a smart contract serves as a pointer to its physical location. To use a contract, nodes just pay Bitcoin to the designated address, and the consensus process handles the rest. Smart contracts eliminate the necessity for intermediaries, enhance traceability, and augment security.

There may be a way to eliminate the distrust that exists between doctors and payers by using blockchain-based smart contracts in healthcare payment systems. To mitigate the occurrence of human errors in the execution of value-based payments, it may be advisable to establish a linkage between reimbursement or penalties and specific health aspects contained in the blockchain medical record. The utilization of smart contracts may result in a reduction of administrative expenses as the patient's insurance provider is notified of billing and claim settlements [39, 40].

Finally, insurance businesses may benefit from blockchain technology because it promotes trust and transparency in transactions. By accepting inputs from several sources without altering any data, blockchain has the potential to enhance claims processing [40]. The integrity or verification of stored data may be ensured with the use of a blockchain architecture [41].

11.5 Blockchain solutions for pharmaceuticals

11.5.1 Drug traceability

Over 15% of pharmaceuticals supplied in developing nations are counterfeit, which is a huge issue for the healthcare business. Counterfeiting costs the pharmaceutical industry an estimated $200 billion a year [24]. The visibility, security, and traceability provided by blockchain may help combat the issue of counterfeit drugs. To combat counterfeiting, the system employs characteristics like confirmation of authenticity and point-by-point tracking capabilities. Before making a purchase, the customer may check the legitimacy of the medication [42]. The utilization of blockchain technology enables the recording of medication effects on a patient in a database for future statistical analysis, as well as the monitoring of pharmaceuticals from production to delivery to the patient [42].

11.5.2 Clinical trials

In a controlled setting, clinical trials provide a wealth of information on a new drug's safety and efficacy. The procedure is time-consuming and costly, and it is not free of corruption. To guarantee that the outcomes of the clinical study are not tampered with, it is essential to have a system that allows anybody to check the clinical reports. The utilization of blockchain technology in clinical studies may prove advantageous as it guarantees the integrity of data and authenticates the validity of documents. In a dispersed network, only authorized users may change data [24].

11.5.3 The healthcare supply chain

The implementation of blockchain technology is being observed in the pharmaceutical industry to monitor the journey of chemicals, raw materials, and components from their origin to the end-user [24]. Blockchain technology may be used by pharmaceutical research organizations to safeguard medical supply chain data. It is anticipated that the implementation of blockchain technology will enhance the traceability and authenticity of the pharmaceutical supply chain [43–45]. As prescription pharmaceuticals gain wider usage, blockchain technology has the potential to effectively monitor all the adverse impacts associated with them. The implementation of blockchain technology within the pharmaceutical industry enhances the security of data sharing. Modum.io, a start-up based in Zurich, is utilizing sensing and blockchain technology to enhance the pharmaceutical supply chain. The development of MODSense, a system that utilizes blockchain technology to monitor the temperature of fragile items in the pharmaceutical supply chain, was a collaborative effort between Modum.io, SAP Software Solutions, and Swiss Post. By avoiding tampering with the temperatures collected, MODSense lets interested parties know exactly how a product was treated while in transit [46]. Vaccine administration, clinical research, medical samples, and perishable food might all benefit from this strategy. Bayer is also employing blockchain technology to track commodities throughout its supply chain. As a consequence of improved technology, the pharmaceutical supply chain was able to locate items more rapidly, resulting in increased efficiency and higher security [47].

11.5.4 Public health

The significance of population health data, referring to data on the health of various populations, became particularly important amidst the COVID-19 pandemic. As a means to increase public health and wellbeing When it comes to battling a broad range of health issues, population health is one of the most effective ways to do it. With the US Affordable Care Act (ACA), healthcare professionals and patients alike were encouraged to work together to improve patient outcomes and care coordination. A full population health record system, such as the COVID-19 pandemic, would be essential to quickly equip relevant organizations with the information they need regarding probable outbreaks [48]. It might be necessary for the implementation of blockchain technology in the public healthcare system. The distributed ledger technology of the blockchain makes it feasible to get a comprehensive picture of healthcare trends. The rise in opiate overdoses is a significant public concern. Blockchain technology may be used to build an industry-wide database of illicit drug purchases. For example, the vendor may utilize analytics to decide how many opioids to provide a dispenser.

11.5.5 Organ transplant

Another example of how the healthcare business is being transformed by blockchain is in the field of organ transplantation. Organ transplantation is a difficult procedure. Because organs decay quickly, they must be donated by someone with the appropriate blood type. According to the University of Michigan Transplant Center, it is possible to perform a heart or lung transplant in less than 10 h. Organs that may save lives are being wasted because of a lack of a well-organized system. Over 120 000 patients are on the transplant list, and 22 of those patients die each day as a result. Blockchain technology is being used by the world's first decentralized database for organ donation, Organ Tree, to link organ donors, patients, and healthcare institutions. The utilization of blockchain technology by Organ Tree has increased the number of matches and acceleration of the transplant process [49].

Organ transplants in The United Arab Emirates (UAE) will integrate blockchain and AI for the first time in the world. Dhonor Healthtech, a renowned national firm specializing in global healthcare blockchain solutions, and the UAE have linked together. One of the most important goals is to donate organs as safely and efficiently as possible. Further goals include developing standards for improving the matching of organs, verification of organs with patients, and optimizing transplants utilizing AI along with blockchain. When it comes to organ transplants, blockchain, and AI may help hospitals streamline the procedure [50].

11.6 Strategic values and implementation challenges

Numerous industries have not yet adopted blockchain technology, which is currently in its development stage. Very few blockchain-based business concepts have found success. As a result, it is more difficult to make an informed judgment on whether or not to invest in blockchain technology in the future. It is possible to assess blockchain technology on its own merits as both a fundamental technology and a means of solving innovative issues, as detailed in the parts that follow.

11.6.1 Addressing innovation challenges and providing opportunities

According to MIT, prosperous enterprises achieve innovation by incorporating the needs of individuals, the capabilities of technology, and the prerequisites for financial prosperity. To produce innovation, these organizations combine marketing, design, and technical views [51]. The following are three characteristics of their products and services (figure 11.1):

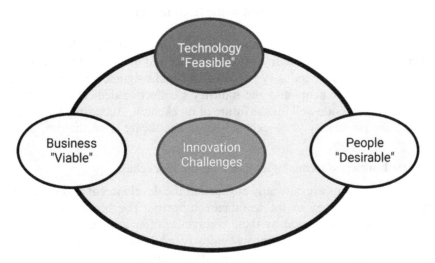

Figure 11.1. Innovation challenges.

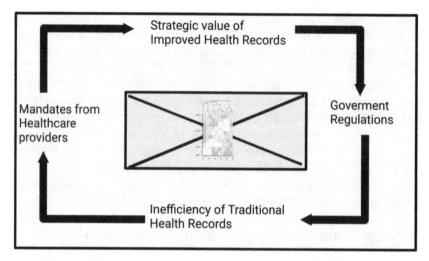

Figure 11.2. A look at the strategic advantages of using blockchain for healthcare.

- Is there another solution? What is the benefit of using this solution?
- Do you think there is a genuine unmet need? How critical is this requirement?
- Is it possible to make a profit? Is it both efficient and effective?

The implementation of blockchain technology in the healthcare industry has the potential to address the three key challenges of innovation. This could result in significant advantages for the healthcare business. It is a possible option for healthcare practitioners, as well as the desired one for patients. An integrated healthcare information system may be achieved by using blockchain technology, as outlined in this study [22]. It keeps track of all the data and work that has been dispersed [52]. The system is capable of handling a wide range of healthcare data difficulties and extracting the greatest value from the data acquired on a variety of levels.

The utilization of blockchain technology in healthcare has been shown to enhance interoperability, patient autonomy, and the caliber and quantity of medical research data [53]. The healthcare industry is poised to benefit significantly from the recent technological advancements and the industry's collective dedication to standards and security, which bode well for the future of blockchain. According to the graph in figure 11.2, the popularity of blockchain-based healthcare is on the rise.

11.6.2 New healthcare technologies based on the blockchain

Multiple organizations are currently engaged in the development and dissemination of blockchain technology in the healthcare industry. The blockchain-based platforms and software developed by these companies offer a secure means of storing digital records within the healthcare industry. Additionally, they enhance the sharing and utilization of medical information, safeguard the integrity of health records, and address the issue of drug traceability and counterfeiting. Furthermore, blockchain technology is utilized by them. Numerous health-related blockchain solutions and prominent corporations provide customized blockchain solutions for diverse applications [54–56].

11.6.3 Disadvantages and difficulties in implementing

A recent literature review analyzed the potential advantages, disadvantages, and impediments associated with the implementation of blockchain technology within the healthcare sector.

The advantages of blockchain technology include its flexibility and responsiveness, as well as its efficient performance and minimal latency with infrastructure [57]. EHRs may also be exchanged securely over the dispersed network. Patients were not aware of the new technology since it was too expensive and complicated. There was also a lot of buzz around it [58]. Apart from the legal, sociological, and technical limitations, scholarly literature has identified the absence of evaluation in the real world as an obstacle to the acceptance of technology. The potential challenges and related solutions for implementing blockchain technology in the biomedical and healthcare domains have been investigated [13].

In numerous sectors, blockchain technology is currently in its early stages. The expeditious implementation of the aforementioned may encounter various challenges. Within the realm of business, information is absent regarding the utilization of blockchain technology. Academics and industry experts agree that blockchain technology is not a magic bullet for all of the industry's ills [53, 57]. The successful functioning of blockchain technology necessitates the resolution of several challenges, encompassing technological, governance, administrative, and societal domains. The development of economic and social structures will rely on innovative foundations rather than disruptive ones because it is a core technology [9].

Regardless of the level of innovation or disruption that a blockchain approach may possess, it is crucial that it is customized to meet the specific healthcare needs of stakeholders such as customers, patients, providers, and regulators [18]. The next sections go into further detail about these issues.

11.6.4 Technical

The technology behind blockchain is still in its infancy, and it is constantly being improved upon. In the beginning, the technology will cost institutions more money than they can afford [22]. Addressing concerns such as limited scalability, absence of standardization, degradation of information quality, and integration with pre-existing legacy systems is imperative. The time it takes to validate fresh blockchain transactions is also a concern [5]. Additional implementation concerns related to the requirement of a network comprised of interconnected computing nodes that offer the required computational capacity for block construction upon every transaction entry, unverified technological advancements, and hidden charges associated with administering such a system. The cost of running a blockchain is directly proportional to the number and amount of transactions that are sent across the network [59, 60]. Before the migration of the current electronic health system to blockchain technology, it is crucial to resolve concerns on software, hardware, implementation, and support [61]. In addition, data with a high temporal resolution does not perform well on the blockchain. When it comes to complicated data, technology has challenges [60]. This includes sophisticated text, photos, and graphs.

11.6.5 Organizational

An EHR is already in place, and it is capable of keeping a very detailed record of a patient's whole medical history. As a result of governmental incentives, many prestigious academic institutions, and huge health systems have invested millions of dollars in EHRs. At this point, urging hospitals, clinics, and doctors' offices to switch to a blockchain digital ledger is not cost-effective [52]. To replace the current record-keeping system with a massive network of connected 'blocks' of data, there aren't enough incentives to use blockchain technology. Although the present system cannot be replaced with blockchain, it may be improved with it. The majority of patient health records would not be stored on the decentralized ledger.

However, a tiny quantity of information about a given patient or treatment would be kept in each 'block' [6]. Finding a method for storing current record data on the blockchain is still another challenge to overcome. A national standard for storing demographic information must be agreed upon by all parties. Organizations must establish a standard for describing the data that can be provided. Moreover, much as with the introduction of new technology, the deployment of blockchain has organizational difficulties, including the management of personnel participating in the transformation process [62].

11.6.6 Regulations and privacy

The dependence of blockchain technology on governmental regulation and cultural factors represents a notable limitation. Regulatory issues concerning blockchain have not yet been resolved by government institutions, and the use of the technology by global healthcare actors will need major buy-in [22].

11.6.7 Drivers for adoption

When it comes to calculating the return on investment (ROI) of blockchain, there are many unknowns. Blockchain-based healthcare's commercial advantages will take time to materialize. What are the 'drivers' for a person's ability to adapt? To get healthcare providers to accept the new technology, there must be a financial incentive. Calculating a company's ROI is not always an easy task. Despite the hype, blockchain is not a cure-all for existing medical record issues, and it cannot be implemented instantly. However, the present healthcare system might benefit from the use of blockchain in several specialized areas [6, 63].

11.7 Summary and conclusion

As per the present section, the exploration of blockchain technology in the healthcare sector is still in its developing phase, however, the volume of proposed remedies is progressively on the rise. With its revolutionary approach to decentralized administration, increased security, and an indelible audit trail, blockchain technology was promoted in this chapter as a paradigm shift. As part of its healthcare investigation, the study looked at several blockchain use cases and their applications. The results of the study indicate that the implementation of blockchain technology can improve the security, provenance, interoperability, and integrity of healthcare data. Because of its decentralized structure, openness, and immutability, the blockchain may help maintain these activities as more affordable for everyone involved. The utilization of technology has been discovered by researchers to facilitate the security coordination and integration of information from multiple healthcare providers, enhance patient engagement, ensure the availability of patient data, enable secure and direct communication between patients, and promote family health management. The implementation of blockchain technology has the potential to facilitate healthcare researchers in obtaining genetic codes and enhancing the supervision of medication supply chains. It is imperative to re-evaluate the interconnections among all stakeholders involved in the healthcare industry, encompassing healthcare practitioners, patients, and the pharmaceutical domain. Before the implementation of a blockchain-based maintenance of the healthcare system, it is essential to conquer legal, technical, and regulatory obstacles. Despite being a developing technology, blockchain holds significant promise for the healthcare industry. Though it has not been accepted by the healthcare industry as a whole just yet, this technology's scope will only expand in the future. Currently, there is a lack of studies on the topic, and additional study in real-world applications is required.

References

[1] Clim A, Zota R D and Tinica G 2019 Big data in home healthcare: a new frontier in personalized medicine. Medical emergency services and prediction of hypertension risks *Int. J. Healthc. Manag.* **12** 241–9

[2] Attaran M 2022 Blockchain technology in healthcare: challenges and opportunities *Int. J. Healthc. Manag.* **15** 70–83

[3] Horgan D *et al* 2020 Digitalisation and COVID-19: the perfect storm *Biomed. Hub* **5** 1–23

[4] Kamble S S, Gunasekaran A, Goswami M and Manda J 2018 A systematic perspective on the applications of big data analytics in healthcare management *Int. J. Healthc. Manag.* **12** 226–40

[5] Gordon W J and Catalini C 2018 Blockchain technology for healthcare: facilitating the transition to patient-driven interoperability *Comput. Struct. Biotechnol. J.* **16** 224–30

[6] Pirtle C and Ehrenfeld J 2018 Blockchain for healthcare: the next generation of medical records? *J. Med. Syst.* **42** 172

[7] Chen H S, Jarrell J T, Carpenter K A, Cohen D S and Huang X 2019 Blockchain in healthcare: a patient-centered model *Biomed. J. Sci. Tech. Res.* **20** 15017

[8] Attaran M and Gunasekaran A 2019 *Applications of Blockchain Technology in Business: Challenges and Opportunities* (Cham: Springer) Springer Briefs in Operations Management (BRIEFSOPERMAN)

[9] Iansiti M and Lakhani K R 2017 The truth about blockchain *Harv. Bus. Rev.* **95** 118–27

[10] Zheng Z, Xie S, Dai H, Chen X and Wang H 2017 An overview of blockchain technology: architecture, consensus, and future trends *2017 IEEE Int. Congress on Big Data (BigData Congress)* pp 557–64

[11] Nian L P and Chuen D L K 2015 Introduction to bitcoin *Handbook of Digital Currency* (Amsterdam: Elsevier) pp 5–30

[12] Mougayar W 2016 *The Business Blockchain: Promise, Practice, and Application of the Next Internet Technology* (New York: Wiley)

[13] Kuo T T, Kim H E and Ohno-Machado L 2017 Blockchain distributed ledger technologies for biomedical and health care applications *J. Am. Med. Inform. Assoc.* **24** 1211–20

[14] Naga Rani K, Pravallika K, Sk N, Poojitha T and Greeshma K 2022 Block chain technology in healthcare: challenges and opportunities *Int. J. Healthc. Biol. Sci.* **3** 51–5

[15] Hillestad R, Bigelow J, Bower A, Girosi F, Meili R, Scoville R and Taylor R 2005 Can electronic medical record systems transform health care? Potential health benefits savings and costs *Health Aff.* **24** 1103–17

[16] Kamal R and Cox C 2019 How has US spending on healthcare changed over time *Health Spending* https://www.healthsystemtracker.org/chart-collection/u-s-spending-healthcare-changed-time/#item-usspendingovertime_7 (accessed on February 2022)

[17] Romero R A and Young S D 2022 Ethical perspectives in sharing digital data for public health surveillance before and shortly after the onset of the COVID-19 pandemic *Ethics Behav.* **32** 22–31

[18] Mackey T K, Kuo T T, Gummadi B, Clauson K A, Church G, Grishin D, Obbad K, Barkovich R and Palombini M 2019 'Fit-for-purpose?'—challenges and opportunities for applications of blockchain technology in the future of healthcare *BMC Med.* **17** 1–17

[19] Attaran M and Gunasekaran A 2019 Blockchain-enabled technology: the emerging technology set to reshape and decentralise many industries *Int. J. Appl. Decision Sci.* **12** 424–44

[20] Rosenbaum L 2019 Anthem will use blockchain to secure medical data for its 40 million members in three years *Forbes* https://www.forbes.com/sites/leahrosenbaum/2019/12/12/anthem-says-its-40-million-members-will-be-using-blockchain-to-secure-patient-data-in-three-years/?sh=51c32a636837

[21] Hoy M B 2017 An introduction to the blockchain and its implications for libraries and medicine *Med. Ref. Serv. Q.* **36** 273–9

[22] Yaeger K, Martini M, Rasouli J and Costa A 2019 Emerging blockchain technology solutions for modern healthcare infrastructure *J. Sci. Innov. Med.* **2** 3–6

[23] Albassam A, Almutairi F, Majoun N, Althukair R, Alturaiki Z, Rahman A, AlKhulaifi D and Mahmud M 2023 Integration of blockchain and cloud computing in telemedicine and healthcare *Int. J. Comput. Sci. Netw. Secur.* **23** 17

[24] Saranya R and Murugan A 2023 A systematic review of enabling blockchain in healthcare system: analysis, current status, challenges and future direction *Mater. Today Proc.* **80** 3010–5

[25] Agbo C C, Mahmoud Q H and Eklund J M 2019 Blockchain technology in healthcare: a systematic review *Healthcare* **7** 56

[26] Cheng E C, Le Y, Zhou J and Lu Y 2018 Healthcare services across China—on implementing an extensible universally unique patient identifier system *Int. J. Healthc. Manag.* **11** 210–6

[27] Prados-Castillo J F, Guaita Martínez J M, Zielińska A and Gorgues Comas D 2023 A review of blockchain technology adoption in the tourism industry from a sustainability perspective *J. Theor. Appl. Electron. Commerce Res.* **18** 814–30

[28] Li H, Zhu L, Shen M, Gao F, Tao X and Liu S 2018 Blockchain-based data preservation system for medical data *J. Med. Syst.* **42** 1–13

[29] Zhang A and Lin X 2018 Towards secure and privacy-preserving data sharing in e-health systems via consortium blockchain *J. Med. Syst.* **42** 140

[30] Silvestri S, Islam S, Papastergiou S, Tzagkarakis C and Ciampi M 2023 A machine learning approach for the NLP-based analysis of cyber threats and vulnerabilities of the healthcare ecosystem *Sensors* **23** 651

[31] Davis J 2018 1.4 Million patient records breached in UnityPoint Health phishing attack *Healthcare IT News* https://www.healthcareitnews.com/news/14-million-patient-records-breached-unitypoint-health-phishing-attack

[32] Raghupathi W, Raghupathi V and Saharia A 2023 Analyzing health data breaches: a visual analytics approach *Appl. Math.* **3** 175–99

[33] Mishra P, Khandelwal B and Dewangan B K 2023 Analysis of blockchain security applications in electronic health records standardization *Recent Adv. Comput. Sci. Commun. (Formerly: Recent Patents Comput. Sci.)* **16** 19–30

[34] Bouras M A, Lu Q, Zhang F, Wan Y, Zhang T and Ning H 2020 Distributed ledger technology for eHealth identity privacy: state of the art and future perspective *Sensors* **20** 483

[35] Tang Y M, Chau K Y, Ho G T S and Wan Y (ed) 2023 *Revolutionizing Digital Healthcare Through Blockchain Technology Applications* (IGI Global)

[36] Roux A V D 2007 Neighborhoods and health: where are we and were do we go from here? *Rev. Epidemiol. Sante Publ.* **55** 13–21

[37] Hughes L S, Phillips R L, DeVoe J E and Bazemore A W 2016 Community vital signs: taking the pulse of the community while caring for patients *J. Am. Board Fam. Med.* **29** 419–22

[38] Giancaspro M 2017 Is a 'smart contract' really a smart idea? Insights from a legal perspective *Comput. Law Secur. Rev.* **33** 825–35

[39] Luu L, Chu D H, Olickel H, Saxena P and Hobor A 2016 Making smart contracts smarter *Proc. of the 2016 ACM SIGSAC Conf. on Computer and Communications Security* 254–69

[40] Lorenz J T, Münstermann B, Higginson M, Olesen P B, Bohlken N and Ricciardi V 2016 *Blockchain in Insurance—Opportunity or Threat* (McKinsey & Company) pp 1–9

[41] Zhou L, Wang L and Sun Y 2018 MIStore: a blockchain-based medical insurance storage system *J. Med. Syst.* **42** 149

[42] Haq I and Esuka O M 2018 Blockchain technology in pharmaceutical industry to prevent counterfeit drugs *Int. J. Comput. Appl.* **180** 8–12

[43] Bocek T, Rodrigues B B, Strasser T and Stiller B 2017 Blockchains everywhere—a use-case of blockchains in the pharma supply-chain *2017 IFIP/IEEE Symp. on Integrated Network and Service Management (IM)* 772–7

[44] Shanley A 2017 Could blockchain improve pharmaceutical supply chain security *Pharm. Technol.* **1** s34–9

[45] Vecchione A 2017 Blockchain tech could track pharmacy supply chain *Drug Top.* **161** 21

[46] Murray A, Kim D and Combs J 2023 The promise of a decentralized internet: what is Web3 and how can firms prepare? *Bus. Horiz.* **66** 191–202

[47] Risso L A, Ganga G M D, Godinho Filho M, de Santa-Eulalia L A, Chikhi T and Mosconi E 2023 Present and future perspectives of blockchain in supply chain management: a review of reviews and research agenda *Comput. Ind. Eng.* **179** 109195

[48] Nash D B 2015 Trending in 2015: population health *J. Healthc. Manag.* **60** 246–8

[49] Moorlock G and Draper H 2023 Proposal to support making decisions about the organ donation process *J. Med. Ethics* **49** 434–8

[50] El Khatib M, Al Mulla A and Al Ketbi W 2022 The role of blockchain in e-governance and decision-making in project and program management *Adv. Internet Things* **12** 88–109

[51] Ouyang C H, Chen C C, Tee Y S, Lin W C, Kuo L W, Liao C A, Cheng C T and Liao C H 2023 The application of design thinking in developing a deep learning algorithm for hip fracture detection *Bioengineering* **10** 735

[52] Roehrs A, Da Costa C A and da Rosa Righi R 2017 OmniPHR: a distributed architecture model to integrate personal health records *J. Biomed. Inform.* **71** 70–81

[53] Ekblaw A, Azaria A, Halamka J D and Lippman A 2016 A case study for blockchain in healthcare: 'MedRec' prototype for electronic health records and medical research data *Proc. of IEEE Open and Big Data Conf.* 13

[54] Yadav A S, Singh N and Kushwaha D S 2023 Evolution of blockchain and consensus mechanisms and its real-world applications *Multimedia Tools Appl.* 1–46

[55] Abdollahi A, Sadeghvaziri F and Rejeb A 2023 Exploring the role of blockchain technology in value creation: a multiple case study approach *Qual. Quant.* **57** 427–51

[56] Balakrishnan A, Jaglan P, Selly S, Kumar V and Jabalia N 2023 Emerging trends of blockchain in bioinformatics: a revolution in health care *Distributed Computing to Blockchain* (Amsterdam: Elsevier) pp 389–404

[57] Baltruschat L M, Jaiman V and Urovi V 2023 User acceptability of blockchain technology for enabling electronic health record exchange *J. Syst. Inf. Technol.* **25** 268–95

[58] Dubovitskaya A, Novotny P, Xu Z and Wang F 2020 Applications of blockchain technology for data-sharing in oncology: results from a systematic literature review *Oncology* **98** 403–11

[59] Hajian A, Prybutok V R and Chang H C 2023 An empirical study for blockchain-based information sharing systems in electronic health records: a mediation perspective *Comput. Hum. Behav.* **138** 107471

[60] Ichikawa D, Kashiyama M and Ueno T 2017 Tamper-resistant mobile health using blockchain technology *JMIR mHealth uHealth* **5** e7938

[61] Angraal S, Krumholz H M and Schulz W L 2017 Blockchain technology: applications in health care *Circ.: Cardiovasc. Qual. Outcomes* **10** e003800

[62] Karafiloski E and Mishev A 2017 Blockchain solutions for big data challenges: a literature review *IEEE EUROCON 2017—17th Int. Conf. on Smart Technologies* 763–8

[63] Aloini D, Benevento E, Stefanini A and Zerbino P 2023 Transforming healthcare ecosystems through blockchain: opportunities and capabilities for business process innovation *Technovation* **119** 102557

Printed in the USA
CPSIA information can be obtained
at www.ICGtesting.com
JSHW060712031123
51216JS00004B/90

9 780750 358378